# THE
# EAST INDIA COMPANY'S
# ARSENALS &
# MANUFACTORIES

# THE EAST INDIA COMPANY'S ARSENALS & MANUFACTORIES

BRIGADIER-GENERAL H. A. YOUNG,
C.I.E., C.B.E.

DIRECTOR OF ORDNANCE FACTORIES
IN INDIA, 1917-1920

**The Naval & Military Press Ltd**

published in association with

**FIREPOWER**
**The Royal Artillery Museum**
Woolwich

Published by
**The Naval & Military Press Ltd**
Unit 10 Ridgewood Industrial Park,
Uckfield, East Sussex,
TN22 5QE England
Tel: +44 (0) 1825 749494
Fax: +44 (0) 1825 765701
www.naval-military-press.com

*in association with*

**FIREPOWER**
**The Royal Artillery Museum, Woolwich**
www.firepower.org.uk

*In reprinting in facsimile from the original, any imperfections are inevitably reproduced and the quality may fall short of modern type and cartographic standards.*

# PREFACE

HAVING served for 28 years in the Indian Ordnance Department, during the greater part of which period I was in, or directly connected with, the Indian Ordnance Factories, I wished very much, on my retirement from the Army, to learn something of the early histories of those factories. This desire was whetted by the slight researches I had to make when the Royal Society of Arts asked me in 1923 to read a paper dealing in some way with the work of the Indian Ordnance Factories. For some years, for various reasons, I was unable to undertake the necessary careful and extensive reading and research. Eventually I was able to start the work in earnest, and I was fortunate enough to obtain the very valuable assistance of Miss L. M. Anstey in my researches among the records of the India Office. Much time was spent in the examination of the various series of manuscript records in the India Office Library, and also in the Indian Institute at Oxford and in the Libraries of the East India United Service Club and the Royal United Service Institution. I cannot claim to have exhausted the subject, and I can only hope that these sketches, for they are only sketches, may be of interest, at least, to those connected with India or to those who may desire to learn something of a little-known branch of the Indian Army. I have striven for accuracy, but, if there are errors, I can only plead that I have verified every statement to the best of my ability. I am indebted, also, to Sir Richard Burn, C.S.I., and to Professor Kenneth Mason, M.C., for much valuable advice and assistance.

H. A. Y.

*Exmouth*
*February*, 1937

# NOTES

THE pagoda in use in Madras till 1818 was equal to 3½ rupees, and there were 46 fanams to the pagoda. The value of the rupee has varied greatly: up to 1873 it was worth from 2*s*. to 2*s*. 3*d*., after that year it sank at times to as low as 1*s*. In 1899 it was fixed at 1*s*. 4*d*., and in 1927 at 1*s*. 6*d*.

A candy was roughly equal to 500 English pounds weight.

A maund varies, but is usually taken as equal to 80 pounds weight.

A lakh or lac is 1,00,000.

15 sicca rupees were equal to 16 Company or sonat rupees; the sicca rupee was abolished in 1836.

Mistry, a native foreman or skilled worker.

Sirdar, a native overseer.

Sircar, a native clerk.

## CONTENTS

## APPENDIXES



## INDEXES

# I

# INTRODUCTION

I BEGAN a paper on 'The Indian Ordnance Factories and Indian Industries', which I had the honour of reading to the Royal Society of Arts in January 1924, with the following words: 'The production and supply of military equipment is a by-way of History but little explored by the historian. The earliest armies obtained their weapons from the nearest forest or beach and nobody thought it necessary to describe the forest or beach, and the fashion thus set has been followed down to quite recent times. The last great war has made us realize, however, that, while an army may march on its stomach, a nation fights with its factories.' Those words are perhaps a suitable beginning to this attempt to describe the means by which the East India Company provided its troops with military equipment.

The subject has never been dealt with before, though there are a few allusions to manufactories and arsenals in the histories of the Presidency artilleries and armies, and some further information can be gleaned from other works, such as those on Fort William, Fort St. George, and old Bengal. But all that can be gathered from such printed sources is scanty in the extreme, and sometimes not strictly accurate. These sketches, therefore, are mainly based on the original manuscript records in the India Office, a wonderful mine of information, though none too easy a one to work, owing to the many series which have to be consulted. Besides the Dispatches to and from the Court of Directors, there are Court Minutes and the Consultations of the various Councils and Boards to be searched before a complete story can be constructed. It must also be remembered that in the early days eighteen months or even two years might elapse between the consideration of a subject in India and the receipt of the orders of the Court.[1]

The very existence of any military manufacturing establishments in India seems to be unknown to modern writers. There is *A History of the Army Ordnance Services*, published a few years ago, in which, in a chapter on the Indian Ordnance Department dealing with the period under the East India Company, appears the amazing statement that 'munitions were bought from the British Board of Ordnance'. Nothing could be farther from the truth, as, for many years before the end of the Company's administration, they had manufactories of their own, under their own officers, from which supplies of gunpowder, brass ordnance, gun-carriages and other vehicles, percussion caps, bullets, and many other stores were obtained. Moreover, the Grand Arsenals were equipped with laboratories, workshops, and armouries, while many stores were procured from local sources. The only important articles of military equipment which the Company never attempted to manufacture were fire-arms, though even these were sometimes purchased in India and were made in many of the Indian States. The author of *The Military Engineer in India* makes no mention of a distinguished officer of the Bengal Engineers, Captain G. Hutchinson, who was the first Director and Superintendent of the Company's Gun Foundry, who went to Europe to study the art of gun-founding, and who built and equipped the Foundry at Cossipore. Another writer, the author of *The History of the Indian Medical Service*, though he has chapters devoted to services other than purely medical, omits any reference to the services of medical officers in Bombay and Bengal who were Agents for the manufacture of gunpowder. Actually in

[1] In 1754 the *London* left England on 24 January and arrived at Madras on 30 September, a good passage. In 1854, however, Lieutenant A. M. Lang, Bengal Engineers, left Southampton on 20 June, arrived at Alexandria on 4 July, left Suez on the 8th, and arrived in Calcutta on the 31st. This was called the Overland Route and had been adopted as the result of a favourable report by a House of Commons Committee in 1834.

Bombay a Surgeon, Helenus Scott, was probably the first to put manufacture of gunpowder in that Presidency on a really satisfactory basis. Moreover, the ignorance of the officers of the Indian Army concerning the factories, in which so much of their equipment was made, and the arsenals, from which they drew their supplies of military stores, was, in my time, simply amazing.[1]

My original intention was to sketch the history of each of the present Indian ordnance factories, connecting them with the early manufactories of the East India Company, but I soon found it simpler and more interesting to compile the histories of the Company's manufactories and to link them briefly with those now existing. In other words, I am confining my sketches practically to the period of the Company's existence. It became clear, however, that no history of the manufacturing establishments would be complete without some description of the storing and distributing agencies—the Presidency Ordnance Departments with their arsenals and magazines. Finally I could find no account of the system of Military Administration under the Company, and some description of this seemed to be necessary to complete the picture.

I think it is essential for any one who reads these sketches to realize that the East India Company began as a company of traders and long continued as traders, and the merchants in those early days were prepared to take great risks for large rewards, but they were most critical of expenses and above all of military expenses. The Company shared to the full their countrymen's dislike of the 'Military', and in the seven-

[1] The statement of the author of *The War Office* (published in 1935), referring to the Home Ordnance Factories, that 'The Factories execute the orders of the Service Departments, as well as of India, . . . for guns, mountings, rifles, ammunition, tanks, vehicles, bombs, and other warlike stores' is distinctly misleading. There are warlike stores which India does not yet manufacture; but by far the greater part is supplied by the seven well-equipped factories which she maintains for the purpose, and from which she obtains guns, gun-carriages, rifles, ammunition, vehicles, explosives, harness, saddlery, accoutrements, and many other articles. A large number of these stores are made from the raw materials, which as far as possible are obtained in the country.

teenth century they did not even think it safe to have soldiers in any post higher than that of lieutenant and desired that captains and superior officers should be drawn from among their civil servants. When an expedition was sent out from England in 1685 to enable hostilities to be commenced against 'the Soobadhar of Bengal', six companies of infantry were sent with subaltern officers only, as it was intended that Members of Council in Bengal should act as captains. In 1710 the Court sent orders to Madras reducing the pay of a lieutenant to £4 a month and of a private to 21 shillings—not very attractive rates. Owing to the difficulty of obtaining recruits in England, whole companies of Swiss and other foreigners were sent out, while the enlistment in India of 'Armenians, Caffres and Blacks' was suggested, the Court pointing out that every man sent from England cost the Company £30. Another difficulty was the heavy mortality on the passage out: in 1709, for example, out of a draft of 30 men only 9 arrived. One draft sent to Madras in 1752 consisted of 3 officers (gentlemen), 5 cadets (labourers), 2 cadets (gentlemen), 1 cadet (watchmaker), and 60 men, all being Swiss or Germans. Owing to the low rates of pay and the bad conditions, there were constant desertions of both officers and men, tempted by the greater opportunities offered in the service of an Indian State. Mutinies from interference with pay and allowances were not infrequent, while corruption and peculation were rife.

While the Court were always urging economy in military expenditure, which too often meant cutting down essentials rather than a reduction in non-essentials, they were not entirely unmindful of the claims of their troops, and sometimes endeavoured to make their Councils more careful of the interests of the soldier. In a letter which they wrote to Madras in August 1791 on the subject of the expenses of the Mysore wars they referred to the pay of the troops, and said: 'Pay must never be in arrears while there is a rupee in your Treasury and every other article of expenditure for civil services or Salaries or otherwise must yield to their superior and irresistible claims in the first instance.' They noted that the King's troops had been paid two months in advance in gold purchased at a premium, while their own men had remained 12 to 20 months in arrears and were paid in the debased currency of the provinces. It is doubtful, however, whether the Court's injunctions had any very lasting effect, and the pay of the Company's troops was often much in arrears. One gets, however, the impression not only from this but generally from the records that the Court of Directors of the East India Company were rather more human and less bound by regulations where the soldier was concerned than their Councils in India, or than the Government of India which succeeded them.

When we read of the various ways in which the civil and even the military servants of the Company augmented their salaries, we must remember that those salaries were for a long time meagre in the extreme, and of themselves afforded little attraction for men to face the undoubted risks and hardships of life in India. Some of those ways were not illegal, being often governed by rules or customs authorized or condoned by Government. As we shall see in the chapters which follow, private trade was, up to a point, allowed, commissions were given on all contracts and purchases, government servants were permitted to take contracts, while there were other sources of profit available, licit and illicit. But was strict honesty any more apparent elsewhere in the British Dominions during the eighteenth century?

Soldiers also had ways of making money: in *The Nabobs of Madras*, by H. Dodwell, it is stated that Clive was allowed 6 fanams daily for each man victualled for field diet or batta —the diet being 1½ lb. beef or mutton, 1 lb. biscuit or 1½ lb. of rice, and 2 drams of Batavia arrack. This was very profitable, and he quotes Orme as saying that Clive made £40,000 out of it. He says that Clive was generous and did not keep all the contract, giving the one for the garrison of

Fort St. David to a friend, and also allowing another to have the contract for the provision of coolies and bullocks. He gave the batta at Trichinopoly to Captain Dalton, who reckoned the profit on 212 men for 31 days at Rs. 909, as he gave the men 4 fanams a day in lieu of provisions.

Not many soldiers had such opportunities, but there was one source of profit to them which deserves mention: this was prize-money, which often was considerable and not always approved by Government. An early example of this was at the capture in 1781 of the Fort of Bidjeghur by a force under Major Popham. The total value of the spoil was estimated at 25 lakhs of rupees, which was divided among the captors on the spot, a proceeding highly disapproved by the Governor-General, Warren Hastings; but all efforts made by Government to recover any part failed. Major Popham's share was Rs. 2,94,000, a subaltern received Rs. 11,239, while even a sepoy had Rs. 50. Presents were often given by Indian rulers for distribution among the troops in recognition of their services or to avoid looting. After the defeat of the Rohillas in 1794 the officers of the army considered that Rampoor should have been looted, so instead the Nawab presented 11 lakhs of rupees for distribution among the troops and another lakh for the families of the officers who had fallen. A colonel's share was Rs. 16,400, a captain's Rs. 3,936, a conductor's Rs. 1,312, while a lascar was given Rs. 21.

The corruption of the eighteenth century was undoubtedly the cause of the flood of certificates, declarations on oath or on honour, checks and counterchecks, which have plagued generation after generation of officers, worrying the honest and amusing the careless, and which vastly increased clerical work and the cost of administration without improving military efficiency. In 1803 the Military Auditor-General in Bengal agreed with the Agent for the Manufacture of Gunpowder at Ishapore that the confusion and delay in his accounts had been due to 'Separating the Responsibility of the Accounts from the Executive duty of the Agency'. In 1864 the Inspector-General of Ordnance in Bombay represented to Government that the establishment of the gun-carriage factory could be reduced if the accounts were simplified. Even down to recent times the accounts of the ordnance factories were compiled in an office in Calcutta, and a superintendent had no means of ascertaining his costs till twelve months or more after the close of a year's working.

Another matter may be fittingly referred to in this introduction, for the principle enunciated in a letter from Bengal to the Court, written in 1817, was too often followed down to the Great War, with costly results. This letter referred to the manufacture of guns in India and urged that India needed special patterns dependent on climate, gun-carriage materials, and draught capacity, and other countries should not be followed blindly. Even the Presidency artilleries followed different ideas in their equipment, but later money has been spent to little purpose, in the sacred name of economy, to avoid the expense of new equipments. Much money was expended, for example, at Cossipore in 1859–61 in an attempt to rifle the existing brass ordnance and later in converting cast-iron guns to rifled ordnance by the Palliser system. In more recent times special guns, howitzers, and equipment were obtained differing from those in use in the British Army. But perhaps the most serious of all was the neglect before the War to follow England in the alteration of the rifle and in the method of packing its ammunition in bandoliers, with the result that the infantryman of an Indian Division advancing to the attack in Mesopotamia could not carry additional rounds, while the passing of ammunition to him in a narrow trench was most difficult. It is thought that one of the important attacks for the relief of Kut was defeated mainly by an insufficient supply of rifle ammunition to the men of the Indian Division, owing to the absence of ready-packed bandoliers.[1]

[1] When India was asked to supply bandoliers, the reply was that they could not

While one cannot help noticing many instances of false economy, it must be obvious that there were often reasons which forced the authorities in India to reduce military expenditure. The Court were often greatly alarmed at the cost of their military establishment, and made regulations, possibly wise in intention but unduly rigid and hampering in action. It was, however, most difficult, and it has nearly always been difficult, to induce any military authority to cut the best possible coat from the cloth available. The Civil Government should know what cloth is available, and it is for the army to make the best use of it, but they often waste too much of it on non-essentials. However, in the last resort, it is Government which has to call the tune and which often has information not available to the soldier. There was a great outcry in India when Lord William Bentinck arrived in 1828, with the strictest orders from the Court to obtain the greatest possible economy in expenditure. He appointed committees to investigate every item of expense and himself reviewed the major questions. He found, amongst other matters, that when the Court sanctioned in 1824 the gradual substitution of horses for bullocks in the field batteries of Artillery there were only five troops of Horse Artillery, whereas there were eleven of these in 1829. On a review of the political situation and the forces of the Indian States he decided that these did not call for any more horsed batteries then, and he replaced the bullocks in the two field batteries at Dum Dum and decided to postpone any further horsing of batteries. He informed the Commander-in-Chief that this was necessary from financial considerations of the most pressing nature. The historians of the Bengal Artillery are loud in their condemnation of this step, and go so far as to say that the horsing was ordered by the Court but the Governor-General paid no attention to it, and state that one

be supplied; but England would be asked to provide—the reason being that the sealed pattern had glove-clip buttons on the pockets, which were not obtainable in India; unfortunately the authorities did not realize that in an emergency and on service any sort of button would answer the purpose.

high official noted that 'we won India with bullocks and why should we not keep it with bullocks?' Lord William Bentinck had correctly judged the political position, and no serious war occurred till 1839.

It is perhaps necessary to point out that the East India Company constituted three Presidencies in India. The term 'Presidency' was used originally to denote a settlement governed by a President and Council, but eventually, as territories were acquired, it had a wider use, and the three great divisions of British India became known as the Presidencies of Bengal, Bombay, and Madras. But for a considerable period during the Company's rule, owing to the imperfect and often dangerous means of communication by land, travel between Calcutta, Madras, and Bombay was mainly undertaken by sea. In 1818, for example, Colonel Low, on transfer from Poona to Cawnpore, went by sea from Bombay to Calcutta and thence by river, the journey lasting six months in all. Moreover, there were many different factors, such as the nature of the country, the characteristics of the peoples, their languages and their customs, which militated against the development of the Presidency armies and their administrative services on identical lines.

## II

## MILITARY ADMINISTRATION UNDER THE COMPANY

In endeavouring to give some account of Military Administration under the East India Company, I am confining myself to that part which is concerned with the provision and distribution of military stores, as distinct from command, training, discipline, and feeding.

In the early days of the Company, however, the Council at each Presidency exercised all military functions, including that of command, and themselves dealt with every matter however petty, and this continued up to nearly the middle of the eighteenth century. Supplies of munitions were ordered by them from various officials, such as the Master-at-Arms, the Gunner, the Storekeeper, and the Paymaster, often by contract, either with or through those officials, who, in any case, were allowed a substantial commission for their trouble. Then, as territories were acquired, forces increased, and political, revenue, and other business grew, committees were formed, which often included officers and others not being members of the Council.

In April 1754 the Court wrote to Bombay directing the appointment of a Committee of Secrecy, consisting of the President, the Second in Council, the Commander of the Troops, the Major, and the Superintendent of the Marine, and this Committee first met in March 1755, though with different members. Its object was the preparation of, and the carrying into operation of, plans for the crushing of the growing power of Angria, which had become a great menace to trade. This Committee became a 'Select Committee', which, with some interruptions, remained in control of military operations and political negotiations, till, in August 1775, it became a Secret Committee of the whole Council.

In January 1785 the Court's orders were received, consequent on an Act of Parliament of 1784, placing the whole power in the hands of a Governor with a Council of three members. Somewhat similar procedure was also instituted in Madras and Bengal, but it must be understood that these committees were concerned with government rather than with administration.

The usual committees which dealt with military administration were the Committee of Stores and the Committee of Works; Bombay had for some years another committee, the Powder House Committee, for the control of the manufacture of gunpowder. Bengal in 1766 set up a Committee of Inspection 'to examine the state of the several Departments, Civil and Military, and to establish such legislation as they shall judge necessary to the due execution of those offices'. This Committee seems to have continued up till 1774, but it must have been superseded for military business by the Military Committee which was set up in March 1771, composed of the Governor as President, with four Members of Council and the Commander-in-Chief. Under the control of this Military Committee were placed the Chief Engineer, the Military Storekeeper, the Naval Storekeeper, the Master Attendant, the Military Paymaster-General, the Paymaster to the Works, and the Storekeeper to the Works.

The Works were those connected with the building of new Fort William, in which there had been considerable peculation, as witness the story of Captain John Brohier, who had been transferred from Madras to Calcutta in 1757 at Clive's request as Chief Engineer. In 1760 he was placed under arrest 'because he intended privately to quit the settlement', when there were grave charges against him. He asked for a court martial and offered to pay Rs. 76,000 towards what he considered to be the defalcations of his servants, but he escaped to Ceylon, where he entered the Dutch service. The trouble may be understood from the report of the new Engineer, who stated that only two-thirds of the workmen were present who had been charged for and there were many false charges for materials. The Court were 'inexpressibly concerned' at the statement that the money plundered was at least one-third of the whole cost and were most annoyed that the persons concerned had been allowed to leave.

Another story connected with the building of Fort William is of interest as it shows how officers, at this time, were remunerated. Captain F. Martin, the new Chief Engineer, applied in 1763 to be appointed Superintendent of the Brick Manufactory, stating that the perquisites attached to it were more than twice his salary as Chief Engineer. However, a friend of the Council was appointed, so Martin was given instead the newly raised company of artillery, or rather he was given the pay and perquisites attached to its command. In 1768 he was given the command of all the artillery with the rank of lieutenant-colonel, and he held both appointments for a short time till he was relieved as chief engineer by Captain Campbell,[1] and went home with, it is said, a large fortune.

The first real attempt at an organization for the control of military expenditure in all its aspects was made by General Sir John Clavering, the Commander-in-Chief in Bengal. In a long and detailed minute which appears in the Bengal Public Proceedings of March 1775, he reviewed the expenses of the Bengal Army and noted the very heavy disbursements for military stores. He proposed the establishment of a Board of Ordnance to control, among other matters, the making of contracts and the custody and issue of stores, and he set out the procedure in considerable detail. He advocated the appointment of a Commissary of Ordnance with a Deputy and two Conductors to Magazines at Berhampore, Dinapore, and Chunar Ghur, to be dependent on, and to be paid by, the Board. Each brigade ordered into the field to have a Deputy Commissary of Ordnance with Conductors. He proposed that the Board should consist of the

[1] See note below, p. 19.

Governor-General, the Commander of the Forces, one Member of Council, the Commissary-General of Comptroll, the Commanding Officer of Artillery, the Chief Engineer, the Commissary-General of Stores, and the Military Storekeeper, with a secretary and assistants. The Quartermaster-General was added to the Board shortly after, and, apparently, instead of there being one Member of Council any Member could attend if he so desired.

All returns, indents, and vouchers, also all proposals for new works, were to be sent to the Board, and no stores were to be issued from the magazines without an order from the Board. It is interesting to note that the certificate which had to be signed at the end of each indent, which ran thus: 'I do hereby certify, in persuance of General Orders, that the articles specified in this Indent appear to me indespensably necessary for the service of the Battalion, according to the best of my knowledge and belief after the most careful examination', was still in use at the end of last century, with the substitution of the words 'on my honour' for 'in persuance of General Orders' and with the insertion of the word 'personal' before 'examination'.[1]

The Court were highly pleased with the institution of this Board, but Colonel Pearse, Commandant of Artillery, objected to it as taking away from him the control of the supply of his equipment, and he also complained in 1781 of having to send petty returns of grease and bits of leather while on service, and also of being asked for the annual survey of equipment, which would have entailed halting the army for a week. It must be stated, however, that Colonel Pearse was far from being a friend of Clavering's, and in a letter of his he went so far as to attribute the formation of the Board to a personal motive on the General's part to lower him. Clavering has been described as 'an honest, straight-forward man of passionate disposition and mediocre abilities', but it

[1] In 1895 I was expected to sign such a certificate on an indent made out in triplicate for a few annas' worth of oil for a guard-room lamp.

seems absurd to suppose that his able and exhaustive minute had for its object an attack on the position of his Commandant of Artillery.

Military historians have condemned the Board: one says, 'it threw the arrangements for equipment into the hands of the Commissary of Stores and the Military Storekeeper, who, from being themselves contractors or connected in interest with contractors, were the least fitted'. The procedure was undoubtedly cumbrous and the Board absurdly large, while authority, even in the smallest detail, was centralized in it; but centralization, unfortunately, characterized military administration in India for considerably more than a century after the institution of Clavering's Board of Ordnance. In 1802 only the Governor-General in Council could authorize the purchase of two wood sentry-boxes for the Gun-carriage Agency yard at Cossipore. A few years before the Great War, only the Government of India could sanction the extension of a travelling allowance of eight annas a mile to Indian clerks, on transfer, between their residence and a railway station, to cover similar journeys between residence and a steamer wharf!

Bombay formed a Board of Ordnance and Committee of Indents in 1779, composed of the Commanding Officer, the Military Storekeeper, the Principal Engineer, and the Commandant of Artillery, with a secretary and also an executive officer—Lieutenant D. Carpenter, Commissary of Stores, but it does not seem to have had the same powers as the Board in Bengal. Madras retained its Committees of Stores and Works and did not form a Board of Ordnance: its Committee of Works was formed in May 1754 on the death of Lt.-Col. C. F. Scott (see Chapter XI). It was composed of two Civilian Members of Council and the Engineer (Captain John Brohier), and administered for many years the business of fortification and buildings.

In September 1785 a change was ordered by the Court. They directed that, in each Presidency, there should be a

Military Board in place of the existing Boards and Committees. It was to be composed of the Commander-in-Chief, the senior officer at the Presidency, the senior officer of Artillery, the Chief Engineer, the Adjutant-General, the Quartermaster-General, and the Commissary-General, the latter being the equivalent of the Military Auditor-General of later times. While many details were left to be settled by the Councils, it was clearly ordered that this Military Board was not to be independent of the Council. It was to be a 'Board of Reference and Report' and it was to scrutinize every item of military expenditure, but was to have nothing to do with discipline or the distribution of troops. This Military Board was duly formed in 1786 in Bengal and Bombay; but though Madras also formed one in the same year there were prolonged discussions regarding its regulations and procedure which seem to have continued up to 1797. General Geils of the Madras Artillery objected both in 1794 and 1797 to many of the changes, and he demurred especially to 'the removal of the charge of stores from the Company's civil servants, who are generally men of property, and putting the charge under military officers who frequently are not so, at least until they have made a campaign as Commissaries'. In the case of civilians, he said, there was a fortune to answer for any loss from embezzlement or neglect—a nice commentary on the honesty of both civilians and officers! An incident in 1792 may be an example of profits made by Commissaries in a campaign, for in July the Madras Council suspended Captain Bell, Commissary of Stores at Trichinopoly, till the Court's orders were known, for neglect and breach of duty as Commissary of Stores in the late war by expending large sums of money without producing satisfactory vouchers for any part. General Geils objected to the abolition of the civilian military Storekeeper and the placing the charge of military stores in the hands of commissaries and deputy commissaries.

In 1830 the Military Board in Bengal was reconstituted to

consist of the Chief Engineer, the Commandant of Artillery, two stipendiary members, and one civilian, who curiously enough was the Chief Magistrate of Calcutta, *ex officio*. It was given control of the Ordnance, Public Works, Canals, Commissariat, and the Stud, but by 1845 it had shed its Chief Magistrate. In Madras the Military Board was not reorganized till 1839, when it had the same members as in Bengal but without a civilian member. In Bombay there was a curious action by the Governor, Sir John Malcolm, who, without reference to the Governor-General or to the Court, suspended the Military Board from 1 January 1830. He wrote a minute saying that the members of the Board had quite enough to do in their own jobs, and moreover it was wrong to have the Commander-in-Chief in controversy with members of his staff. He ordered that the Commandant of Artillery was to be vested with authority over the Ordnance Department and also over the gun-carriage and gunpowder manufactories, and for this he was to have an Ordnance Assistant and the necessary office establishment. The Commandant cannot have been vested with much authority, as in 1834 he could only recommend to Government the request of the Agent for Gun-carriages to be allowed to purchase a clock for the Manufactory.

The Court, in a letter dated in July 1831, expressed great surprise and some disapproval of the action taken by Bombay, but wrote that they would await a further report after there had been some experience of the new system. In March 1834 the Bombay Council wrote that they regretted the abolition of the Board and they considered the extra work entailed on Government rendered necessary either the appointment of a stipendiary Board or the appointment of some responsible military officer as Secretary to Government in the Military and Naval Department, and they preferred the latter course. Actually, with the approval of the Governor-General, a military officer was appointed as Secretary to Government, and the Court were so informed. More correspondence followed with the Court and with the supreme Government, with the result eventually that Bombay was directed to re-establish the Military Board on the lines of that in Bengal, and this was done in 1840. The Board was composed at first of the Chief Engineer, the Commandant of Artillery, and one stipendiary member, but shortly afterwards the Military Auditor-General was added. All these Boards had, of course, a secretary and a considerable office establishment, and usually an assistant secretary as well.

We get some idea of the method of working in the Bengal Military Board from a letter from the Court to Bombay, dated in July 1840. They wrote that the Board was divided into two Boards: the one for Public Works consisting of the Chief Engineer, the Chief Magistrate, and the two stipendiary members, while the one for Ordnance was composed of the Commandant of Artillery and the two stipendiaries. The stipendiary members were usually lieutenant-colonels, chosen from any branch of the Presidency Army.

Then came the end of all boards, as Lord Dalhousie wrote in a private letter dated in February 1855, in which he said:

> 'Before I left Calcutta I had the satisfaction of issuing a General Order abolishing the Military Board. When I came to India this Board was omnipotent and omnipresent. It managed everything and marred everything. It had under it the Commissariat, the Ordnance, the Powder Factory, the Gun Foundry, the Department of Public Works, the Studs and divers other things. One by one, I have got the departments withdrawn and now the Board itself, supposed to be immortal and unvulnerable, is dead and buried. So may all Boards perish.'

In his minute dated in July 1854 he said that, with the approval of the Court, all the departments except the Ordnance had been removed from the control of the Military Board and 'now only the Ordnance remained to occupy the time of the Board, its Secretary and its establishment'. He therefore proposed to place the Ordnance Department under a single head as in the case of the Commissariat and the other departments, but he could not agree to its being placed under the Commandant of Artillery, even had the head-quarters of the artillery remained at Dum Dum. He proposed to create the appointment of an Inspector-General of Ordnance and Magazines to have the entire charge, power, and responsibility as the Military Board had, but audit would be transferred to the Military Auditor-General. There would be no extra expense, as the existing Principal Commissary of Ordnance would be appointed Inspector-General on the salary the stipendiary member of the Board had and the same as the Chief Engineer, i.e. Rs. 2,250 a month with the pay of his rank. The Deputy Principal Commissary of Ordnance would be retained on his present salary, but the word 'Deputy' would be dropped. The Governor-General admitted that three years before he did not advocate the abolition of the Board, but experience had removed all desire to continue it. He asked, therefore, for authority to abolish the Board, and he expected it would be a great reform, beneficial throughout all internal administration.

The Court wrote to the Government of India in February 1856, 'desiring that the Governments of Madras and Bombay in concert with the Government of India, should proceed to consider the measures to be taken for withdrawing from the Military Boards the remaining portion of their duties and for entrusting those duties to separate and responsible Chiefs of Departments agreeably to the system authorized and established in Bengal'. They observed that this would involve in each Presidency the creation of one appointment, viz. that of Inspector-General of Ordnance and Magazines.

It is now necessary to point out that in the development of the Presidency Governments the Court was insistent that the authority of the Council was supreme over all Boards. Thus the Military Board had to obtain the sanction of the Council for any action they might wish to take outside the somewhat narrow limits of the duties of reference and report. Thus there grew up inevitably in each Presidency

Secretariat a branch to deal with the references from the Military Board and to record and convey to the Board the decisions of Government. This branch had sooner or later a secretary to Government of its own and became the Military Department of the Presidency Government. In the beginning the secretary was a covenanted civilian, but before long the post was given to a military officer, with military assistants. In 1811, for example, both Bengal and Madras had a civilian secretary, while Bombay had a civilian who was secretary in the Military and Commercial Departments and also secretary to the Military Board. In 1842 each Government had a lieutenant-colonel as secretary to Government in the Military Department; in Bombay he was also secretary in the Naval Department, which was joined to the Military Department.

*Note to page 12, line 19*

Captain A. Campbell was at first a Royal Engineer and became Chief Engineer in Bengal from 1767 to 1773. In these six years he amassed considerable wealth. He became a Member of Parliament in 1775, but on the outbreak of the American rebellion he raised at his own expense the 71st Regiment of Highlanders and took it to America as its Lieutenant-Colonel. Later he became Governor of Jamaica and from 1785 to 1789 was Governor of Madras. He died in 1791 and was given a public funeral in Westminster Abbey.

## III

## THE EARLY ORDNANCE OFFICERS

I USE the term 'ordnance officer' as a generic one, covering all military officers and civilians connected with the receipt, storage, and distribution of military equipment, though the term was not used much in the days of the East India Company.

When the fortification of any settlement was undertaken, it obviously became necessary to have some official to take charge of the military stores connected with the armament of the works and the equipment of the garrison. The first to have this charge was 'The Gunner', the head of the gun-room crew, and there is a Bengal record of December 1718 stating that the Trustees of the estate of Captain Henry Harnett, deceased, had put in an account of the Gunner's stores, the balance of which had been taken over by Captain John Jones. Captain Jones had been commander of 'several ships for many years and as he had behaved himself well' he was appointed Head Gunner to succeed Harnett. This is typical of the military appointments at that time. These stores included shot, powder, and various articles of equipment. Then, when the gun-room crew was abolished on the formation of a regular company of artillery in each Presidency in 1748, a Military Storekeeper was appointed whose duties were much more extensive than those of the Gunner, but this will be dealt with at length later on.

The records contain, however, many appointments of a more definitely military nature, more nearly resembling those of ordnance officers of a much later date than is to be found in the civilian appointment of a Military Storekeeper. In Madras in 1756, for example, Mr. Charles Milton, described as one of the Conductors of His Majesty's Artillery, undertook to regulate the Military Storehouse at Fort St. George, and in May 1757 he was granted a gratuity of 250 pagodas for his trouble, while the Engineer was ordered 'to draw out a plan of the Military Storehouse to serve as a model for methodizing the Military Storehouse at Fort St. David', where the Military Storekeeper had apparently got his stores into a muddle. Milton went out to Madras with the detachment of the Royal Train of Artillery which accompanied Colonel Adlercron and his regiment, the 39th Foot. He is shown as Assistant Paymaster and 1st Clerk of Stores on the passenger list of the *London*, which arrived at the end of September 1754. After his work in the storehouse he was Assistant to the Military Storekeeper at Madras, till in 1760 he was sent as Commissary-General of Stores to Colonel Coote, and he signed the inventory of stores captured at Pondicherry in 1761. Milton was allowed a salary of 10 shillings a day in addition to pay and he was given two civilian assistants on 5 shillings, plus batta of 4 rupees a day, and he was permitted to select conductors. Milton was succeeded as Assistant to the Military Storekeeper by Mr. Robert Fletcher, who was entertained as a monthly writer for the purpose. Fletcher was transferred to the Army as an ensign in September 1757, and had a very extraordinary career. As a lieutenant he was summarily dismissed in January 1760 for having written an insolent letter to Government. He apologized and was reinstated, at the request of Colonel Coote, for good service. He was transferred to Bengal as a major in December 1763. In 1766 he was tried by court martial and cashiered for his share in the Officers' Mutiny. Being a man of wealth and influence the Court restored him to the service, and he rejoined at Madras in 1771 a full colonel. He was so obstructive that he had to resign and go home, pleading his privilege as a Member of Parliament. However, he returned again in 1775 as Commander-in-Chief and intrigued against the Governor. He died in December 1776 at sea on his way to Mauritius.

In July 1768 Lieutenant Isaac Manoury of the Madras

Artillery, after having served during the previous year as Clerk of Stores with Colonel Smith in Mysore at a salary of 4 shillings a day, was appointed Commissary of Stores with the Army in the field on 10 shillings a day, plus, of course, his pay and allowances. A year later it was decided to appoint officers for the better care of military stores. Manoury was appointed Commissary of Stores at Fort St. George, Captain-Lieutenant De Morgan was made Deputy Commissary at Vellore, and it was proposed to post another artillery officer to Trichinopoly, both the Deputy Commissaries to have a salary of 5 shillings a day.

Manoury had been recommended for the post of Commissary by the Field Deputies who had been sent by the Madras Council to watch over Colonel Smith, and there is an interesting story about them. Not only did Smith have to leave a considerable detachment to protect them, but as they shared in the contract for feeding his European troops and in that for the provision of transport they hampered him in every way by deficiencies in supplies. The matter came to the notice of the Court, owing to complaints by various officers, so they wrote very strongly to Madras in March 1770. They signed their Dispatch, as usual, 'your loving friends', but they did not disguise their extreme displeasure. They pointed out that no tenders had been called for since 1761, when these contracts had been given to Mr. Call, the Engineer, and, they went on, 'the advantages of the Council (you say) were small, therefor Mr Call proposed that the Members thereof should become Joint Subscribers for carrying on the Business of the contract'. They said they were amazed that not one of the Council had honour or virtue enough to reject the proposal. (Apparently, the victualling contract not being sufficiently profitable, the one for the provision of bullock transport was added to it.) The Court added that Colonel Smith and other officers had written strongly on the wretched bullocks and on the way the men were forced to buy food at prices much higher than the bazaar rates, but the Council had ignored all such representations. Mr. John Call was the Engineer who carried on the reconstruction of the defences of Madras after Captain Brohier left for Fort William in 1757. He became third in Council in 1767, though the Court objected to what they described as an amalgamation of the offices of a civil servant and an engineer. Call sailed for England in February 1770, and when he died in London in 1801 he was Lieutenant-Colonel Sir John Call, Bart., F.R.S., and a partner in the banking house of Pybus, Call & Co. He also made money at Madras by private trade through Captain J. Hume at Fort St. David, who sent him oil-seeds, while Call sent wax candles, tea, and ginghams in return.

In May 1758 the Bengal Select Committee thought it highly necessary that their military stores should be kept in good order, so they appointed Captain-Lieutenant William Jennings of the Artillery to be Commissary of Military Stores, as 'we esteem it impossible for a civil officer'. He was also appointed Director of the Laboratory, and his salary was fixed at Rs. 120 a month.[1] As there was no room in the fort, it was decided to appropriate the building known as the Court House for the laboratory and the stores, the rent, apparently Rs. 900 Arcot a year, being continued to the churchwardens for the use of the 'Charity Stock', and the Mayor was directed to find another house for his Court. The laboratory was removed to the old fort in 1760. Jennings had been in the Madras Artillery and went to Bengal at the end of 1756 in command of a detachment of artillery; he transferred to the Bengal Artillery in 1757 and commanded the artillery at the battle of Plassey; he was one of the officers who voted against immediate action. He could not have held the appointment of Commissary for long, as he was soon promoted captain and given command of the Bengal Artillery.

[1] 'Salary' was the term used to denote what is now called staff pay; it was always in addition to regimental pay and allowances.

Later, in 1758, Clive sent a Bengal civilian, Mr. John Johnstone, who was Storekeeper to the Works at Fort William, to Vizagapatam, in advance of a force under Colonel Forde. Stubbs calls him Commissary of Ordnance, while Broome says he was appointed Political Assistant to Colonel Forde and Commissary to the force; evidently he had many duties besides those usual to a Commissary of Ordnance with a force in the field. Though a history of the Ordnance Department is not directly concerned with the career of this particular 'early ordnance officer', yet Johnstone's history is of considerable interest, as it is one of very varied activities and gives an insight into the ethical standards of the period.

Mr. John Johnstone, the fifth son of Sir James Johnstone, Bart., M.P., was elected a Writer for Bengal in December 1750, his securities being his uncles, Lord Elibank and the Hon. Alexander Murray. He was appointed to the Dacca factory as Assistant in September 1754, and reached Fultah after the capture of Calcutta in June 1756. There he attached himself to the artillery as a volunteer and served as such at the battle of Plassey, where he did good service, though he was not commanding the artillery, as has been stated. He was also with Major Coote in July 1757, when he not only assisted Lieutenant Kinch, who commanded two 6-pounder guns, but acted also as Coote's secretary. He was back in Calcutta in October, when he was appointed Storekeeper of the materials for carrying on the works of Fort William, on a salary of Rs. 1,000 a year for his trouble, his pay as a Factor being £15 per annum. However, he wrote that he would prefer to remain in the military, but nothing happened on this except that in February of the next year he was given a commission as lieutenant in what was called an independent corps of the servants of the Company and the inhabitants. Then in July 1758 he was ordered to Balasore as head of affairs there, but it may be that he did not go, as he arrived at Vizagapatam in September. He was present at the battle of Condore on 8 December, when he served with the

Grenadier Company of the Bengal European Regiment, and was wounded. He must soon have recovered, as Forde sent him in March of the following year to negotiate with Salabut Jung, in order to gain time. He was at Midnapore in 1761 as Chief, and two years later he was Chief at Burdwan. A Dutchman, William Bolts, who had been brought up in trade, arrived in Calcutta in 1760 as a Factor in the Company's service, and he very soon entered into partnership with Johnstone and another civil servant, William Hay. These three started an extensive private trade, evading the payment of any duties to the Nawab and using all the power of the Company to further their trade. The profitable nature of this trade may be judged from the fact that Bolts is said to have made £90,000 in six years. In 1764 the Court, having heard of the way in which Cossim Ally Cawn, the Nawab, was being defrauded, wrote to Bengal in February that they had dismissed Johnstone, Hay, Amyatt, and Major Carnac, and they were to be sent home in the following season. However, in May they thought better of Johnstone's case and wrote that they had thought proper to restore him to his rank and station on the Council, the only reason given being 'on account of his former services'. So Johnstone returned to his post at Burdwan till, in February 1765, he took his seat on the Council and was then chosen to head a deputation to negotiate with the successor to the late Nawab, Meer Jaffer Khan. Johnstone obtained presents to a huge amount, his share being Rs. 2,37,000, with Rs. 50,000 to his younger brother Gideon, who was not even in the Company's service. Lord Clive arrived in Calcutta in May with special powers for himself and for a Select Committee, and a struggle ensued between the Council, headed by Johnstone, and the Select Committee, with the result that Johnstone and others resigned. Johnstone applied for passages for himself and his wife towards the end of September 1765 and went home to commence a fight with the Court and with Clive. In May 1766 he was dismissed the service and rendered incapable of re-employment for receiving money from the Subah and his ministers to place him in the Subahship, and the sum of Rs. 3,37,500 was demanded from him, as well as all other money and effects received as presents, and a Bill was filed in the Court of Chancery against him. Johnstone had already defended himself to the Council in Bengal, stating, with regard to the presents he had received, 'That where they are not the price of unworthy service and no trust betrayed for them, the acceptance of them is in no way improper; and, in the present case, as being previous to the execution of the deed of covenant, as warrantable as in time past by any one who had received them.' However, in May 1767 the General Court of Proprietors decided that various prosecutions against their former servants on account of presents received before signing the covenants on 9 May 1765 were to be abandoned. They repeated this decision when the Court of Directors, fortified by legal advice, asked for a reconsideration. The fact was that Johnstone and his friends had very great influence, while most of the Proprietors were hostile to the Directors, on account of the latter's opposition to an increase in the dividend.

In *The Sons of Bare Betty*, by Colonel the Hon. Arthur C. Murray, there are some interesting letters written by John Johnstone's uncle Patrick, Lord Elibank, to his natural son, William Young, who arrived in Bengal in 1765 as a Writer. In one letter he states that he had written to John Johnstone to assist Young, as he might find desirable, and in another he refers to the conduct of the Company in lessening the profits of their servants. Lord Elibank remarked that he had been greatly hurt by the fall in India Stock and he disapproved of the management. Young told him that he would return home as soon as he had made a competency, on which his father remarked that less than £40,000 did not pass for a competency; but in a later letter said that less than £100,000 would not do. By the end of 1779 Young reckoned himself to be worth £36,000, but hoped to reach his aim in

1785 (apparently £40,000). Lord Elibank referred to the Court of Directors as, in general, a parcel of rascals, but admitted that he was liable to suspicion from his connexion with the Johnstones, who were obnoxious to Lord Clive and his party. He urged Young to correspond with Governor Johnstone, an elder brother of John, who was a Member of Parliament, and he mentions his friendship with General Clavering. Young was in London in 1787, having left India in the previous year, and he died in 1824. One of his sources of profit was an opium contract, which he and Patrick Heatly had for four years from December 1785, and from which the partners expected a profit of at least a lakh of rupees a year.

Clive, soon after his arrival in Calcutta, made all members of the Civil service sign formal covenants binding themselves not to accept presents or pecuniary rewards from any native authorities, and later made the military officers sign also. There was much opposition, and, in some cases, signature was delayed till presents had been obtained. In his view, moreover, the Court agreeing, private trade outside the Company's territories had never been allowed, except on the conditions laid down by the native rulers for their own subjects. In a letter which he addressed to the Court in September 1765 he stated that

> 'Luxury, Corruption, Avarice and Rapacity had possession of the principal posts. Affairs could not be managed by men whose views did not extend beyond a year or two. They set all orders at defiance knowing that they could acquire a Fortune or at least a comfortable Independency before resentment could reach them. A competency should be allowed to all from the time of their arrival in India; but they should not hope to be able to return home till they had reached the rank of Councillor, when the prospect should open to them of returning in a few years with an independent fortune.'

Clive instituted a monopoly of salt, betel-nut, and tobacco, to be carried on by a Committee for the benefit of the services. A duty was first to be deducted for the Company and the remaining profits to be shared among the higher officials and senior officers. In 1766 there were 60 shares, each about Rs. 10,000, of which the Commander-in-Chief had 3, the two colonels of brigade 2 each, two lieutenant-colonels each two-thirds of a share, and majors one-third. The plan was accepted by the Court with evident reluctance, and there was a good deal of correspondence about the accounts and the amount received by the Company, but it was continued under various pretexts till September 1768. Clive in his letter referred to above stated that he could only mention three servants of obvious integrity, and in a letter to a member of the Select Committee he said that he feared the Military were as far gone in luxury and debauchery.

It does not seem that Clive's efforts to eradicate corruption, luxury, and avarice produced lasting results, for, after his retirement from India and until Lord Cornwallis started his campaign against these vices, large fortunes were still being acquired by doubtful means. It must, however, always be remembered that the Company itself was largely to blame by reason of the miserable pay allotted to its servants. In Madras in 1756, for example, Charles Bourchier, aged 28, was Military Storekeeper, Rental General, and Scavenger with pay of £40 per annum, though he had diet money, quarters, and servants, but the position of Military Storekeeper was a profitable one. In fact the pay of a civil servant was usually a very small proportion of his total receipts, and the case of Mr. D. C. Ramsay, a Bombay civil servant, is a good example of this. In 1793 he was a senior merchant with monthly pay Rs. 26, diet money Rs. 30, servants Rs. 54, house-rent Rs. 40. He was stationed at Surat and had Rs. 500 a month as Agent for building and repairs, he was also Commissary of Supplies at the Magazine, with a salary of Rs. 50, plus 10 per cent. on the cost of all stores supplied by him.

Even Warren Hastings indulged in private trade to supplement his somewhat meagre emoluments; but this trade seems to have been legitimate, as it was within the Company's territories and did not conflict with the Company's interests. In 1743 the Dacca Council complained of his Agent making illegitimate use of the Company's sepoys, but in his reply he stated that they had been employed only for the protection of his Agent's life, who was engaged in collecting a great number of timbers belonging to him and to other gentlemen, which were scattered on the river between Dacca and Backergunge. One of the sources of the fortunes made by the old 'Nabobs' was the sale of passes for internal trade to the Indian merchants of Calcutta; all civil servants could obtain such passes, and even juniors made fortunes from their sale.

During a great part of the eighteenth century the post of Military Storekeeper was one of considerable importance and profit, William Hickey describing it as the most lucrative one in the Company's service. He was referring to Major T. T. Metcalfe, who is stated, in an article in *Bengal Past and Present*, as having obtained the post of Military Storekeeper 'by most perseveringly courting the heads of Government'. In the life of his distinguished son Charles, Lord Metcalfe, it is mentioned that Major Metcalfe, when an ensign of only three months' service in Bengal, in a fit of the blues wanted to resign, but, the conversation at breakfast taking a pleasant turn, a hearty fit of laughter got the better of 'his blue devils'. (It is not uncommon for an Englishman in India to have a fit of the blues before breakfast, and it is not unknown for the affliction to continue after his retirement to his native country.) Major Metcalfe is said to have acquired an income of £4,000 a year, and after his return to England he obtained a seat on the Court of the East India Company in 1789. He became a Member of Parliament and was made a Baronet in 1802, as a staunch supporter of William Pitt. Hickey says he bought his baronetcy.

The post of Military Storekeeper was, however, rarely held by any one not a covenanted civilian, usually of some standing, and it carried with it a commission of varying amount on everything which was purchased or manufactured for military use. It is probably correct to say that the early Military Storekeepers were the ordnance officers of their day: they undertook the provision of such stores as could be made or procured in the country, and for a time they stored and distributed them, but laboratory work was the duty of the artillery. The establishment of grand arsenals at the Presidency forts greatly curtailed the duties of the Military Storekeepers, as the Commissaries of Stores at these arsenals became responsible for storage and issue and to some extent for manufacture in the arsenal workshops. Moreover, the institution of the system of Agencies for the construction of gun-carriages in manufactories belonging to the Company still further rendered the Military Storekeepers unnecessary.[1]

Madras, for example, had a succession of Military Storekeepers up to 1795, all of whom, with the exception of Captain Bryan Scottney, whose tenure of the post lasted from 1778 till 1786, were covenanted civilians. Scottney had a varied career. He was commissioned as ensign in the Madras European Regiment in April 1754, and was on service under Stringer Lawrence. He went to Bengal with the Madras troops under Clive at the end of 1756, when he was commissioned as captain. He complained of repeated super-

[1] In India an arsenal has always been an establishment for the receipt, storage, and issue of military equipment, and not a manufactory, as the Royal Arsenal at Woolwich is. The Indian arsenals have, it is true, certain armoury and other workshops, but these are intended for repair work, though small quantities of minor stores are often made in them. A magazine was originally the place of storage of the equipment required by a field brigade should it have to proceed on service, and it held also the artillery train. The term 'magazine' was later extended to denote all places, outside the Presidency towns, in which military equipment was stored for the use of troops operating in, or stationed in, their vicinity. Eventually, on the recommendation of the Special Ordnance Commission of 1875, only the buildings which actually contained ammunition and explosives were called magazines, and the storage places of general military equipment became known as arsenals in the case of the larger and more permanent establishments, or as depots for those of a minor nature. In 1875 there were actually 34 arsenals, magazines, and depots in India.

session and was allowed to resign in October 1758, when he went to England, but he was later allowed to return to Bengal as a free merchant, and in 1761 he was an Alderman of Calcutta. In a letter dated in December 1761 the Court authorized his reinstatement as captain, but not to have a company till a vacancy occurred. He does not seem to have re-joined, and in August 1765 he was still a free merchant and was trading at Patna, when the Select Committee notified all such merchants that permission to reside and to trade in the Dacca District would be withdrawn in October. This action was the result of Clive's efforts to stop the scandals caused by Johnstone, Hay, Bolts, and others trading in the Nawab's territories. In August 1767 Scottney applied to the Council at Fort William for a passage to England, and apparently remained at home till in December 1773 the Court allowed him to proceed to Bengal and to reside there for three years to settle his affairs. He arrived in England again early in 1777, and, in a petition to the Court referring to his services and to his losses, stated that he was resident in Madras, and asked for an appointment there, either in the Civil Service or as Military Storekeeper. For some reason not discovered the Court in February 1777 appointed him to succeed Mr. George Dawson as Military Storekeeper, and in their letter to Madras they expressed the opinion that there were many advantages in having a military officer as Military Storekeeper. By October 1782, however, the Court, as they so often did, changed their minds, and when approving of a salary of 1,500 pagodas a year to the Military Storekeeper 'positively directed that on the death or removal of Scottney, the post was to be filled by one of the Council as formerly'.

In 1786 the Military Board allowed Scottney 30 per cent. on his bill for beds for two Danish 13-inch mortars, but in the same year he had trouble over his accounts, as he could not supply vouchers for charges amounting to 61,411 pagodas, and there were other objections. He had handed over his post to Mr. Petrie in July, and a few months later the Council agreed to accept Scottney's affidavit to the validity of the charges in his accounts, unsupported by vouchers, corroborated by oath of the Commissary-General of Stores and of the conductors that the vouchers had once existed. This, they said, was on account of his upright conduct and the peculiar situation of the times. In January of the following year, however, the Council noted that Scottney had reported the finding of many of the missing vouchers.

There was considerable trouble in Madras in 1790 consequent on investigations ordered by Lord Cornwallis, the Governor-General. Mr. T. Lind was removed from the post of Military Storekeeper owing to various scandals, and a Paymaster, Mr. Willis, was found to have disbursed 21,221 pagodas for which he could not account. Willis was called upon to refund a part of the money within a month, but he absconded, and all Government could do was to file a suit against him in case he ever returned. The Military Board, as a result of the investigations, proposed that the Military Storekeeper should have a salary of 300 pagodas a month in lieu of all perquisites and that contracts should be given for all stores not made up in the arsenal. The Acting President of the Council, Mr. G. Oakley, in his minute on the subject, said the position of Military Storekeeper was extremely lucrative, as he had, besides his salary, very considerable profits from the provision of capital stores, on which he was allowed to charge 15 per cent. as commission. Mr. Oakley said further that the prime cost of these stores was not ascertained by any declaration upon honour or oath, but certain prices were fixed by different authorities, and on these the 15 per cent. was charged; moreover, there was a great probability that the Storekeeper had an advantage in the fixed prices, and Government was ignorant of his total emoluments.

There was a curious struggle in Bengal about 1779 between the Military Storekeeper, Mr. G. Livius, backed by Francis and the Commissary of Stores, Lieutenant-Colonel Green, supported by Warren Hastings. Both Livius and Green were also contractors and each made charges of fraud against the other. A survey was ordered by the Board, but both fixed locks on the storerooms. Hastings, however, ordered the Storekeeper to remove his locks, in spite of the contention of Francis that the Storekeeper was the obvious check on the Commissary. It appears that the commission on the contracts was usually 15 per cent., but was sometimes as much as 30 per cent.

In Bombay in 1743 it was ordered that, in accordance with the directions of the Court, the Paymaster was no longer to charge 10 per cent. on the stores he supplied, but it is clear that this order either disappeared or was disregarded, and we actually find in 1790 the Military Storekeeper drawing a commission of 25 per cent. on the cost of all that he obtained for the troops. The Bombay Government protested very strongly in 1793 against the orders of the Governor-General to place all military stores in the charge of a military officer in place of a civilian Military Storekeeper. They said the charge had always been held by a Member of Council, till in 1785 the number of Members was reduced and they were not permitted to hold such posts. Mr. Crokatt was then appointed, and on his succeeding to the Council, Mr. Seton was given the post at the express command of the Court. They further stated that the commission of 25 per cent. was established in July 1772 as compensation in lieu of salary, and no orders had ever been received from the Court to reduce it to 10 per cent. It must indeed have been a blow to have such a wonderfully profitable appointment abolished, still they did their best to make up for it, for though they certainly appointed a Military Commissary of Stores, they appointed Seton as Agent for Stores with a salary of Rs. 20,000 a year. Crokatt had been accused of having taken a commission of 40 per cent. on certain stores, but the Council, of which he was a Member, would not agree that he had done so. Bombay was certainly not behind any other Presidency in the feathering of civilian nests, though they did say that Seton's salary was not to form a precedent, and he was to supply such stores as were not provided by contract at the actual cost upon honour.

The fact was that the efforts of Lord Cornwallis were having effect, and the Military Storekeeper was losing his very profitable job. But the councils did not give up a good appointment readily, and each Presidency created a new appointment, as in Bombay, of an Agent for the supply of military stores; but it had to be on a fixed salary, 500 pagodas a month in Madras, Rs. 1,500 in Bengal, and Rs. 20,000 a year in Bombay (soon reduced to Rs. 10,000), with no commission, and supply to be at cost certified on honour. This appointment did not last very long, and in Bombay, on its abolition, it was noted that stores were supplied on contract at 20 per cent. less than the rates specified in the book of rates at which the Agent used to supply. Thus from the early part of the nineteenth century local stores, which were not obtainable from the Government manufactories, seem to have been mainly supplied on contracts placed and controlled by the Military Board, with much saving to the Company.

Apart from the commissions which were allowed at one time to the Agents of the Company's manufactories and to Commissaries of Stores there were many opportunities of making money open to military officers. Here are some examples. In 1778 Major C. Morgan, the Quartermaster-General in Bengal, was also the Contractor for Boats, though under the regulations of the Board of Ordnance the Quartermaster-General was to be the check over the Contractor. In Madras, in 1802, officers commanding units were granted a monthly sum for the provision of tentage and carriage, a practice which was abolished in 1808. Major M. W. Browne of the Artillery, while holding the appointment of Deputy Principal Commissary of Ordnance from

1809 to 1821, was also one of the Agents for army clothing, and only relinquished this latter appointment when the Court abolished such pluralities in 1821. At Bombay in 1812 the Adjutant-General was also the Agent for clothing the army.

# IV

# THE PRESIDENCY ORDNANCE DEPARTMENTS

EACH Presidency developed its own Ordnance Department, but there were differences in organization, in the methods of control, and in the rate of progress towards its establishment as a separate part of the Presidency Army. Besides the sources of information mentioned in the Introduction, there are two others of great value in this connexion. They are: first, the East India Registers published by authority in England, containing the civil and military lists for each Presidency; and second, the manuscript Annual Statements sent by each Presidency to the Court, containing the names, rank, position, pay, and allowances of all officers, with much other information concerning military expenditure. The earliest Registers I have seen are those for 1795, 1799, and 1804, while the earliest Annual Statements are those for 1784–5 Bengal, 1790–1 Bombay, and 1793–4 Madras. It is not always possible to reconcile Register and Statement, and the earlier ones are not very easy to follow, as an officer may often appear in more than one place.

In general, the officers employed as Commissaries and Deputy Commissaries of Stores or of Ordnance and those in charge of manufactories were drawn from the Presidency artilleries. At first the officers of the grand arsenals were called Commissaries of Stores, while those on service or at magazines 'in the field', i.e. at out-stations, were usually called Commissaries of Ordnance, though this was by no means universal. Wars were frequent from the middle of the eighteenth century, and these entailed the appointment of officers, usually taken from units of artillery not engaged, as commissaries with the forces and also the formation of magazines in existing forts for the use of the troops holding the captured territory. This explains the very large number of minor magazines or depots which were scattered over India up to well on in the nineteenth century, many of them being in the charge of conductors.

Though the term 'Ordnance Department' was often used in correspondence and also in the Annual Statements, it does not appear in the East India Registers till 1804 for Bengal and Madras, and not till 1818 for Bombay, and in the latter case only for conductors. The appointment of officers was in the hands of the Governor, but they were not for a long time in any sense permanently appointed to the Department, and they were often allowed to proceed on service with the battalion of artillery, returning later to their ordnance post. This happened also to officers in charge of manufactories.

In 1823 Bengal ordered that the Superintendent of the Gun Foundry must vacate the appointment on promotion to major-general or regimental colonel if an engineer. Agents for Gun-carriages and Gunpowder, and the Superintendent of the Gun Foundry, if artillery, must vacate on promotion to lieutenant-colonel, regimentally. Bombay made a similar order in 1834 and Madras in 1849. This system died out, however, soon after the Mutiny. Bengal, which was the first to institute a real organized department in 1818, laid down that an ordnance officer must vacate when promoted major unless he had reached the grade of Commissary; in 1806 the rule was that 'the situation of Deputy Commissary was incompatible with the rank of Captain'. Madras organized its department in 1821, with the stipulation that no officer under the rank of field officer could be appointed as Principal Commissary of Ordnance. Bombay seems to have followed the Madras practice when it appointed a Principal Commissary in 1835. The officers of ordnance continued on their regimental lists and received promotion accordingly, and could, in due course, become Commandant of the Regiment and obtain promotion to still higher rank. This meant, of course, that ordnance officers and the Agents at the manufactories remained quite definitely officers of the artillery, in close touch with their fellows and with the needs of the Army. For example, there is the case of Captain Archdale Wilson, who was Superintendent of the Gun Foundry from November 1841 till August 1845, when he vacated the post on promotion to lieutenant-colonel. He was in command of the army at the end of the siege of Delhi in 1857, and when he died was Lieutenant-General Sir Archdale Wilson, Bart., G.C.B.

The three Presidencies only came into line in 1844–5, when their Ordnance Departments were reorganized with a fixed establishment of the different grades and became known as the Ordnance Commissariat Departments. It was not, however, till the abolition of the Military Boards from 1855 to 1857 that the Presidency Ordnance Commissariat Departments were placed under the control of Inspectors-General of Ordnance and Magazines, having full powers over their departments, including the manufacturing establishments, subject only to Government and corresponding direct with the secretary to the Presidency Government in the Military Department.

The question of retirement was one of great interest to officers serving the Company; and according to Stocqueler, in *The British Officer*, published in 1851, retirement on full pay was allowed after 22 years in India, or 25 including 3 years' furlough. But pay did not include allowances, nor staff pay, and there was no provision for retirement due to the effects of the climate or of wounds, except from the Fund established by Lord Clive in 1766. This fund was started by him with a legacy of 5 lakhs of rupees left to him by the Nawab Meer Jaffer Khan, and it provided for a pension of 10 shillings a day to a lieutenant-colonel not possessed of £3,000, or 7 shillings and 6 pence to a major not possessed of £2,500, and of 5 shillings to a captain not possessed of £2,000. A widow was allowed half these rates. There was always a tendency for officers to remain in the service after they had become entitled to the pension, thus seriously blocking promotion. The Court had issued an order in 1798 making all officers about to retire on pension declare on oath that they had not received any pecuniary or other gratification or compensation for so retiring. But when officers petitioned against this in 1837, the Court said that they had not enforced the regulation for forty years, and they did not propose to interfere with the practice of inducing time-expired officers under the rank of lieutenant-colonel to retire. Buckle states that for many years the officers of the Bengal Army had procured the retirement of their seniors by the donation of a sum of money, varying in amount according to the value of the step and the abilities of the donors. He further states that in 1828 the officers of artillery established a fund by monthly contributions from all captains and subalterns to provide for two retirements annually. Both in Bombay and Madras the system of buying out senior officers obtained; for example, Brevet Lieutenant-Colonel P. Anstruther, C.B., Madras Artillery, Superintendent of the Gun-powder Manufactory, was purchased out in 1858 for Rs. 31,000.

Conductors were appointed in the early days both from the ranks of the army and from the European civilian inhabitants; later, when an organized department was formed, appointments were made, in the first instance as sub-conductors, and the entry of civilians ceased. For example, in 1783 Mr. Bartles and Mr. Hossack, with Sergeant-Majors Chapman and Dautes, were appointed conductors. Gallantry on service often led to appointment to the Ordnance Department; at the storm of Rachore in 1796, for instance, the forlorn hope was led by Conductor Lindsay, with twelve artillerymen under Sergeant-Major Murphy, and Lindsay was rewarded with a commission in the Artillery, while Murphy was appointed a Conductor of Ordnance. At the storm of Zamina in January 1805 and of Karawal in February, Corporal Cross of the Artillery was mentioned for gallantry; then, at Dalra in March, he with five other artillerymen led the sepoys to the assault. Cross was appointed to the Ordnance Department, in which he served till placed on the invalid pension establishment in 1845, when he was, after fifty-one years' meritorious service, promoted captain. He died at Penang in December 1859, aged 83—not a bad record for an artilleryman in India. Commissions in the Invalid or Veteran Corps were the usual reward for conductors, and most of the assistant and deputy assistant commissaries were officers on those establishments.

There were also park, laboratory, and magazine sergeants on the establishments of the arsenals and magazines, and usually a number of magazine and laboratory men as well, all drawn from the ranks of European units and given extra pay. Then there were also a number of men employed in the arsenal workshops and in the manufactories as foremen and superior artificers, who were also drawn from the ranks of European units. Very rarely up till the time of the Mutiny were civilians engaged as foremen.

Both in manufactories and arsenals there was a permanent establishment of native artificers and labourers, with, of course, a large number of non-permanent men, and there does not seem to have been any difficulty in obtaining the numbers required. For a long time the clerical staff was provided for by a lump-sum grant to the officer in charge which included provision for stationery also.

The Presidency Ordnance Departments remained distinct till the abolition of the separate Presidency armies, when an Indian Ordnance Department came into existence, with a Director-General of Ordnance stationed at the head-quarters of the Government of India. Major-General T. E. Hughes became the first Director-General of Ordnance on the 1st April 1884, and under him, directly administering the arsenals, depots, and factories within their Presidencies, were three Inspectors-General of Ordnance. The one for Bengal had his head-quarters at Calcutta, the one for Bombay had his at Poona, and the Madras one at Fort St. George. On the 1st February 1890 the Charge of the Inspector-

General of Ordnance at Calcutta was considered to be too large and it was split into two, with two Inspectors-General, one having his head-quarters at Rawal Pindi. In 1894 the establishment of the Indian Ordnance Department was:

1 Director-General of Ordnance.
4 Inspectors-General of Ordnance.
1 Deputy Director-General of Ordnance.
4 Assistant Inspectors-General of Ordnance.
5 1st Class Ordnance Officers.
7 2nd ,, ,, ,,
10 3rd ,, ,, ,,
13 4th ,, ,, ,,
(Ten of these two latter classes were Assistant Superintendents of Factories.)
9 Superintendents of Factories.

# V

## THE BENGAL ORDNANCE DEPARTMENT

It is not easy to fix any date for the beginning of the Indian Ordnance Department, but Bengal seems to have taken the lead, and possibly 1765 may be taken as the year in which the first attempt at any definite organization was made. In that year Lord Clive reorganized the Army in Bengal and he established a depot at the head-quarters of each brigade in the field, in charge of a deputy commissary, with two conductors, under the orders of the officer commanding the artillery with the brigade. The deputy commissary, who was not a commissioned officer, and the two conductors were a part of the staff of the artillery company. These depots at Monghyr, Allahabad, and Bankipore contained the equipment of the trains of artillery, but, according to Stubbs, they could not be regarded as proper magazines.

The establishment of a grand arsenal, as for many years it was called, was obviously a great step forward. In India the term 'arsenal' has always been used for a main place of storage for military equipment. It received stores from England and from local manufacture or purchase, it had work-shops for repairs and laboratories for making up ammunition, and it distributed equipment to the troops. Usually magazines for the storage of gunpowder were attached to it, though not always under the same control. A military officer, called at first a Commissary or Commissary-General of Stores, was in charge with a staff of deputy commissaries, conductors, and others. The grand arsenal at Fort William was in use in 1769, when Major Du Gloss was Commissary of Stores, and Warren Hastings is said to have had the armoury rearranged in 1777. Fort William itself was begun in 1757, but was not completed till 1781, at a cost, so Lord Curzon states, of nearly two millions sterling.

It will be convenient to deal at some length with the evolution of the Bengal Ordnance Department, leaving the other Presidencies to be taken up more briefly later. Bengal was fast becoming the most important of the three Presidencies, and progress usually lagged a bit in Madras and Bombay, owing partly, no doubt, to the location of the Governor-General at Calcutta.

The organization based on General Clavering's minute of March 1775 established magazines at the fixed stations of Berhampore, Dinapore, and Chunar Ghur, each with a commissary of ordnance, a deputy commissary, and two conductors, and provided that this staff were to be appointed and paid by the Board of Ordnance, and were to receive all instructions from the Board, but that, under the general regulations of the army, they would be subordinate to the commanding officer at the station, and be under the immediate control of the commanding officer of the artillery. It is evident that for many years the commanding officers of artillery had considerable authority over the magazines. For example, an order was issued in 1790 to the effect that commissaries and deputy commissaries of ordnance at the magazines were to perform the business of making up stores and ammunition, and all laboratory work, under the direction of the commanding officers of artillery at their respective stations. The grand arsenal was much more directly under the control of the Board.

The deputy commissaries and conductors were not borne on the rolls of the artillery companies for long, and it is evident that the deputy commissaries appointed by Lord Clive and the commissaries and deputies appointed under General Clavering's proposals were civilians, not belonging to the covenanted service, for in 1782 the Court wrote expressing disapproval of Europeans being appointed to posts which could be filled by covenanted servants or military officers, of whom there were a number unemployed. In consequence of this the Council ruled that persons not in the Service holding the posts of commissaries or deputy commissaries of ordnance must be removed, and further decided in August 1783 that commissaries of ordnance must in future be artillery officers.

The Board of Ordnance then annulled the appointments of four commissaries and three deputy commissaries, all civilians except one lieutenant of infantry, and they fixed the new establishment at:

Berhampore—Deputy Commissary Mr. R. Copplestone and 2 conductors.

Patna—Commissary Lieutenant R. Sands, Artillery, Deputy Commissary Mr. J. McCabe, and 2 conductors.

Buxar—One conductor.

Chunar Ghur—Commissary Captain V. W. Hussey, Artillery, Deputy Commissary Mr. J. Roquier, and 3 conductors.

Cawnpore—Commissary Lieutenant J. Burnett, Artillery, Deputy Commissary Mr. W. Bartles, and 2 conductors.

Futty Ghur—Commissary Lieutenant A. Robertson, Artillery, and 2 conductors.

Midnapore—Deputy Commissary Mr. D. Baker and 1 conductor.

In addition there was at the Expense magazine at Calcutta Deputy Commissary Mr. G. Shaw with three conductors, while four conductors were allowed for the grand arsenal under Lieutenant-Colonel P. Duff, the Commissary of Stores.

Then in 1785 came one of the recurrent calls for economy in military expenditure, and the number of commissaries of ordnance was reduced to 2 with 4 deputies. However, by 1790 there were 7 deputy commissaries and there were 19 conductors. In 1799 the numbers had again increased, and there were 3 commissaries at Chunar, Cawnpore, and the Expense magazine, 8 deputy commissaries at Midnapore, Monghyr, Berhampore, Futtyghur, Fort Marlborough,[1]

[1] Fort Marlborough was in Sumatra. In 1684 the Company established a settlement at Bencoolen, and built a fort called York. In 1714 this was removed to a

Buxar, Chunar, and Dinajpur, while there were 23 conductors. In 1804 we find the Ordnance Department as a separate heading in the Register, but the numbers were 3 commissaries, all artillery, with 7 deputies, 1 being artillery. In November 1810 Lieutenant-Colonel H. Grace went to Cawnpore to command the artillery in the field, and he started at once to improve the condition and working of the magazines, which were left, it was stated, too much under the control of the warrant officers and sergeants of the department for lack of sufficient officers.

The first real organization came in 1818, when a General Order was issued dated the 19th of May, directing the organization of the Ordnance Department on the lines of that of the Commissariat Department. It was called the Ordnance Department of the General Staff, and the establishment was to be:

1 Principal Commissary of Ordnance for the Chief Arsenal with a salary of Rs. 1,200 a month.

1 Deputy Principal Commissary of Ordnance for the Chief Arsenal, salary Rs. 600 a month.

6 Commissaries of Ordnance—Agra, Allahabad, Cawnpore, Delhi, Fort William with Dum Dum, Nerbudda Field Force; 3 on a salary of Rs. 500 and 3 on Rs. 400.

6 Deputy Commissaries, 3 being commissioned officers at Rs. 250, for the Army in Rajputana, Penang, and Chunar; 3 warrant officers at Rs. 250 with full pay, batta, and house-rent of a lieutenant.

3 Assistant and 3 Deputy Assistant Commissaries at Rs. 200 and Rs. 120, plus pay, batta, and rent of an ensign.

more healthy site and renamed Fort Marlborough. From 1703 to 1785 it was a Presidency under a Governor and Council, but in 1785 it was reduced to a Residency under the Presidency of Fort William, in Bengal. It was handed over in 1825 to the Dutch in exchange for Malacca. It cannot have been much of a fort, as in May 1773 Major M. Johnston, writing to the Court, headed his letter—'Marlbro' Village, for fort there is not the least vestige of'. He wrote to call attention to the entirely defenceless condition of the settlement, and also to complain of the want of courtesy shown by the civil servants to the military officers.

The commissioned officers were to have as usual the pay, full batta, gratuity, and house-rent of their regimental rank. They were eligible for appointment to the department after five years' service in the artillery, to begin as deputy commissaries, and they would have to vacate on promotion to major if they had not reached the grade of commissary. This organization ended the separate position of the arsenal at Fort William, the Commissary of Stores becoming the Principal Commissary of Ordnance, a post to be held by the senior in the department, but it did not carry with it any direct control over the department, which still remained with the Military Board.

In 1824 there was a revision of the establishments of the magazines, mainly in an increase of European and Indian artificers with a decrease in the numbers of lascars and magazine men. But the Court were asked to approve the appointment of an Inspector of Ordnance with general supervision and control over the Ordnance Department, as had once before been recommended by the Military Board. In 1827 the Court approved the revision of establishments and also the proposed new appointment, but the appointment was not made, and in January 1830 the Court were informed that, considering the heavy expense of the department, it was not thought expedient to make it. It was at this time that Lord William Bentinck was reducing military expenditure, wherever he found it to be possible. It was thought that frequent inspection of magazines by commandants of stations accompanied by the senior officer of artillery, as well as by occasional committees of survey, would answer the purpose equally well.

It was not till the end of 1844 that Major Delafosse was appointed Principal Commissary of Ordnance and Inspector and was relieved of the executive duties of the Fort William arsenal, which were to devolve on the Deputy Principal Commissary of Ordnance. Major Delafosse was to be stationed at Allahabad and to exercise control over the department from there; but it is evident that his control was limited to inspection and report. The designation of the department was, at the same time, changed to Ordnance Commissariat Department, and its establishment consisted of the Principal Commissary and Inspector, 6 commissaries, 5 deputy commissaries (2 being warrant officers), 5 assistant commissaries, and 2 deputy assistant commissaries, with 40 conductors.

The final step was taken when the following order was issued by the Governor-General on the 9th February 1855:

'. . . the Military Board to be relieved from the Superintendence of the Ordnance Commissariat Department from the 30th April, 1855, and that Department to be placed under the direct control of an officer to be designated the Inspector General of Ordnance and Magazines, on whom is to devolve all the duties of the Military Board, except the duties of Audit which are to be taken over by the Military Auditor General.'

Lieutenant-Colonel A. Abbott, the Principal Commissary of Ordnance, was appointed Inspector-General from the 1st May, and the establishment of commissioned officers was fixed at 1 Principal Commissary of Ordnance (the former Deputy), 6 commissaries, and 4 deputy commissaries. The head-quarters of the Inspector-General were to be in Fort William.

We must now go back to the early days of the grand arsenal at Fort William and extract some items of interest from the records. In 1784 Lieutenant-Colonel P. Duff of the Artillery was Commissary of Stores, and, in addition to the establishment of the foundry (see Chapter XIII), he had 4 European masters—carpenter, gunsmith, painter, and cooper—each at Rs. 50 a month, 453 men of various trades, 424 lascars, and 2 native doctors. In 1788 the Commissary of Stores was Major C. R. Deare, Artillery, and he had an assistant commissary, 4 conductors, 3 park and laboratory sergeants, 6 European laboratory men, 2 European smiths, 1 carpenter, and 1 cooper. Of Indians he had 5 coopers, 53 smiths, 65 carpenters, 13 sawyers, 11 painters, 22 brassmen, 204 sicklegars (polishers or cleaners of small arms), 11 sail-makers, 32 armourers, 13 chucklers (leather-workers), 344 magazine men, and the foundry establishment. In 1790 Lieutenant-Colonel Deare gave over charge temporarily of the arsenal to Lieutenant Humphries, the secretary to the Military Board, and took command of his battalion of artillery for service in the second Mysore War; but he was killed on the 13th September 1791 at Sattimungalum.

The idea that no one in the Army could do his duty unless he was in an expensive and uncomfortable fancy dress was as firmly fixed in the minds of the military authorities of the Company as it has ever been since their day. In 1787 European overseers in Fort William had to be clothed in green, with red facings and white lace, and they had to wear this uniform at all times. What a dress for the foundry over-seer in a Calcutta hot weather! In 1789 orders were issued that deputy commissaries, not being commissioned officers, were to wear a long plain blue frock coat with capes, round cuffs, and facings of the same colour, and plain gilt buttons, four on the cuffs and ten on each lappel. Conductors were to have the same but without lappels. These 1789 orders were cancelled by a G.O.C.C. of the 18th June 1814, which laid down that conductors must wear a plain blue frock coat without lappel, but with scarlet cuffs and collar, yellow ordnance buttons, ten at equal distance at the breast, sleeves and skirts slashed, one button on the cuff and one on the sleeve, a plain embroidered buttonhole on cuff and collar, but without skirt ornaments. The deputy commissary, not being a commissioned officer, to have the same coat, except that the buttons at the breast to be by twos, and two instead of one on the sleeve and skirt, with the addition of a plain gold epaulette and suitable skirt ornaments. Both conductor and deputy commissary to wear a plain cocked hat and black feather, with regulation sword. In 1787 Lord Cornwallis insisted on the wearing of uniform on all occasions.

Early in March 1789 there was a very serious fire in the arsenal at Fort William. It started in some workshops which had upper stories used as store-rooms. All the camp equipment, several thousand stands of arms, and a number of gun-carriages were destroyed; more than 200 carriages were saved. Colonel Pearse, the Commandant of Artillery, in a report on the occurrence, not only pointed out the danger of combining workshops and store-rooms, but mentioned the fact that the arsenal was full of dwelling-houses. He proposed that the Water Gate of the Fort should be allotted to the Commissary of Stores, with some addition, in lieu of his apartments within the arsenal. I do not know if this suggestion was acted on then, but the Water Gate contained the quarters of the Ordnance officer in charge of the arsenal in 1908, and had certainly been his residence for many years.

From 1770 till the post was changed to that of Principal Commissary of Ordnance, the Commissary of Stores was usually a senior major or a lieutenant-colonel of the Bengal Artillery, but from 1792 till 1807 the appointment was held by a lieutenant of the Bengal Engineers. From 1792 to 1796 Lieutenant W. Golding was Commissary, and received batta Rs. 120, gratuity Rs. 24, pay Rs. 93, with an established allowance of Rs. 1,336. Lieutenant T. Anbury succeeded when Golding died, and became eventually a major-general and K.C.B., dying at Saugor in March 1840.

A very serious fire was discovered in the arsenal on 25 July 1832, about half an hour after it was closed. It broke out in two separate godowns separated by a brick wall, in charge of two different conductors. A Committee of Inquiry, by a majority, considered it to be the work of incendiaries, but the cause was never discovered. The loss of stores was estimated at sicca Rs. 8,56,613–11–4½. The Council at its first consultation on the matter directed a letter of thanks to be sent to Captain Young of the ship *Fergusson* for the voluntary assistance of himself and his crew in fighting the fire, and as a token of appreciation presented him with a piece of plate and Rs. 1,000 for distribution to his crew. Colonel G. Swiney was the Principal Commissary of Ordnance at this time, and Major R. Powney was town and fort major and was specially mentioned for his exertions on this occasion.

On the night of 24 July 1839 an attempt to set fire to the arsenal was discovered, and investigation showed that several of the native workmen came under strong suspicion, and though no legal proof could be obtained they were dismissed; they included the men of the lascar guard and the Sicklegar mistry who were on duty that night. The investigations were held to show that sufficient precautions for the safety of the arsenal had not been enforced. The Committee of Inquiry did not attach blame to the Principal Commissary of Ordnance, Lieutenant-Colonel R. Powney, for the defects, as the system, such as it was, had been of long standing. The Court, however, did not agree, and considered Colonel Powney to blame for not having inquired into the arrangements of the office for which he was responsible, and held him to be liable to censure. They sent out a copy of the rules in force at the Royal Arsenal at Woolwich for instruction.

In the *Handbook of India*, published by Stocqueler in 1844, there is some account of the Fort William arsenal. It states that the armoury usually contained 60,000 stands of arms and 20,000 swords. It had a workyard with 30 forges constantly at work, a grand magazine entirely for small-arm ammunition, containing ready made 1,200,000 rounds, while the ordnance yards usually contained between 3,000 and 4,000 pieces of brass and iron ordnance, independent of those mounted on the works, which were 619, from 12 to 32-pounders. Shot and shell were seldom below 1,800,000, ready prepared, exclusive of more than 14,000,000 loose shot for grape and canister. The principal magazines for gunpowder were at Duckinsore and Pultah.

When the Mutiny broke out in May 1857 the Bengal Ordnance Department had magazines or depots at Allahabad, Agra, Ferozepore, Delhi, Multan, Peshawur, Saugor,

Lahore, Jhelum, Cawnpore, Phillour, Pegu, and Rangoon. Those at Allahabad, Saugor, Delhi, Multan, and Phillour were guarded solely by native troops, and at most of the others the actual guard was native, though British troops were in garrison. Delhi and Cawnpore were captured by the Mutineers, but the others were saved, in some cases with difficulty.

At Delhi the Ordnance Depot contained only a small magazine, the main one being at the farther end of the cantonments. Lieutenant G. D. Willoughby of the Bengal Artillery was the Deputy Commissary in charge of the depot, and he had under him Lieutenants G. Forrest and W. Raynor, with Conductors J. Buckley, G. W. Shaw, and J. Scully, Sub-Conductor Crowe, and Sergeants Edwards and Stewart. When the outbreak occurred guns were prepared and a train laid to the magazine, the native establishment fled or assisted the assailants, two of the small band were killed, so Willoughby gave the signal to Scully, who had volunteered for the duty, and the train was fired by a portfire. The destruction among the assailants was very great, but only Willoughby, Forrest, Raynor, and Buckley managed to escape. All four were recommended for the Victoria Cross, Forrest and Raynor were promoted to the rank of captain, and Buckley was given a commission as lieutenant. Willoughby was murdered a few days later on the road to Meerut. Phillour was secured by a company of British troops from Jullundur. The Lahore fort, with its magazine, was nearly lost, but was saved by strong measures. Saugor and Multan were saved without much trouble. At Ferozepore a company of British infantry ejected the native guard, but had then to repulse an attack by the native regiment. At Allahabad the situation was for a time most critical, and the arsenal and magazine were of the greatest importance. So critical was the position that Lieutenant W. C. Russell of the Bengal Artillery, the Commissary of Ordnance, laid a train to the principal magazine. The fort was saved, however, by the expulsion of the native infantry company by Lieutenant J. Brasyer with his company of Sikhs. Brasyer had received his commission from the ranks of the Bengal Artillery. Allahabad was soon after made secure by the arrival of Colonel Neill.

Cawnpore had a magazine full of guns, stores, and ammunition, which were in a large walled enclosure, near the river, and which could have been made impregnable against native attack. Unfortunately General Wheeler would not use it, as there was a native guard on it, which he did not like to remove. The Assistant Commissary of Ordnance in charge, Lieutenant Reilly, was ordered to blow up the magazine at the last, but was unable to do so by himself and perished.

One curious incident should be mentioned. Lieutenant-Colonel F. R. Bazely, Principal Commissary of Ordnance, who had gone home in May 1856 on sick leave, returned and went to Cawnpore in September 1857, just before the advance on Lucknow, which he was allowed to accompany as a volunteer. He was killed in the assault on the 25th, his body being found a few days later not more than 300 yards from the Baillie guard gate.

# VI

# THE MADRAS ORDNANCE DEPARTMENT

THE arsenal at Fort St. George was begun in 1770 on the site of the Artillery Park, in the south-west angle of the fort; it was designed by Colonel P. Ross, Chief Engineer, and was built under contract by Mr. J. Sullivan, who had arrived in Madras in June 1765 as a Writer at the age of 17. The estimated cost was 28,000 pagodas, and it was completed in November 1772. Madras sought the help of Bengal in arranging the store-rooms, and Major John Green, Bengal Artillery, went there early in 1771 for the purpose, but in April he wrote to Government to say that he could do nothing till the arsenal and other buildings were completed and fit for the reception of arms and military stores, so he was returning to Bengal by the first ship; Green was later the Commissary of Stores at the Fort William arsenal.

A Commissary-General, or, as later he was called, a Commissary of Stores, was in charge of the arsenal, but all stores procurable by manufacture or purchase were supplied by the Military Storekeeper. In 1786 Lieutenant-Colonel J. Moorhouse, Artillery, was Commissary-General of Stores, with a seat on the Military Board, till he went on service with his battalion and was killed at the siege of Bangalore in March 1791. The establishment of the Fort St. George arsenal in 1794, under Major G. Hall, Artillery, Commissary-General of Stores, consisted of two deputy commissaries —Lieutenant J. G. Scott, Artillery, and Mr. B. Bishop— four conductors, four sergeants, and one matross. At the magazine at Trichinopoly there was a Commissary and a Deputy Commissary of Stores. There were also magazines at Vellore, Tanjore, Masulipatam, Kistnagherry, and Vizagapatam, each with a lieutenant of artillery as Inspector of Stores. Supply at Fort St. George was under Mr. J. Du

Pré Porcher, Military Storekeeper, with a salary of 500 pagodas a month.

In 1799, besides the arsenal at Fort St. George with a commissary and a deputy, there were considerable magazines at Trichinopoly and Amboina, each with a commissary. There were other magazines at Vellore, Kistnagherry, Vizagapatam, Ganjam, Chittledroog, and Malacca, each under a deputy commissary. In addition there were no less than seventeen minor magazines mostly under a conductor, owing to the extensive operations being undertaken in Mysore.

A dreadful scandal occurred in Seringapatam in 1801 in the Ordnance Department. In June Sir Arthur Wellesley wrote a dispatch in which he said he was much taken up with an inquiry into complaints about the Store Department. He said one colonel had taken saltpetre from the godown and sold it at his house, the Commissary had been guilty of false musters, and he wrote, 'You cannot conceive what a scene of villainy has come out.' Further, he said that the Dubash had come forward with a general confession of all the villainies in the Store Department since the capture of Seringapatam. A third officer was found to have known of the robberies and to have participated in them. As a result two lieutenant-colonels and one captain-lieutenant of the Madras Artillery were dismissed by sentence of General Courts Martial in September and October 1801. In the *Memoirs of George Elers*, the author says that the three officers were tried for 'peculation and defrauding the Company at the Arsenal of bell metal &c., to a large amount, Colonel Wellesley prosecuting them'. He also adds a bit of scandal: he says 'F' was appointed in place of one of the dismissed officers, 'bringing a very young and rather pretty wife' to whom 'Colonel Wellesley, who had then a very susceptible heart, paid pointed attention, which gave offence to his A.D.C. but not to her husband'. This sorry case of fraud shows that the corruption of the eighteenth century was dying hard.

In 1811 all the store lascars were formed into 32 companies, each consisting of 1 Syrang, 2 Tindals, and 50 lascars; 3 of the companies being allotted to the gun-carriage manufactory at Seringapatam. The number of commissaries and of other grades varied from time to time, and in 1819 there were 11 commissaries; but a definite organization on the lines of that established in Bengal in 1818 was instituted in 1821. A Principal Commissary of Ordnance was appointed for the Fort St. George arsenal, with 7 commissaries for Fort St. George, Secunderabad, Nagpore, Masulipatam, Bellary, Seringapatam, and St. Thomas's Mount. There were also 3 deputy commissaries, officers, at Jaulna, Vellore, and Trichinopoly, with 3 more, warrant officers, at Cannanore, Bangalore, and Quillon. The establishment also included 3 assistant and 3 deputy assistant commissaries, warrant officers. Artillery officers were eligible for appointment to the department after 3 years' service, all vacancies being filled by Government by selection. The staff allowances were fixed at Rs. 1,050 for the Principal Commissary, Rs. 450 for the 4 senior commissaries, Rs. 350 for the 3 juniors, Rs. 250 for a deputy commissary, Rs. 200 for an assistant, and Rs. 150 for a deputy assistant commissary. It will be noted that, as usual in India at that time, the conditions and rates of salary were not the same as in Bengal.

From January 1831 to September 1840, as a measure of economy, the Principal Commissary of Ordnance was also Superintendent of the gun-carriage manufactory, drawing the staff salary of the latter only, viz. Rs. 1,400 a month. He had a Deputy Principal Commissary of Ordnance who was also Deputy Superintendent, who received a salary of Rs. 700 a month out of the former salary, Rs. 1,050, of the Principal Commissary. Another economy had been effected in 1832, when the armoury of the Fort St. George arsenal was fitted with glass windows, allowing the discharge of 50 out of the 150 Chickledars (same as Sicklegar in Bengal), employed on keeping the arms clean.

The next reorganization was effected in 1845, when the

department became the Ordnance Commissariat Department, with an establishment of a Principal Commissary of Ordnance on a staff salary of Rs. 1,000 (fixed in 1838); 6 commissaries at Masulipatam, Trichinopoly, Hyderabad, Fort St. George, Bangalore, and the Nagpore Field Force; 5 deputy commissaries for Vellore, Cannanore, Bellary, Tenasserim, and Penang; 1 assistant and 4 deputy assistant commissaries, and 30 conductors. The arsenal at Fort St. George had then an establishment consisting of the principal commissary, a commissary and a deputy assistant commissary, 10 conductors, 14 sub-conductors, 13 store sergeants, 1 laboratory sergeant, and 1 laboratory corporal. It had also 422 lascars and 146 workmen.

In Madras, as in Bombay, the commanding officers of artillery had powers over the Ordnance Department; in the field the Ordnance establishments were under the 'superintending control' of the senior officer of artillery, while in cantonments he could not issue any orders to the commissary, but was able to visit the arsenal or magazine at any time and to call for information, and was to report anything amiss. These regulations were modified in 1851, when all officers in charge of arsenals, magazines, and ordnance depots at outstations were placed in direct communication with the principal commissary on all matters connected with making, storing, and issue. It was not, however, till the abolition of the Military Board and the appointment of an Inspector-General of Ordnance and Magazines, which had effect from 1st May 1857, that the department became independent and was administered by a head having full authority and responsibility.

Madras in those days had the greatest number of ordnance establishments of any Presidency, a great contrast with the present day. Even in 1853 there were magazines or ordnance depots at Bangalore, Masulipatam, Nagpore, Saugor, Bellary, Cannanore, Penang, Moulmein, Malacca, Singapore, Palamcotta, Secunderabad, Trichinopoly, Vizagapatam, and Vellore, besides the grand arsenal at Fort St. George.

# VII

## THE BOMBAY ORDNANCE DEPARTMENT

In September 1779, when Bombay established a Board of Ordnance, Lieutenant D. Carpenter of the Infantry was appointed Commissary of Stores on an allowance of Rs. 4 per day. It is evident, however, that he was merely an executive officer of the Board for the purpose of receiving indents from the quartermasters of corps and preparing from them a general monthly indent on the Military Storekeeper, who was still the equivalent of an ordnance officer.

In 1790 at Bombay there was a Military Storekeeper, Mr. D. Crokatt, drawing a commission of 25 per cent. on the cost of all stores he supplied, with an assistant on Rs. 30 a month, and a European establishment at the Military Store Depot, consisting of 2 overseers, a master smith, a master carpenter, and a master cooper. There was also at Bombay a lieutenant of Infantry, successor to Carpenter, as Commissary of Stores. Then there were Military Storekeepers at Tellicherry, Tannah, and Surat, all civilians, drawing a commission of 25 per cent. and having a small European staff. On service with the Southern Army there was a Commissary of Ordnance, Major R. Jones, Artillery, with an allowance of Rs. 984, a deputy commissary, Captain J. Hawkes, Artillery, and 3 conductors.

In July 1793 an advertisement was published that the Honourable President in Council, 'having determined to fit up the different Apartments in the Castle for a general Arsenal and to build such new ones as are deemed necessary', called for proposals for contracts. The arsenal was completed in March 1794 at a cost of Rs. 44,673. It is clear that this action was taken as a result of orders from the Governor-General that military stores must be placed in charge of a military officer. Captain J. Hawkes, Artillery, was appointed

Commissary of Stores at the arsenal, with a salary of Rs. 700 a month, from 1st July 1793, and Lieutenant W. Abernethy was made his deputy on Rs. 300. The salaries were later reduced to Rs. 600 and Rs. 200. At the same time as those appointments were made the posts of Director and Sub-Director of the Laboratory were abolished, and the appointment of Commissary of Arms and Accoutrements was discontinued.

The establishment then fixed was: Department of Ordnance and Stores at the Presidency, a commissary and a deputy commissary of stores, a deputy commissary for the laboratory and the expense magazine, 2 conductors, 3 laboratory and magazine sergeants, 4 laboratory men, 1 European carpenter, 1 European smith, with 200 Indians. There was also for Cannanore, which was called the Grand Magazine for the Coast, a deputy commissary with a conductor, a magazine sergeant, 2 laboratory men, and 60 Indians. The magazines at Calicut and Surat had each a deputy commissary. But in addition to the staff shown under Ordnance and Stores there were covenanted civilians who retained the profitable work of the supply of stores. At Bombay there was Mr. Seton, shown as Military Store Agent on a salary of Rs. 1,666 a month, while at Cannanore, Calicut, and Surat there were Commissaries of Supplies who received Rs. 100 or Rs. 50 as pay plus 10 per cent. on the cost of all stores they supplied, and they drew, in addition, the pay and allowances of their civil standing. The deputy commissaries at these magazines were all lieutenants, and received a staff salary of Rs. 150 a month. There were also minor magazines at Tellicherry, subordinate to Cannanore, at Palaghat under Calicut, and at Tannah, each in charge of a conductor.

In February 1797 it was ordered that the general arsenal was to consist of two branches: (1) Ordnance and Laboratory Branch; (2) Military Store Branch. The first was to include all that was formerly under the Commandant of Artillery and the Director of the Laboratory, i.e. guns, shot, shell, laboratory, gunpowder, magazine, ammunition, &c.;

the second, all that was formerly under the Military Storekeeper, viz. armoury, accoutrements, camp equipment, &c. The Commissary was to report each morning on (1) to the Commandant of Artillery, and on (2) to the Quartermaster-General. It was also laid down that Commissaries of Ordnance in the field were to be concerned only with receipt and issue and to have no interest directly or indirectly with the supply of stores. Major Jeremiah Hawkes, the first Commissary of the Bombay arsenal, met his death in March 1800 in a curious manner. He was crossing an arm of the sea near Bombay in his palanquin, when the bearers became frightened at the rising tide and dropped the palanquin. Though Major Hawkes was a good swimmer, he was overpowered by the tide and unfortunately drowned.

In 1798 the official list for the Bombay arsenal shows two divisions: Receipt and Issue Branch, and Supply Branch. In the latter there was a civilian Agent of Stores, John Morris, on a salary of Rs. 833 a month, with an office establishment of 15, costing Rs. 274. In the Receipt and Issue Branch there was a Commissary of Stores, salary Rs. 600, 2 deputy commissaries on Rs. 200 each, 4 conductors at Rs. 50 plus house-rent of Rs. 10, 3 sergeants on Rs. 20 plus Rs. 4 rent, 10 laboratory men on Rs. 6 plus Rs. 4 rent, also 70 permanent artificers costing Rs. 619 a month. There were 3 companies of store lascars each having a Syrang at Rs. 13, 4 Tindals at Rs. 9, and 70 lascars each Rs. 5–3–60. Rs. 286 a month was allowed for writers, peons, lights, and stationery. Twenty gallons of arrack were allowed each month for the Europeans employed in the magazine at a cost of Rs. 40. By October 1799, however, the Supply Branch had disappeared, and stores were supplied on contract at 20 per cent. less than the rates specified in the book of rates at which the Agent used to supply.

While the Department of Ordnance was referred to in correspondence, there was no mention of it in the printed registers till 1830, though from 1818 there was a list of conductors under such a heading, officers being shown in the Artillery list. In October 1830 the Governor noted that the principal arsenals were Bombay, Bhooj, Surat, Baroda, Poonah, Sevendroog, with sub-depots. He proposed Bombay, Ahmedabad, Ahmednugger, and Belgaum, the latter having been recently transferred from the Madras Presidency. The establishment to be, for Bombay, 1 commissary and 2 deputy commissaries, 3 commissaries and 2 deputy commissaries being allowed for the other three. The salary of the Commissary at Bombay had some years previously been raised to Rs. 833–5–3 a month, but the Governor now proposed to make it Rs. 1,000 and to make other alterations in rates. The Governor-General, however, did not approve of several of the proposals, including the increase in salaries, and he especially disapproved of the companies of store lascars. He could not understand the use of a company to the gun-carriage manufactory, and he said there were no such men in the Bengal magazines, where the work was done by men on Rs. 6 a month with a Sirdar on Rs. 12 for each 10 men; moreover, neither clothing nor pensions were allowed in Bengal to such men. The action taken by the Governor did mean, however, the definite appearance of the Bombay Ordnance Department, with an establishment of a senior commissary at the Presidency, 3 commissaries for Ahmedabad, Belgaum, and Poonah, 4 deputy commissaries, 2 for Bombay and the others for Ahmednugger and Surat. There were also 3 deputy assistant commissaries and 17 conductors.

It has been shown in Chapter II how the Bombay Government in 1830 suspended the Military Board and placed the Ordnance Department and the manufactories under the control of the Commandant of Artillery, but had to re-establish the Board in 1840. The Commandant seems to have been most unwilling to relinquish his authority over the department, but eventually orders were issued defining the situation. In February 1844 commanding officers of artillery were authorized to inspect arsenals and depots within their area and to report the result to the Military Board, but it was stressed that commissaries were responsible to the Board, and the commanding officers of Artillery while 'possessing powers of inspection had none of interference'. It seems a somewhat difficult position for the ordnance officer, but was probably not so bad as it appears, for the officers of the Ordnance Department were artillery officers and were not removed from the Regiment, frequently becoming themselves, in due course, commanding officers.

In 1845 a further step in reorganization was taken, the department becoming the Ordnance Commissariat Department on much the same lines as in Bengal and Madras. It was given an establishment of a Principal Commissary of Ordnance, 3 commissaries, 3 deputy commissaries, 1 deputy assistant commissary, all being officers; also 2 deputy assistant commissaries, warrant officers, and 19 conductors. Bombay Arsenal had the Principal Commissary, 2 deputy and 2 deputy assistant commissaries, 10 conductors, 7 sub-conductors, 5 store sergeants; also 4 artificer sergeants—painter, turner, armourer, and saddler, 3 gunners, and 4 laboratory men. The Principal Commissary and his deputies were each given a conveyance allowance of Rs. 60 a month.

The final step was taken in 1856, when the Military Board was abolished and an Inspector-General of Ordnance and Magazines, Major-General F. P. Lester, was appointed by G.O. dated 28th August 1856. He was to correspond direct with the secretary to Government in the Military and Marine Department. Audit was to be in the province of the Military Auditor-General, with an artillery officer of not less than ten years' service as Ordnance Assistant. The salary of the Inspector-General was fixed at Rs. 1,600 a month consolidated, with the pay proper of his rank. The Ordnance Assistant was to have Rs. 350, plus pay, garrison allowances, and Presidency house-rent.

# VIII

## GUNPOWDER MANUFACTURE IN ENGLAND AND INDIA

THE East India Company in its early days had little interest in munitions of war, except for the equipment of its ships, though it exported weapons, powder, and shot for purposes of trade, and sometimes as presents for eastern potentates, while small quantities went to India for the personal use of its servants. Gunpowder was usually bought from the King's Powder Maker, the price in 1600 being eightpence a pound, but supplies from this source ceased when King James wanted all he could get for his war with Spain. India was, however, rapidly becoming the chief supplier of saltpetre, for which the King was almost the only customer, at his own price; so as an encouragement the Company was granted a licence in 1626 to make powder for its own use. They erected mills at Egham, near Windsor, in spite of opposition from Evelyn, the King's Powder Maker, but they soon had to close those mills, as King Charles complained that they disturbed the royal deer.

The company then rented mills at Chilworth, near Guildford, and appointed Edmund Collins, a survivor of the Amboyna massacre, to be their Powder Maker. Evelyn, however, continued his opposition and obtained an interdict, but by July 1635 Collins was making powder not only for the Company but for the King also. Then came trouble over the lease, and, Collins dying in the middle of 1636, the Company became anxious to get rid of the business, so in February of the following year they assigned the lease to one Cordell, who had a contract with the King, and thus relinquished their attempts to make gunpowder in England.

They had then to depend on Evelyn for their supplies, or they had to buy them, as they sometimes did, from the

Continent. They had purchased some in Danzig in 1626, but unfortunately the troops of the King of Denmark seized their store, and the Court of Directors bewailed a loss of £161 and the stoppage of supplies. The Company must have heard from their factors in India that gunpowder was being manufactured in, and could be purchased in, that country, so their disappointment at their failure to establish mills of their own in England would naturally turn their thoughts to the encouragement of manufacture in their settlements abroad.

Gunpowder was certainly made in India early in the seventeenth century, as all the materials were easily procurable, and powder, of a kind, was not difficult to make. It required no elaborate plant, nor any great skill, and, in many of the Indian armies, powder workers were among the camp followers, while women often made powder for their men's matchlocks. The ordinary country hand flour-mill was used for grinding the ingredients, and, so long as the powder was quickly used, which in those days of constant warfare it would be, lack of proper refining or of expert manipulation did not greatly matter.

Gunpowder was being manufactured at Masulipatam, on the Coromandel Coast, about 1610, saltpetre and charcoal being obtainable locally, while sulphur came from Sumatra. The Dutch were making it at Pulicat, their earliest settlement in India, which dated from 1609, and from thence it was distributed to their other factories. There is a record, dated in 1660, of the British factors at Surat buying gunpowder from Calicut, as they found it to be very dear in Surat, where there was only one man who made and sold it.

In all three Presidencies, sooner or later, manufacture of gunpowder by or for the Company was established in some form or other. Mills were set up either by the local Council or by their servants acting as contractors. The buildings, plant, and methods were for a long time of the crudest description, copied from those of the native powder makers. Mat, or as they were usually called straw, sheds were the buildings, grinding was done by hand with wooden pestles and mortars, and the ingredients were sifted in leather sieves. The workers were mainly quite unskilled and were mostly women and boys, sometimes pressed into the service, and they invariably bolted after an explosion—and explosions were not infrequent. The overseer was an Indian powder maker, though there was usually some European supervision, but only to keep the work going; and whoever might be in charge, whether contractor or manager, profit, not always legitimate, was his main object. Cheapness seems to have been the aim of the Council, and to its members and to its servants powder seems to have been powder, however made and of whatsoever quality it might be. Certainly up to the latter part of the eighteenth century the business of providing gunpowder for the Company's forces was conducted in the most haphazard manner, with the natural result of indifferent quality and sometimes of excessive cost.

In England matters seem to have been little if any better. Fortescue says that 'Mr. Walton's Powder Mills at Waltham were purchased in 1787 by the nation for the manufacture of its own gunpowder. Mills at Faversham had been bought for the same purpose in 1759, but had been little used, as throughout the American war powder was obtained from private manufacturers, with bitter complaints from Admiral Barrington in 1779.'[1]

As will be seen later, the main obstacles to the manufacture of good powder in India were, first, the difficulty of obtaining skilled workers from home, and second, the deep-rooted objection of all the Presidency Councils to the expenditure necessary to provide proper works and plant.

In the following three chapters I sketch the history of the Company's powder works in the three Presidencies, but it must be understood that the manufacture of gunpowder in

[1] Powder-mills are said to have been in existence at Waltham Abbey about the middle or end of the sixteenth century. The first gunpowder factory in Scotland is stated to have been erected at Stobsmill in 1794; it had water-power driving 10 water-wheels, and employed from 50 to 60 men.

India was not confined to these works. The major Indian States before their subjection to the British power maintained their own powder manufactories, while the smaller ones could purchase it from local makers or even from the Company. Travancore and Beerbhoom, for example, are said to have made excellent powder in the middle of the eighteenth century. The quantities of powder found in the fortresses captured by the British forces were often very large. For example, when Seringapatam was taken in 1799 some 520,000 pounds of powder were found in the fort. It is certain that when the British power covered the whole country, manufacture of powder in organized works ceased, except in those belonging to the Company. But during the Mutiny the Rebels were still able to make it in many places, such as Fatehgarh. The Mutiny, of course, threw a heavy burden on the Company's works, and it is evident that no powder could be sold; and this probably accounts for the existence in 1858 of a powder works at Khandala, belonging to Mr. Faviell, contractor for the railway from Bombay, where in February an explosion occurred killing twenty men, women, and children and injuring many others.

## IX

## THE BOMBAY GUNPOWDER MANUFACTORY

THE records seem to prove that Bombay had the first powder works belonging to the Company. In 1668 the Council at Surat, then the seat of Government, asked the Court to send out a powder maker able to contrive a powder mill, or to send a mill; they said that powder made by local powder men was bad and expensive and they added that they could 'sell a lot round about'. They further asked that he should be sent as a hired servant under articles. The Court replied that they would send if they could find a man; but it is evident that they did not find one.

Bombay, however, had a powder maker, an Indian, who in 1669, it is recorded, promised to make 30 maunds of powder a month. A year later Surat was ordering the dispatch of 1,000 maunds of saltpetre from Karwar to Bombay, where it was said to be much needed for the manufacture of powder. Seven years later the President of the Council at Surat wrote to Bombay:

'One Mungi Dugi who now takes his passage to the Island hath made some propositions to us touching the construction of a new mill and other engines for making powder better and at far cheaper rates than now you make it on the Island. We have referred Mungi unto you to discourse with him, and, if you judge it convenient, to employ him.'

A mill was built for him to the south-west of the Castle, between the Church and Apollo gates, about the site of the present Secretariat. It seems evident that this replaced an older one, which it is possible was taken over from the Portuguese in 1665.

An interesting side-light on the primitive methods of dealing with gunpowder at this time is contained in a letter dated in April 1677, from Bombay to Surat:

'We had lately an unfortunate accident befallen us and yet we have reason to bless God for his deliverance from a greater mischief. It was thus—The Storekeeper as customary had sent up some powder to dry upon the north-east bastion. It was about two o'clock in the afternoon, when one of our corporals, by name Stanton, took an old Bandalier, or leather pistol case and filled it with wildfire, intending to tie it to a dog's tail then in the guard. Coming to the gate, the dog not being in the way, he took the bandalier . . . and flung it towards the Judge's old house. The wind being very strong the bandalier blew upon the bastion and fired the drying powder, 35 barrels, all English. Eight coolies and one sentry . . . were all burnt to death, whereof six were blown into the ditch and the parade and some limbs were carried over the fort. . . . We had this day a Council of War upon the Corporal. Having examined . . . we could not find him guilty of any wilful treacherous design. Still that an officer into whose hands our lives are sometimes entrusted should be so wretchedly careless . . . we cashiered him from ever more bearing arms, and to run the gauntlet three times for an example to all.'

The records are silent till February 1731, when a Bombay Consultation notes:

'There having been frequent complaints made of the hardship of pressing People to work in the Powder House and it being likewise represented that the Powder is not so good as it might be made were the materials better mixed, which it is impossible to do by the Methods that have been hitherto practiced, which is employing Women and Boys to beat the said Materials in Wooden Mortars. It has therefore been proposed to make two Mills to be worked by Buffaloes which will much better answer the purpose and free the Inhabitants from a Grievance . . . . The General Storekeeper to whom this affair was recommended, lays before the Board a Plan and Calculate.'

This was for two mills to cost Rs. 1,400 with a powder house to contain them at Rs. 1,200, the existing powder house being, it was stated, 'not only grown very crazy but is likewise very dangerous'. It was estimated that 'by a moderate computation the said Mills in two years will be paid for and the Powder rendered much better than at present', and it was agreed that 'the Land Paymaster give Directions for setting about the said house and mills with the utmost expedition'. In spite of this order nothing was done till in 1734 yet another plan was put forward, this time by Mr. Archibald Campbell, First Lieutenant of the *Princess Caroline* galley, who had just been appointed Clerk of the Works on Rs. 30 a month and also Master of Arms at Rs. 40. The proposed mill was to have 24 pestles to be worked either by buffaloes or by wind. It was decided to adopt the plan, the house to be made in such a manner that, in case the buffaloes did not answer, a spire could be erected on the house for a windmill. It was erected on Old Woman's Island, now Colaba; but it was never used, as it was too far away for the work-people, it had no fresh water, and moreover there were no store-houses. A curious story, ending with the sale of the premises in 1747 for Rs. 600.

The next step was to obtain from England, in 1741, a model for a new mill, and one was erected on a site close to the old powder house near the present Secretariat. This mill proved satisfactory though the Court thought the powder should be cheaper; but they admitted in 1747 that it was superior to European powder, and in 1749 ordered that it should be supplied to Bengal and the Coromandel Coast. The Bombay Government pointed out in reply that a handsome profit was made on the brimstone and saltpetre supplied to the contractor. The increasing demand rendered necessary the provision of a second house; but there were the usual delays, and it was not till March 1753 that the Court sent out models of the different parts to enable the Bombay workmen to construct a proper powder mill. They also engaged John Cairn, skilled in the burning of charcoal, to serve on the works at £60 a year. Even then there were objections to the site, confined as it was by the sea on one side and by the town on the other. However, the work was done in 1754; but a year later the Court had to sanction new buildings to replace those blown up.

In a hundred years methods of manufacture altered but

little, the main change being the substitution of buffaloes for manual labour in working the mills. At first, manufacture was under an Indian powder maker, controlled by the Storekeeper, the latter being allowed a commission of Rs. 2 per barrel, though the Court objected to this. In 1744 a test of all gunpowder in store was carried out by the Gunner and the Bombardier under a Committee of the Council. They tried all powder made since 1738 in comparison with the stock of European powder, with the result that, while the home powder ranged 514 feet, the Bombay powder only ranged 56½ feet! They also tried powder recently made by Doctor Gregorius Meisters, a free merchant, and this ranged 472 feet. Meisters was promptly given a contract, from February 1745, and a small dwelling-house was built for him near the works; but he died in June of the following year. This contract with Meisters started a new era, under which contracts were made with Europeans at a price which allowed a bonus for a greater range than the stipulated minimum and which provided for an independent proof.

The contract made with Captain Isaac Ainsworth, the Gunner, dated in June 1746, was for two years, renewable by mutual agreement; the Company to supply him with best refined saltpetre at Rs. 14 per bag of two Bengal maunds, good brimstone at Rs. 65 per Surat candy, together with the necessary utensils, and to be at all charges in keeping them, as well as the buildings, in good repair. The Company supplied the cattle but Ainsworth had to feed them, and he had sole charge of the workers, who were appointed at rates fixed by him. He was to be paid Rs. 20 per barrel of 100 lb. delivered and accepted. Proof was to be made by a Committee of the Council, minimum 150 feet, with 1 oz. of powder from a 4½-inch mortar, with a shell of 8 lb. 1 oz. Under 150 feet was to be rejected or taken at a lower price, all that exceeded this 'to be paid in proportion to its goodness'. At a proof in the following September the range was 402 feet, and Ainsworth was paid a little over Rs. 28 a barrel.

In June 1747 it is noted that

'Captain Isaac Ainsworth, Our Gunner being lately dead, it is agreed that Captain Hugh Cameron, who is well acquainted with the Theory of that Art and in all respects the most proper person upon the Island, have charge of that Post; but to hold the same only Provisionally as we have reason to expect from our advices home . . . that the Honorable Company will send out some person to act as Bombardier who may likewise be proper for that of Gunner.'

Cameron was Ensign in the 3rd Company of Infantry in 1738, was appointed Master Gunner in September 1748, and became 1st Captain and Chief Engineer of the Artillery Company in April 1749; but transferred again to the Infantry in October 1750. Captain Ainsworth's widow was allowed to carry on the powder contract with Cameron till it expired in June 1748, and it was decided that the Storekeeper with the Captain Commandant should form the Committee for the trial of powder. The widow married Mr. John Spencer, the Accountant-General, and he carried on the contract with Cameron till it expired, when it was given to Mr. Samuel le Blank, Ainsworth's brother-in-law, for two years. His contract specified 300 feet as the necessary range and the price was fixed at Rs. 24 a barrel, and it was later extended for a further two years.

When le Blank died, at the end of his contract, the head workman offered to make powder, if all the materials were supplied to him, on a pay of Rs. 30 a month. This offer was accepted; but it was 'thought highly proper to appoint a Covenanted Servant to prevent embezzlement and to see that the labourers attend the work'. Mr. W. Delagarde was appointed, under the Storekeeper; but when he became, himself, acting Storekeeper, Captain Walton supervised the works. On Walton's resignation from ill health the works and stores were handed over to de la Garde, who remained in charge till he died at the end of 1759, with the exception of some eight months when he was acting Chief at Ghereah. He was styled Superintendent of the Powder Works, the first to have that title, and he complained that he served in the business at little private advantage. He was a Senior Merchant on £40 a year with £100 a year as Superintendent. He also had a house as Superintendent of the Powder Works, described as being near the hospital, outside the town wall, and very commodious.

When Delagarde died, a Committee was appointed to inquire into the management of the works and the quality of the powder made. This Committee found that various irregularities had occurred, including the sale of powder to His Majesty's ships, and that the powder was bad, so they recommended that the Powder Works should be managed by a Committee with a Covenanted Servant as assistant at the usual salary. The Council did not claim payment of the overcharges, as the family had been left badly off; but they issued strict orders that no one was to make or sell powder except on the Company's account under severe penalties.

In 1760 a Powder House Committee was appointed, the members being Messrs. Byfield, Spencer, and Holford, all senior merchants, with Mr. Beaumont as assistant, and this system of management continued till May 1789. It must be noted, however, that there was always an Indian powder maker, whose pay was usually Rs. 30 a month, and de la Garde had complained in 1759 that one Manuckjee Manuvah was appointed powder maker and not he, and no more could be expected of the Superintendent than the care of stores and keeping the men up to the work, yet all defects were put on to him and not on to the powder maker. There is evidence that plant and methods were somewhat improved under the management of the Powder House Committee; but no great advance was made, one reason being, no doubt, the frequent changes in the personnel of the European supervision.

The Committee soon made representations regarding the danger and inconvenience of the saltpetre houses, and in 1764 various alterations were made; but it was becoming evident that the position of the works was most dangerous. The

Chief Engineer reported in 1766 that they were within 833 yards of the centre of the town, were close to the new fortifications between the Apollo and Church gates, and would afford cover to an enemy in an approach to the Marlborough and Stanhope bastions. The Committee of Surveys reported that

'We have pitched upon a spot of ground which we esteem in every respect very commodious for the Powder Works. It is situated to the north of the entrance to the Mud Dock at Mazagon on a rising ground, well sheltered from the salt sprays. A very good tank for the cattle lies contiguous thereto, stones for erecting the buildings are in great plenty within 50 to 60 yards and chunam kilns on the spot.'

The removal of the works to this site was strongly recommended to the Court.

A curious incident is recorded in the Bombay Diary of 13 January 1768, which emphasized the danger of too much powder near the town:

'About nine o'clock this morning a small magazine adjoining the ramparts that contained about 27 barrels of gunpowder . . . was unhappily blown up through the unparalleled villainy of Solomon Hart, who was Quartermaster Serjeant and was this morning broke by sentence of a Court Martial and destroyed himself in the explosion. By this unhappy accident some lives were lost and many private houses much destroyed.'

The removal of the works had been approved in principle by the Court as far back as 1764; but it was not until October 1768 that the removal of one of the mills was ordered to be carried out, at once, and the other to be moved as soon as the first was in work. Additional buildings were constructed in 1779 costing Rs. 19,028, in order to increase output by about 1,000 barrels each season, and from 1769 for a hundred years the Bombay gunpowder manufactory was located at Mazagon.

In 1786 'a dreadful and ruinous explosion, cause unknown' occurred, three mills being entirely destroyed and nine

Biggaries (labourers) being killed. The cost of repair amounted to Rs. 1,20,805. Another explosion occurred three years later, when one mill was blown up, one man was killed and five injured. The families of the men killed on both occasions were granted a pension of Rs. 3 a month.

In November 1788 the Council decided that all supplies to the Powder House should be furnished by contract, and six months later decided upon a radical change in the system for the provision of gunpowder, and 'resolved to issue notices that we will receive sealed proposals this day sennight for contracting for a quantity of gunpowder for a year's consumption'. The tenders sent in included ones from J. Rivett, J. R. Smyth, and Rustomjee Manockjee. Mr. Rivett had been assistant under the Powder House Committee from 1785 to 1788 and Mr. Smyth had been assistant for a short time. Rustomjee Manockjee was the powder maker on Rs. 60 a month, and he sent in a petition saying that his father Manuckjee Manuvah was powder maker more than fifty years before, and two of his brothers had direction afterwards and died in the Company's service. He stated also that work was so continuous that he could not make any money and asked for an increase in pay, which was refused. Mr. Rivett's tender was found to be 'the most admissible', the price being Rs. 24 per barrel of 100 lb. for a range of 500 feet, the barrels themselves to be Rs. 8½ each. The usual guard was to be provided, but Rivett would stand any loss from explosion.

In May 1789 the Powder House Committee reported that all buildings at Mazagon, known by the name of the Powder Works, also cattle, &c., had been handed over to Mr. Rivett, and in August they sent in their books and dissolved. Mr. Rivett, who was Mayor of Bombay in 1787–8, was Purveyor to the Medical Board when his tender was accepted. He was a member of the Council in 1803 and had before then changed his name to Rivett Carnac. He also dealt in arrack, which he imported from Batavia; in May 1782 his tender for the supply of 110 'leagers' (casks) at Rs. 1–1–60 per gallon was accepted. He held the powder contract for one year only, and was followed by Rustomjee Manockjee, 1790 to 1793, who made 400 barrels in 1790–1 at Rs. 23 per barrel; then came Bomanjee Hirjee, 1794–5, with a contract for 2,000 barrels at Rs. 20 a barrel. Evidently cheapness was at the expense of quality, for in November 1795 a Committee, consisting of the Chief Engineer, the Commandant of Artillery, and Surgeon Helenus Scott, was ordered to investigate methods and to make experiments.

This Committee made a searching inquiry into every detail and found that sea-water was used in refining saltpetre, which led to salt in the powder, and they also found that, at the existing price of materials, it was impossible to make good powder at the contract price of Rs. 20 per barrel. They improved some of the plant and processes, and there is little doubt that Scott was the moving spirit in the matter and the first to attempt to place gunpowder manufacture in Bombay on a sound basis. Government decided in December 1796 that manufacture should be by agency and appointed Scott as Agent at a salary of Rs. 500 a month, under the Military Board. In 1797–8 Scott received, in addition to his salary as Agent, Rs. 496 as Apothecary plus Rs. 50 for house-rent. He had as assistant George Keir, Assistant Surgeon, whose salary was Rs. 60, with pay Rs. 62, gratuity Rs. 24, batta Rs. 60, and house-rent Rs. 24. The establishment allowed for the works was:

> Head Powder Maker—Rs. 60, 1st Assistant—Rs. 25, 2nd—Rs. 23. Head Purvoe—Rs. 30, Purvoe—Rs. 20. Haveldar—Rs. 7–2, 6 Peons—Rs. 5 each. Overseer of cattle and herds—Rs. 20, 15 Herds—Rs. 78–2. Cost of feeding, cleaning, &c., 146 buffaloes—Rs. 1,022. Other charges for materials, hire of labour, &c., estimated at Rs. 3,000 a month.

Helenus Scott was born in 1760, studied medicine at Edinburgh; but went to India as a cadet. He resigned the

Army and was appointed an Assistant Surgeon; but was ordered back to military duty, as the Court objected to such changes. However, thanks to the efforts of the Principal Surgeon, Scott was commissioned as Assistant Surgeon in January 1783. He was Medical Storekeeper in 1800, second member of the Medical Board in 1801, and became President of the Board in April 1806. His retirement from the post of Agent for Gunpowder seems to have occurred on his appointment as President. He had the contract for the supply of arrack, surely a curious one for a medical officer, which in 1799 was for 25,000 gallons. He was in partnership with the Ashburner brothers, one of whom was a senior merchant, in a plantation of sugar-cane on Salsette from which arrack was made, and he was permitted to use the powder works' buffaloes during the rains, feeding them at his own expense, powder manufacture having to cease in the rainy season. This contract was a very profitable one and other officials coveted it, so the Bombay Government took it from him; but on his retirement he appealed to the Court stating that he had lost a lakh of rupees by that action. The Court agreed that he had been deprived of the contract in an irregular manner and granted him compensation. Scott retired in 1810 and practised at home till he died in 1821.

The subject of arrack is not without interest. It is stated that in 1708 the punch houses for the men were often the private speculation of the officers, and every soldier had to take his dram. In 1798 there is shown an allowance of Rs. 40 a month for 20 gallons of arrack for the Europeans employed in the magazine of the Bombay arsenal. In Madras General Orders dated 31 March 1780 it was ordered that commandants of out-stations were to pay the Madras Agent for arrack 5 per cent. commission, and they would then get the profit on the sale to the men. In a later General Order the profits for the year 1788–9 are given as Star pagodas 11,860, which, at 46 fanams to the Star pagoda, came to fanams 545,560. This profit was shared amongst the commandants of garrisons, e.g. Colonel Sydenham at St. Thomas's Mount had fanams 29,571, while General Horne at Trichinopoly drew 74,280, about Rs. 6,190.

A serious explosion occurred in January 1797, when two graining houses blew up, killing nine men. Explosions also occurred in 1804 and 1807. In the last one thirty-two men were killed, and Government refused for ten years to sanction the complete repair of the works, thus reducing output to about one-half.

Medical officers continued to hold the Agency, as a part-time job, till the end of 1821, Surgeon G. Keir succeeding Scott, then J. Inverarity from 1811 to 1817. D. Christie was the last of the Medical Agents for Gunpowder.

The Powder Works not only made powder for the Army and for the Navy, it made it also for sale to Native States. When Government reviewed the position in 1817, it noted that output was only 2,005 barrels, whereas the annual expenditure was 3,078. Extra buildings were sanctioned at a cost of Rs. 56,754 to bring output up to 6,000 barrels annually, in order to replenish stocks and to provide for supplies to Native States. It was stated that in the previous seven years Rs. 1,17,940 had been received from sales at a profit of Rs. 14,523; but nobody from the Native States was ever allowed inside the Powder Works.

In 1813 the Court had informed Bengal that, in future, Superintendents of manufactories must be Army officers, with preference to those of the Artillery; but there was a doubt whether this excluded surgeons, and both in Bengal and Bombay medical officers continued in the Powder Works for a time. However, in Bombay, on the departure of Surgeon Christie for England in December 1821, Captain A. Manson of the Bombay Artillery became Agent, and from then on the management was always in the hands of an artillery officer as a whole-time appointment. The salary was raised to Rs. 600 a month in 1823, when the Indian head powder maker was given Rs. 250 a month plus Rs. 30 for house-rent.

On the night of 18 August 1826 an explosion occurred which did great damage, killing the guard of four men, also one man in a boat and two in the adjacent docks. The cause was not discovered, but as there was no wall round the works and rafts of timber and boats were allowed to lie close to the grounds, and the docks were near by, it was thought that a spark came from the adjacent shipping. Stock of powder in Bombay at the time was found to be 870,500 lb., and it was reported that the quantity of powder in the works was excessive, owing to the lack of barrels and to inadequate magazine accommodation, some magazines being under repair. Moreover, the Agent stated that the older buildings were too solid in construction, while recent ones were better, having slight roofs with walls of split bamboo and mud plaster. He also mentioned that he had no European assistance. The building of an enclosure wall was suggested but was vetoed on the score of expense; and the Military Board and the Police were directed to take steps to prevent boats lying close to the works. In consequence of this explosion Bengal and Madras had to be asked in the following year for gunpowder to meet deficiencies, and Bengal was also asked to allow Lieutenant-Colonel Galloway, the Agent at Ishapore, to send a cylinder mill with full particulars of the buildings and utensils required for it, and this was done.

On 7 June 1840 a serious explosion occurred when lightning struck a corning house, setting it on fire and exploding the 1,250 lb. of gunpowder which it contained. Much damage was done, not only to the factory but also to neighbouring buildings. Fortunately the explosion took place at 7 a.m. on Sunday, when there were no workmen on the premises. Captain Willoughby, the Superintendent, Merwanjee Rustomjee, the Powder Maker, and the Guard were able to prevent the fire spreading to two other buildings containing 800 and 2,000 barrels of powder, being aided by torrents of rain which began to fall soon after the explosion. The occurrence caused great alarm in Bombay and led the

*Bombay Times* to urge the necessity for the removal of the works to a spot more distant from Bombay.

In 1844 a percussion-cap factory was added to the works and a plantation of willow, for charcoal, in the Mahableshwar Hills was approved. The Agent at this time, Lieutenant-Colonel J. Lloyd, C.B., asked for an increase in salary to place him on an equality with the Agents in the other Presidencies; but this was refused, though his salary was only Rs. 600 a month as compared with Rs. 1,000 at Madras and Ishapore. The quarters occupied by the Agent at Mazagon were erected in 1834, near the south end of the grounds, at the expense of Captain Jacob, and it was ruled that they must be purchased at a valuation by his successor, and eventually they were purchased by Government when the works were moved to Kirkee. The Agent drew the house-allowance of his rank, which in 1851 was Rs. 180 a month for Major Willoughby.

Considerable extensions in buildings and plant were authorized between 1856 and 1859, though as far back as 1826 the Committee of Inquiry into the disastrous explosion considered the position of the Works to be dangerous and advocated their removal to a drier climate inland. Major Thew was asked for a report on the subject in 1827, as he had been Agent for Gunpowder to the Peishwa, when he was commanding the Artillery of His Highness at Poona. Thew stated that he had made small quantities of powder in the Cave near the Residency, called the Sungam; but this was unsafe and an accident cost many lives. He then had a building erected between Dapoorie and the Gunnesh Cund Hill; but the Peishwa's Government would not sanction any but the most common machinery. He did not make more than 30 Poona maunds a month, costing Rs. 22 to 26 a maund.

It was not till September 1864 that the commencement of buildings at Kirkee for a new powder factory was ordered. This factory was completed in 1871 at a cost of Rs. 16,26,636, the magazine to store 200 tons being completed later at a cost of Rs. 1,52,075. The old works at Mazagon with the land were sold for Rs. 40,00,000.

This new factory at Kirkee did not last very long. Cordite was taking the place of gunpowder, and in 1896 the experimental manufacture of the new explosive was undertaken in the factory; as soon as it was seen that there were no insuperable difficulties in its manufacture in India, the Kirkee gunpowder factory was doomed. It ceased manufacture in August 1890 and was finally closed at the end of March 1900, when plans were commenced for its reconstruction as an arsenal in place of the old grand arsenal in Bombay Castle.

We may say, therefore, that the modern Cordite Factory at Aruvankadu in the Nilgiris is a direct descendant of the primitive little powder house which about the year 1678 stood near the site of the present Bombay Secretariat, and which may even have taken the place of one which perhaps existed in the days of the Portuguese ownership of the Island.

So the Bombay gunpowder factory at Kirkee became the new grand arsenal. Though the description 'grand' had long been dropped, still it was the successor of the general or grand arsenal which was fitted up in Bombay Castle in 1794. Does India ever change? We can smile at the ineptitude of the Bombay Council which in 1734 erected a powder works on Old Woman's Island, where there was no fresh water and no store houses, so that it was never used. But what are we to think of those who erected the buildings for the new arsenal at Kirkee and of those who flooded the place with stores before a proper system of connecting roadways had been constructed and before the old internal tramway had been made usable? Such was the position of the new Kirkee arsenal at the beginning of 1909, and the cost of unnecessary labour and transport and the value of the stores ruined by exposure in the open must have far exceeded the loss due to the erection of that useless powder house on Old Woman's Island 175 years before.

# X

# THE MADRAS GUNPOWDER MANUFACTORY

GUNPOWDER was manufactured on the Coromandel Coast at least as early as the beginning of the seventeenth century, and it was being made in Masulipatam by native powder makers in 1611, when the British established their Agency there. The settlement of Madras dates from 1639 and Fort St. George from 1664, and there is a record of powder being received from England in 1665. The date of the establishment of a powder mill at Madras is uncertain; but in 1672 the Chief at Masulipatam was ordered to send some teak planks to Madras for the use of the powder mill. In 1680 it is recorded that 'one Naganna undertakes to manufacture gunpowder for the Company at cheaper rates than formerly, viz. 1¼ pagodas per candy for refining the saltpetre instead of 1¾, and 3½ pagodas per candy instead of 5 for making the Powder and finding the Charcoal'. There are also many references in the records of money paid to the Powder Maker, for example, in July 1685, 60 pagodas were ordered to be paid to the Powder Maker on account of making gunpowder for the 'Right Honorable Company'.

The first powder mill in Madras must have been the one situated in old Black Town, near the burial ground; but the works were soon found to be a danger to the town, so at a consultation in March 1682 it was 'concluded upon to build a new Powder House, the other to be sold with the ground of ye old gardens'. In 1683 the Court approved the erection of new buildings on the Island, the old ones to be dismantled and the ground sold. At the sale in 1684 the ground fetched 260 pagodas and the old powder house 146 pagodas. The site was shown on a plan as to the east of Garden Street.[1]

[1] Madras has always called the piece of ground within the two arms of the river Cooum, to the south of the fort, the Island.

Manufacture in this second mill cannot have been very satisfactory in its early days, as it is stated that up to 1703 'gunpowder formed one of the articles of outward-bound investment; but about this time the manufacture of it was so much improved as to preclude the necessity of sending any more'. A letter from Madras to the Court dated in January 1704 says, 'We can now make as good powder for 25 shillings a barrel as the 50 barrels received which cost £5–5 each.' Madras asked, however, for 'one or two good powder makers who might be entertained officers of the military'. The Court replied in 1705 that they were not sending any more powder and were considering sending 'a person to make it with you or in the Bay after the Europe manner as you say the French do'.

From 1728 to 1732 new and, it is said, costly works were under construction on another site on the Island, but they seem never to have been used except as magazines. The old mills continued in use till, in 1737, they were reported as being in a very decayed state, and a year later a survey showed that no part was serviceable, doors and windows being quite decayed, walls and roofs unsafe, and the tank filled up. The report stated that it would be necessary to pull the whole down to save what little of the material could be utilized, and further that the site, being near the town and between the only two roads leading to it, was very unsafe. So in 1739 it was decided to build new works at the north-west corner of the Island at a cost of 2,456 pagodas.

Early in 1741 Fort St. David, which was a fortified settlement on the coast at Cuddalore, purchased in 1690, being threatened by the 'Morattas', asked for powder and for some experienced gunners. They were told that Fort St. George had no skilled gunners and had no gunpowder to spare; but as powder makers were working daily it was hoped to send them some later, if they were not interrupted by the enemy, who made an unsuccessful attempt on Madras itself, at this time.

There was a serious explosion in these works, which were the fourth, at the end of 1741, in which 10 workers were killed and 14 injured. Grants were made to the families of the killed varying from 10 to 22 pagodas, while the injured were given from 3 to 5 pagodas, one who had lost an eye being allowed 10 pagodas, as compensation. The explosion caused a difficulty in obtaining labour, so the Council decided to allow the Powder Maker one pagoda more per candy of powder to enable him to offer better pay to the work-people. It was hoped that this would prevent 'our being under the necessity of forcing them to work in the powder house, which has been a method too often taken, more especially since the late accident'.

In December 1744 Mr. Joseph Smith, the Bombardier and Engineer in charge of the Powder House, asked for additions to accommodate two more stamps, and he also wanted brass or copper to be used in place of iron for bands, nails, and rivets. This was sanctioned at a cost of 540 pagodas; but these mills were destroyed by the French when they captured Madras in 1746.[1] This Mr. Smith had been Gunner and Engineer in Bombay and was sent from there to direct the fortifications at Fort St. George. His allowance was to be Rs. 140 a month. In May 1746 he was appointed by the Naval authorities to act as agent 'for the affairs of the squadron at Fort St. George', but he died soon after. He had a son who was a Captain of Infantry in 1756 and later became Commander-in-Chief.

After the destruction of the mills at Madras by the French, powder was made at Fort St. David, which from 1746 to 1762 was the seat of the Madras Government. Several powder makers went there from Madras and desired to enter

[1] A letter written from Madras after the capture states that the soldiers in garrison were few in numbers and indifferent in quality, that the town was ill provided with ammunition and stores, and that its fortifications were in a ruinous condition, 'the necessity for rigid economy having withheld the means of maintaining . . . in a state of efficiency'. Madras was restored to the British in 1748 as a result of the Peace of Aix-la-Chapelle.

the service of the Council, and as there was a great lack of powder they were engaged, and the Paymaster was ordered to repair buildings at 'Middle Point' for their use. Evidently the production was most inadequate, for in 1750 Bombay was asked to send 7,000 barrels of powder, but they could only send 600 with a further 727 in the following year, and a small quantity was obtained from Calcutta. Moreover, the quality of the powder was indifferent, but the need being so great the Council decided to continue manufacture under the direction of the Military Storekeeper, the powder to be surveyed by the commanding officer. Up to 1752 powder was supplied on contract, Mr. Pybus, the Military Storekeeper, having the contract in that year, when it was decided to have it made on the Company's account, i.e. the Company supplying everything and paying all wages, the Military Storekeeper having a fixed commission on the output.

In May 1752 Captain Brohier, the Chief Engineer, again called attention to the badness of the powder from Fort St. David and represented the necessity for building a powder mill in Madras. He recommended the employment of John de Roos, a Hollander, who had been employed at Pondicherry in making powder but had left on account of some ill usage and had been in the Company's settlements for two years. He believed him to be capable of making good powder, as efforts were being made to induce him to return to Pondicherry. He estimated 3,755 pagodas as the cost of erecting a mill of 16 mortars and pestles. The Council were slow to move, and, when more complaints were made, said they could not understand why it was not as good as that made by the French. Brohier made the obvious reply that it was due to the want of proper mills and 'to the lack of a skillful method of making it'.

It was not till January 1753 that it was decided to utilize the Egmore Redoubt for the erection of a powder mill, at a cost of 7,500 pagodas, and it is said that the materials from the demolished Capuchin Church of St. Andrew's in Fort

St. George were used for the buildings. Meanwhile, more powder was obtained from Bengal; but Brohier reported it as being so bad as to be hardly fit for salutes. Powder was also demanded from England, which moved the Court to action. They wrote in December that they were sending 1,000 barrels in two consignments; but they would not send any more, as the risk was too great, and they remarked that the only need for manufacture at Fort St. George was skill, and they were determined it should be made there. So 'they had procured the most exact models of a Powder House and Mill with all the various parts in their due proportion and of every Machine and Utensil used in the whole process, that you may from them cause Propper Works and Utensils to be made and erected. Said models go by ship Onslow with a very minute description of them and the method of making gunpowder.' They also appointed Mr. William Bishop to be Superintendent of the Powder Works, to be paid £100 over and above his pay as First Lieutenant of the Military to which they had appointed him. They left the decision as to the best site to the Council of Madras.

John de Roos had been engaged and was employed on the erection of the mill, already sanctioned in 1753 by the Council, in the Egmore Redoubt, and also in 'claryfying saltpetre' and other preparations for manufacture. In place of the old hand and foot mills, this mill was to be worked by bullocks, and it was agreed in July 1754 to continue de Roos on a salary of 25 pagodas a month till Bishop arrived, the Military Storekeeper to pay such workers as were required. Bishop arrived soon after and reported the mill to be nearly finished; but he said it would require considerable additions, and he pointed out that there was no residence for him, and as he must be on the spot he asked that, pending the provision of quarters, he might be allowed 'a palankeen, as he cant bear the fatigue of going a Foot'. The Council refused his request, on the ground that they allowed him £100 to execute the business over and above his pay as lieutenant. Brohier recommended the completion of the Egmore works and the erection of Bishop's mill at Fort St. David; but it was decided that de Roos, who claimed that he could make 500 lb. of powder a day, should continue in the management, while Brohier and Bishop were to find another site in Madras for the new mill. Bishop died, however, at the end of 1755, and nothing more was done then in the matter of a new mill.

In December 1755 de Roos offered to enter into a contract to make and deliver gunpowder at 10 pagodas a candy, the mill and all its appurtenances to be maintained by the Company and all materials to be supplied at their charge, all other expenses to be borne by him. The Council thought this would be a saving and ordered a trial. The Powder House at this time had 16 mortars complete, 5 stones for beating saltpetre, one large copper boiler for saltpetre, one iron boiler for brimstone, and two beam scales—not a very elaborate equipment. De Roos promised to deliver 240 candies of good powder a year; but there soon arose a difference of opinion on the quality of his powder, so his contract was stopped and he was offered 25 pagodas a month as pay, to conduct the work on the Company's account as formerly; but he refused, saying that he could make more by other means.

John de Roos having gone, a contract was given to Mr. Alexander Wynch, the Military Storekeeper, at 28 pagodas per candy for cannon and 29 for musket powder, Wynch having told the Council that powder made on the Company's account had cost 62 pagodas a candy! He was to have the use of the Company's mill at Egmore for three months from 1st May 1756 as a trial; but being ordered to Fort St. David, he was allowed to hand over the contract to his successor, Mr. Bourchier. In November of the following year, Bourchier obtained a revision of the terms of the contract. He said that owing to the rise in the pay of the coolies on the fortifications he had to pay his men more, and he estimated the extra cost at 1½ pagodas per candy since March. He also stated that, no saltpetre being available, the works were at a standstill, the monthly charge being 250 pagodas. The Council raised the contract price by 1¼ pagodas per candy and also agreed to pay the monthly charge while the mill was stopped. Saltpetre was said to be expected from Bengal in a month; it must be understood that the contractor had to buy saltpetre and other materials from the Government stores.

The Egmore mill was blown up by the French in February 1759 after the unsuccessful investment of Fort St. George, and according to one historian the works had cost £30,000. The Council lost no time in ordering the Committee of Works to take steps to make powder by hand till such time as a new mill could be erected; but in December, having found that one on the model of that sent out from England five years before was an expensive undertaking, they decided to construct a temporary mill at Egmore for the time being. However, a disastrous explosion occurring in these temporary sheds, the mills were restored, using the plant from England, pending a decision on a better site.

The Council had been in correspondence with the Court on the whole question of the method of making gunpowder, and the Court, in their reply dated in March 1761, asked for a list of ingredients and their proportions, with an account of the whole process employed, and made some suggestions for improvement. Madras then sent a full report by their Engineer, Mr. John Call, who was a member of the Committee of Works, accompanied by the samples for which the Court had asked; but nothing seems to have come from the correspondence.

Meanwhile, in 1763, the troubles in the Carnatic had caused a great demand for gunpowder, and evidently the stocks at Fort St. George and the facilities for manufacture were insufficient. For the siege of Madura powder was sent from Vellore to the base at Trichinopoly. In December it was estimated that 2,500 barrels of powder, of which 500 should be of European make, were needed for recommencing the siege. The Nawab was earnestly asked to send the 2,000 barrels which he had promised and the Storekeeper at Vellore was ordered to continue to make all he could. Vellore had been occupied by the British in 1760 on behalf of the Nawab of Arcot, who had been unable to recover it from a rebel. In it there seems to have been a powder mill, which was utilized by the British under the management of the Paymaster or the Storekeeper. A considerable quantity of powder seems to have been made there, from 1763 to 1765, barrels, brimstone, and wax cloth being sent from Madras. After 1765 it would appear that manufacture ceased, till in October 1771 the President of the Council at Madras informed the Board that he had applied to the Nawab, who had consented to the powder mill being repaired and continued under the management of the British. Manufacture was continued intermittently till 1790, when the Committee of Stores stopped it, as it produced powder much inferior to that made in Madras.

In 1768 a cyclone unroofed the Egmore Mills and it was at last decided to erect new mills, and a site was selected in new Black Town on a piece of ground to the north-west, within the ramparts and west of the Seven Wells. A plan submitted by the Engineer, Mr. Montressor, was adopted; but there was considerable delay, caused by a scarcity of workmen, and it was not till July 1771 that the Committee of Works, of which Warren Hastings was President, reported their completion. There were many accidents in these mills and they were a danger to the town, but they were not abandoned till 1806. The site was then allotted for a Mint, the buildings for which were finished in 1807, when Mr. Benjamin Roebuck became Mint Master. The site is now occupied by the Government Press and the Medical Stores. The Egmore Redoubt site had been appropriated in 1789 for the Madras Male Orphan Asylum.

From the time John de Roos left the service in 1756 up

to early in 1759, gunpowder was supplied on contract from mills owned by and maintained by Government, the actual making being by native powder makers. The Court having disapproved of the contract being given to any of their Covenanted Servants, it was ordered in November 1758 that powder was to be made on the Company's account, under the inspection and direction of the Committee of Works, and the contractor, Mr. Bourchier, was given two months' notice as allowed in his contract. The contract system seems to have returned in 1770; but there was trouble later over prices, and it appears that a few years after 1770 manufacture on the Company's account was resumed. In 1790, at the instance of Lord Cornwallis, the Governor-General, an inquiry was instituted into public expenditure and various scandals were brought to light. Among other matters the cost of gunpowder was investigated, and it was ascertained that the cost per candy, which was pagodas 28 to 32 in 1771 on contract, had risen since 1775 from 38 to 43 pagodas. Mr. Petrie, who was Military Storekeeper from 1786 to 1788, in his defence said

> 'that when the provision of gunpowder first devolved upon him, he found great imperfections and had to study the subject, while the overseers and workmen took pains to keep him in the dark. He saw that the Mills and the materials in use could not produce powder up to proof requirements, and he had condemned 600 barrels, which would have been passed by the modes of deception formerly practised. He constructed a set of mills at his own expense and brought a German overseer from Bengal and a number of men from the powder works at Calcutta. All went well till an unfortunate accident occurred in February, 1788, when he had contemplated resigning but eventually re-erected the works and asked for compensation; but was told to charge the same price as the Storekeeper at Vellore was allowed for his powder.'

He was exempted by Government from any censure.

The explosion to which Petrie referred destroyed two corning rooms and killed the German overseer and 29 men;

3,500 lb. of powder exploded. His story is not quite clear; but apparently in lieu of compensation he was allowed to charge an excessive price for his powder. It is clear, moreover, that powder was being made under the Military Storekeeper on the Company's account, the Storekeeper being allowed 15 per cent. on the cost of production or on a price fixed by the Military Board. The production in 1791 seems to have been about 300 barrels a month.

The first real Superintendent of the Manufacture of Gunpowder at Madras was Mr. Benjamin Bishop, Commissary of Stores at the arsenal of Fort St. George. Madras never called the officer in charge of the gunpowder manufactory an Agent, as did the other Presidencies. Bishop joined the arsenal in 1783 and was appointed deputy commissary in 1791, and from 1795 he acted as assistant to Mr. Porcher, the Military Storekeeper, in the powder mills, getting 15 pagodas a month for this plus 6 for attending the magazines. In 1796 he put forward proposals for making powder on contract, stating that he had attended at the works for some years without advantage and had to pay for conveyance. He offered to make powder for 33 pagodas a candy and said that the existing cost by agency was very high. Government, however, decided in favour of agency and in April 1797 ordered Bishop to take charge and granted him a salary of 60 pagodas a month in addition to his ordinary pay and allowances. As superintendent and commissary, his total emoluments in 1800 came to Rs. 496 a month, approximately—not much compared with those drawn by the Agents in Bengal and Bombay.

The mills in new Black Town, the sixth in Madras, were evidently becoming inefficient by the time Bishop took over charge. In 1799 and 1800 they were under repair and had very few men at work, while in 1798 Bengal had been asked to supply requirements for the ensuing year. Once more the Court were asked for full particulars of the methods of manufacture used in the King's powder works.

There was an explosion in 1802, and a pension of one pagoda a month was granted to the families of those killed. This caused Bishop to ask to be allowed to pay for certain ceremonies, as had been done by former officials in charge, such as the sacrifice of sheep, which the men performed at the beginning of the year of manufacture, on the occasion of an explosion, and on the resumption of work after any accident. The cost was usually five pagodas on each occasion, and the workmen believed their safety to depend on these ceremonies. Government sanctioned this expense; but asked for a report on the state of the mills. This led to a consideration of the whole subject by the Military Board, who reported at the end of 1802 that considerable improvements in manufacture had been effected by Bishop; but that the mills were in a ruinous state. They also recommended a commission of Rs. 2 per barrel to Bishop in addition to his salary; they thought the Rs. 5 allowed in Bengal to be excessive. This commission amounted in 1808–9 to Rs. 4,182.

A site to the north of Black Town upon which was situated the Artillery Butt was recommended for the new mills, the cost of which was estimated at 31,150 pagodas, including the cost of conversion of certain buildings into magazines. Government sanctioned the construction of the new works but not the conversion into magazines, and decided that Bishop, who had recently been commissioned as lieutenant of Artillery, should superintend the construction to plans to be furnished by the Military Board, and should receive the percentage usually allowed to engineer officers employed on building works.

These mills which Lieutenant Bishop commenced to build in 1803 were the seventh and last to be established in Madras, and the site came to be known as Perampore, though originally called Vyasarapady. Bishop may have been a good powder maker but he certainly did not shine as a builder. He had to take leave on account of ill health about the middle of 1803, so the Military Board had to measure the work done by him. They reported that he had deviated seriously from the plans supplied by them, and that many of the buildings required extensive alterations and repairs to make them safe, as their arches had sunk. They said that Bishop had offered to pay for the repairs; but they left this for Government to decide. Considerable extensions to the buildings were asked for by Bishop early in 1805 and were approved in 1806. The Court were not at all pleased with the way the business had been conducted; they approved of the two rupees commission but did not like the constructional work being entrusted to Bishop; later they noted that their disapproval was fully justified, and while they allowed that Bishop's ill health was some extenuation, they said the result was a great waste of public money. Then in April 1809 they wrote that, though powder was cheaper in Bengal, over a lakh of pagodas had been spent on the works, and as the process was known only to Bishop the works must go on. In August of the same year, however, they wrote that they would view any further expenditure on the works with dissatisfaction. They sanctioned 2,000 barrels of powder being obtained from Bengal, owing to the delay in completing the works.

When Bishop went on leave in 1803, Captain T. Fraser, of the Engineers, was appointed to complete the works. In 1806 the old mills in Black Town were given up, because Government wished the new Mint to be got on with, as the machinery for it had arrived from England. By May 1807 Bishop was able to work two mills in the new buildings. In August 1808 a Committee of the Board, consisting of the Chief Engineer, the Quartermaster-General and the Military Auditor-General, inspected the machinery of the new mills and pronounced it complete and satisfactory. They recommended that the Brazier, Mr. Menaud, who had cast the cylinders, &c., under Captain Fraser, should be retained for three months on his salary of 60 pagodas a month, which included the pay of his three apprentices, till a native mistry could take over. This Menaud was a Frenchman who left Brest in 1789 and was employed by Tippoo in Seringapatam. He arrived in Madras in 1799 and was allowed to remain. He was first described as a turner and cutter; but later as an iron-founder or smith. He took the oath of allegiance in December 1808 and was then described as 'a man of family'.

Menaud had set up the brass furnace in the new works and had been successful in casting the large bronze cylinders for the incorporating mills. Though it was anticipated that he would only be required for a further three months, he was retained for six to make spare axles and other parts on a salary of 40 pagodas, and thereafter on 30 a month to keep the plant in a serviceable state, with permission to accept other work. In 1810, however, Government approved of his permanent retention, as Bishop, though he found him not entirely satisfactory, said he was afraid of anything going wrong and could not trust natives for repairs. When Captain Galloway from the powder works at Allahabad visited Madras on his way back from leave in 1815, he saw Menaud and his work; and when he was entrusted with the construction of the new machinery for Ishapore, he asked for his services. Menaud was allowed to go, and he left with his family of eleven in October 1816. Bengal allowed him Rs. 300 a month, and he remained at Calcutta casting the cylinders for Ishapore and Allahabad till 1821, when he returned to Madras, the Court granting him a pension of 25 pagodas a month.

In 1808 Bishop was allowed as his assistant his son, Lieutenant C. M. Bishop, 19th Native Infantry, on a salary of 30 pagodas a month. Soon after his appointment a petition from the workmen, alleging violence from him, was investigated by a Committee of the Military Board; but it was pronounced to be frivolous. However, in June 1812 the young officer was tried by a General Court Martial on a charge of disgraceful language to, and assault and maltreatment of, another young officer living near him, and he was found guilty and sentenced to be discharged. The Commander-in-Chief considered 'the faculties of Mr Bishop's mind to be so much impaired' that he recommended a small pension, equal to the subsistence of a lieutenant of Infantry, which was sanctioned; but he died on passage to England.

Captain Benjamin Bishop retired in 1814 and died in England in 1824, and there seems to be little doubt as to his competence as a powder maker. He wrote an official memoir on the subject in 1801 and a report on the drying of powder in 1802, in which year also he made numerous experiments on charcoal in conjunction with Mr. B. Roebuck. The Court, in a letter dated in May 1812 commending the work of the officers in charge of the manufacture of gunpowder, specially noted the zeal and ability of Captain Bishop at Madras. Lieutenant F. N. Balmain, of the 6th Cavalry, succeeded Bishop as Superintendent of the Gunpowder Manufactory. He was Barrack Master at the Presidency, and one qualification for the post at the gunpowder mills seems to have been his marriage a few months before to the daughter of the Governor, Sir George Barlow. He continued as Barrack Master till 1820 and was Superintendent till 1823.

Captain Fraser, who was on leave in England in 1812, had been directed to study home methods of the manufacture of gunpowder, and had reported that the methods of drying by steam instead of by solar heat, and of burning charcoal in iron cylinders, were great improvements. The Court decided that he was to make himself fully acquainted with the whole apparatus and, after informing Madras, was to visit the other Presidencies for the same purpose. In January 1813 they informed Madras that they had engaged G. Barnes, Millwright, to serve five years on 12 shillings a day, also six other persons on a five-year agreement at 10 shillings a day, to be ranked as Conductors of Ordnance. These had been workmen at Waltham Abbey and the charcoal works at Petworth;

J. Braddock, R. Todd, and W. Taylor were expert at making gunpowder; J. Hattersley, J. Tims, and M. Tims were expert at charcoal burning. The Court said they had paid £40 for each man for expenses at the Boatswain's Mess, and asked that, as they were all young men with no friends in Madras, they might be met by some proper person and put in the way of suitable quarters. The apparatus sent out was to be at the disposal of Captain Fraser.

The Court must have felt that, at last, gunpowder would be made in India of a quality equal to that made at home. They had taken the Engineer officer who had successfully built the new works at Madras, given him every insight into the methods in use at home, they had engaged working experts in the two main branches of the subject, and now Fraser was going out to instruct the Presidency powder makers and to leave with each of them two expert workers. Unfortunately the Court does not seem to have known India or human nature. Bengal and Bombay have never thought much of Madras, nor a great deal of each other, and the officers in the Bengal and Bombay gunpowder manufactories united in condemning the plans of Fraser. Galloway at Allahabad had only to refer to 'extreme and unnecessary expense' to frighten everybody. The result was that Fraser left Madras only to go home on sick-leave, and even in Madras only a part of his proposals were adopted, while the seven experts had a chequered career. Early in 1817 Braddock's father addressed the Court saying that his son was left in a state of inactivity. Late in 1814 or early in 1815, Barnes, Todd, and J. Tims were sent off to Bengal, and the first two were employed in the Ishapore Powder Works, Tims having died on the voyage. Four out of the seven remained; but in 1820 there were only two: Hattersley, who was employed under the Superintending Engineer on Rs. 175 a month, and Braddock, who had found a post in the office of the Accountant-General.

John Braddock had a rather extraordinary career. He was

the son of Mr. John Braddock, Master Refiner of Saltpetre at the Royal Powder Mills, Waltham Abbey, and when the Court sent him to Madras in 1813 his covenant stated that he was to practise and teach the art of making gunpowder. As we have seen, he remained in a 'state of inactivity' till we find him in the office of the Accountant-General in 1820, though it is possible he did have some employment before that year. When at the end of 1824 the officer in command of the Carnatic Ordnance Artificer Corps died, Braddock was appointed Superintendent of the Corps, with the military rank of Deputy Assistant Commissary of Ordnance. He held the post till 1833, when he was transferred to the arsenal at Fort St. George. He had been given the rank of deputy commissary in August 1831 and was appointed lieutenant in the 1st Native Veteran Battalion in 1833. For a short time in 1832 he actually held charge of the gunpowder manufactory, while Major Napier, Native Infantry, who had succeeded Balmain in 1823, was away on other duty; but it was not till the end of 1835 that he was employed on the work for which he was sent to Madras twenty-two years before. In November 1835 he was posted to the works to assist in the renovation and improvement of the machinery, and for a time in 1838–9 he acted as Superintendent till Captain C. Taylor, Artillery, joined. In April 1839 he was appointed in the Public Department as Actuary and Accountant of the Government Bank and Accountant of the Savings Bank; but was to continue under the Military Board to complete the work at the gunpowder manufactory. The Court expressed surprise at the delay in completing the work and did not like Braddock being in two departments. Lieutenant John Braddock, of the Invalid Battalion, died in Madras on 9th September 1840.

The remuneration of the Superintendent was changed several times; Bishop had 400 pagodas a month as salary at the end of his tenure. Balmain, who succeeded him in 1813, had 300, raised to 350 in 1816, and then Rs. 1,400 in 1822.

Napier also drew Rs. 1,400; but from 1838 Rs. 1,000 was the established allowance. In all cases the Superintendent also received the pay and allowances of his regimental rank, which meant that Major Taylor in 1844 drew Rs. 1,610–14 as his total remuneration, while Captain Anstruther in 1845 received Rs. 1,392 in all.

In September 1818 the European clerks in the mills petitioned against being compelled to work on Sundays, and a similar petition was forwarded by 335 native workmen. The Military Board refused the application, but were overruled by Government.

In June 1826, with the close of the Burmese War, the manufacture of powder was suspended, the daily output up till then having been forty 90-lb. barrels. The wastage was high, being 18 per cent. of saltpetre, 3 per cent. of sulphur, 30 per cent. of charcoal, and 4 per cent. of gunpowder. In 1828 the drive for economy, instituted by Lord William Bentinck on orders from the Court, was taken up by Mr. Lushington, the Governor, who reduced the scale of practice ammunition and ordered two of the four mills only to be worked, thus saving Rs. 1,000 a month in establishment charges alone. However, in the season of 1830, eight and a half months, February to the middle of October, the output of the two mills reached 347,535 lb. of powder, with a wastage of 13½ per cent. of saltpetre, 2 per cent. of sulphur, 30½ per cent. of charcoal, and only ¾ per cent. of gunpowder. Stock being sufficient for four years, manufacture was wholly stopped during 1831, one mill being kept in action to prepare saltpetre for private merchants. Discharged men were granted gratuities or pensions according to length of service. Manufacture was soon resumed, and the Superintendent, Major Napier, was in trouble over the deterioration and inferior range of powder made in 1832, for which he was unable to account.

In 1835 it was decided that the mills were defective, and a new metal bed and pair of cylinders were cast under the direction of Braddock for one of them; ploughs being introduced on them which rendered unnecessary the employment of four men for turning the composition. Government then agreed that the other three mills should be completed in the same manner. The Military Board also proposed 'to use pumps or other machinery in place of the present semi-barbarous system of ladling by hand from boilers to cooling pans, requiring the constant employment of two persons to throw cold water over the bodies and limbs of the two boiler men'. In 1840 it was discovered that the size of grain ordered in 1836 had not been followed, with the result that several years of musketry powder on hand were inferior to English powder. All was ordered to be sent to the works to be ground to the proper size, and the assistance of the late Lieutenant Braddock in the matter was acknowledged. In 1843 Major C. Taylor successfully introduced the pressing and glazing of powder which had often been attempted before. Bullocks continued to work the mills until 1863, when the first steam mill was successfully erected.

A description of these, the last powder works in Madras, received from the Madras Secretariat in 1923, should be of interest:

'Notwithstanding its two tall chimneys nothing could be less like the modern conception of a factory than the drowsy old-world pleasaunce at Perambore, still known as the Powder Mills. It dates from the latter part of the eighteenth century[1] and is enclosed by low walls, and shaded by a variety of trees, conspicuous amid which is the great Baobab (*Adansonia digitata*) from Senegal, its huge suede-covered pods filled with a variety of tamarind greedily devoured by squirrels. Entrance is through a gate to south. The interior contains numerous godowns, a number of widely separated bombproof buildings, and some large masonry tanks, where big pink lotus float upon opaque green water. To north a broken stone bridge partly spans a channel, originally it led to a widespread bombproof edifice, over the arched door of which is the sign "Government Fisheries".'

[1] This is incorrect, it was started in 1803.

The manufacture of gunpowder ceased in Madras in 1887, and in 1893 the harness and saddlery workshops were moved from the arsenal in Fort St. George to the powder works buildings. In 1909 all leather work was concentrated at Cawnpore, and the old powder works were handed over to the Madras Government.

## XI

## THE BENGAL GUNPOWDER MANUFACTORIES

NINE years after Job Charnock had established himself in 1690 at Chatanuttee on the river Hugli, the East India Company formed its settlements in Bengal into a Presidency and ordered the construction of Fort William. By 1702 the fort had been made strong enough to ward off attack, guns had been mounted on the walls, men taken from the ships to serve them, and the garrison raised to 120 men. The fort was not completed, however, with its four bastions and its river wall till 1717. Gunpowder manufacture had long been established in Bombay and Madras, while saltpetre was one of the most important articles of the Company's trade in Bengal, thus it was natural to manufacture gunpowder in Calcutta also. It seems evident that the Council had early erected some sort of a powder mill, for in its consultation of 9th May 1704, it is recorded: 'The powder workhouse through carelessness of the workmen blew up, and in it perished Bickerstaff, a soldier who came on the "Dutchess", also eleven Gentues and one Mahometan.' In December 1717 there was, in store, 42 maunds of cannon powder at Rs. 11–8 per maund, 7 maunds of musket powder at Rs. 14, and 8 maunds of European powder costing Rs. 20 a maund.

The records are silent regarding gunpowder till 1734, when we find that the Storekeeper-General was ordered to purchase powder for the use of the garrison. All references from 1735 to 1754 seem to show that the Company did not then possess any powder works of their own in Calcutta and that they were contracting with their own servants for the supply of gunpowder. In a Consultation dated 30th April 1739, for example, it was resolved that 'saltpetre, brimstone, and charcoal should be supplied from the Company's warehouse and that the Gunner and the Master Attendant should be allowed for making the gunpowder' and 'for the hazard of their mill, cattle, &c.' for the current year, for a maund of cannon powder Rs. 5–8, for musket powder Rs. 8, which they allege is the least they can do it for. From 1744, however, the contracts made with the Gunner appear to have been inclusive ones, the rates being Rs. 16–5 for a chest of cannon and Rs. 20 for a chest of musket powder. By 1748 stock had greatly increased, the Gunner reporting that he had 569 maunds of cannon powder, 113 of musket, and 208 of European. The Council ordered half to be sent to Fort St. David, with the Gunner's remarks 'on what good and what indifferent'.

In 1748 the Court ordered the abolition of the gun-room crew and its replacement by a company of regular artillery, and Captain Lawrence Witherington was sent out to be one of the officers of this company. In July of the following year Witherington made proposals for making gunpowder for the Company, and after some delay and his assurance that his terms were the lowest possible, he was given the contract. It seems probable that he had acquired the mills belonging to the Gunner, and that he manufactured powder for the Company from 1749 up to 1753. But his output can have been neither sufficient nor satisfactory. In January 1753 there appears, in a Consultation, the following: 'Having small quantity of gunpowder in provision, resolved that the Fort returns no salutes to any of our country ships', and it was further resolved to purchase some from Hugli and to ask Bombay for a large quantity. The quality was found by Colonel Scott to be inferior both for ordnance and for small arms, and he said he had heard complaints about it all along the Coromandel Coast. Scott also condemned the powder from Bombay, and supply from there was stopped.

Lieutenant-Colonel Caroline Frederick Scott, 29th Foot, A.D.C. to H.R.H. the Duke of Cumberland, was appointed Engineer-General of all the Company's Settlements in the East Indies, with a salary of £400 a year, by unanimous resolution of the Court on 11th October 1752. He was also appointed major of the garrison of Fort William, Commander of all the Company's forces at that Presidency, and Third in Council with the usual salary and allowances. This salary was £250 a year, with allowances for diet, servants, and palanquin, also suitable apartments or payment in lieu. He was allowed 100 guineas for the expenses of his passage and in November was given a present of £400. A passage was provided for himself, two English servants, and a black boy in the *Winchelsea* in December, and he was granted permission to ship wine at the Madeiras. Scott had distinguished himself during the rebellion in Scotland, especially in the defence of Fort William in March 1746, when he was a Captain in Guise's Regiment (6th Foot). Three companies of his regiment with three companies of Argyll Militia, about 500 in all, formed the garrison of the fort, which was armed with eight 12-pounders, twelve 6-pounders, two 13-inch mortars, and ten cohorns. The siege lasted a month before the rebels spiked their guns and retired. Scott is said to have earned notoriety as one of the most ruthless of the English officers in the suppression of the rebellion. He was promoted major in September 1746 and lieutenant-colonel in the 29th Foot in January 1749.

Scott arrived in Calcutta in September 1753, having visited Madras on his way and reported on the fortifications there. He evidently acted with great energy during his short stay in Bengal, for, besides preparing plans for the defence of the settlement (which were never carried out), he made proposals for contracting for the manufacture of gunpowder, which were accepted by the Council. The contract was to be an exclusive one for three years, all materials being supplied by the Company, and Scott to be paid at fixed rates for refining and working them. Scott wrote home in December 1753 that he had bought a large garden with an indifferent house in it for £450 and had begun the erection of powder mills thereon. He said his scheme was not only to make powder for Bengal and for the Coromandel Coast, but also for any one who would buy it, and he hoped that, when he left the country, the mills would be in such good order that the Company would buy them and take manufacture into their own hands. He added that he was told the project was worth a good £500 a year without fraud, though his predecessor was said to have made upwards of £8,000 in five years. In January 1754 he wrote that the gunpowder business would 'cost him a good £1,000 before he turned a farthing' to his advantage, but he believed the contract to be a good one; and in February he wrote that he was extremely well and had been excessively busy all the winter getting his powder mills up, though not finished in spite of driving the workmen all he could. The works were not complete when, in March, he went to Madras at the urgent request of the Council of Fort St. George, and, unfortunately, he died there of a violent fever on 12th May.

The Company had bad luck with their engineer-generals. In 1696 the Court sent out to Madras Captain von Werhinhoffe as Engineer and Miner-General, his commission being dated in April of that year. His salary was to be £100 a year and he was to have accommodation in the Fort and at the general table, taking place next to the chiefs of factories. He went to Fort St. David in March 1698 to construct fortifications there; but four years later he was dismissed as constituting 'a great charge to the Company to no purpose'. Then in January 1748 Captain A. Delavaux was sent out to Fort St. George; but he was found to be unsatisfactory and was charged with misappropriation of funds. He deserted to Pondicherry in May 1749 and was cashiered. The Court then appointed Mr. Benjamin Robins on £500 a year for life, on condition that he served them as engineer-general for five years. He arrived in Madras in July 1750 with six assistants, and found the fortifications in a ruinous state; but before he could do much he died at Fort St. David, twelve months later. The *Encyclopaedia Britannica* says that 'The introduction of rifling owes much to Benjamin Robins', and he was the inventor of the ballistic pendulum for the measurement of muzzle velocity, and the author of several works on gunnery. Captain John Brohier of the Artillery, who had been one of Robins's assistants, took his place pending the arrival of Colonel Scott, and his career, ending with his desertion to Ceylon, is referred to in Chapter II.

The administrators of Scott's estate in India were Ensign William Scott and Captain John Buchanan. William Scott had been granted a commission as ensign in Bengal in November 1752, and went out to India at the same time as Colonel Scott, and was probably a relative. He went to Madras with Colonel Scott in March 1754 in command of a guard consisting of a sergeant-corporal and sixteen men. Captain John Buchanan is somewhat of a mystery. In a recent article in *Bengal, Past and Present* it is stated that he was Buchanan of Craigievern, and that in 1737 he conveyed his land to trustees in security for the burdens thereon and for an advance of £400 towards purchasing a Quartermaster's Warrant in the Royal Regiment of North British Dragoons. Colonel Scott was then a cornet in the same regiment. In the Army List for 1746 John Buchanan appears as an ensign in Major-General St. Clair's Regiment (now the Royal Scots) and was a lieutenant in 1747. The establishment of the regiment was reduced in 1748 and probably Buchanan had to leave. He asked the East India Company for a commission, representing his services in His Majesty's forces, and was made a captain on the Bengal establishment in 1752, proceeding to India in the following year. Some authorities have stated that he married Colonel Scott's niece, who, after the death of Buchanan in the Black Hole in June 1756, met Warren Hastings at Fulta and later became his first wife. Sydney Grier, in *The Letters of Warren Hastings*, agrees that Mary, widow of Captain John Buchanan, was the first wife of Warren Hastings; but states that the little evidence there is, is against the supposition that she was a niece of Colonel Scott, and suggests that Buchanan was his nephew, since he was his principal executor. I have not been able to find any evidence in support of this suggestion.

Scott's executor in England was his brother George Lewis Scott, who was sub-preceptor to His Royal Highness Prince George. Colonel Scott made two wills, the first as he was leaving England in January 1753, leaving everything to his children, and the second before he left Calcutta in March 1754, in which he left his property to 'his dear friend Mrs. Martha Bowdler' (who may have been the mother of his four children, three girls and one boy, all named Scott), or failing her to the children. The boy was named Frederick and is probably the Frederick Scott shown in the Records of the Royal Military Academy as a cadet, who, being only 11¾ years old, was allowed to remain absent till he attained the age of 12, by an authority dated in September 1764. Many children of tender years were entered as cadets at this time, one mentioned in the same authority being only 3 years old. Frederick Scott had been a gentleman cadet since November 1762. Caroline Frederick Scott was commissioned as fire-worker in July 1769, having probably added his father's name of Caroline at some time. He was invalided as a captain in June 1793 and died at Rochester in September 1794.

The action of the Council at Fort William after the death of Colonel Scott is inexplicable. In January 1753 they had noted the deficiency in the supply of gunpowder; a year later they entered into a contract with Scott for its manufacture, but he died before he could produce any, and in June 1754 they invited tenders for a new contract. Yet in July they decided that 'as the Gentlemen on the Coast had not asked for any gunpowder and there was a large stock in the Magazines, they would defer making or contracting for any at present'. Scott's executors endeavoured to sell his mills, which were on the site known as Perrin's Garden, to the Council, but at first without success; so Buchanan bought and finished them and made powder for sale to the shipping. In November 1755 the Council again invited tenders, when

Buchanan offered to sell the mills for Rs. 4,000, and to make powder at actual cost plus a yearly recompense; he stated that they had cost Scott Rs. 6,000, and had cost him, Buchanan, Rs. 734 to finish. At last, in February 1756, the Council agreed to buy them and to allow Buchanan Rs. 700 a year to oversee the manufacture. Four months later the procrastination and ineptitude of the Council had its reward, when Calcutta was captured and the tragedy of the Black Hole caused the death of Buchanan, Witherington, William Scott, and many others. Roger Drake, in his remarks on Holwell's report on the siege, said they had 700 maunds of gunpowder, about one-third being damaged, and he had moved for the purchase of Scott's mills and recommended that Buchanan should have the making of powder, two months before the Council agreed; and he also commented on the superiority of the powder which Buchanan had made.

For the next twenty years the Company maintained their own powder mills at Perrin's Garden, which took its name from Captain Charles Perrin, a free mariner, master and owner of several ships trading on the coasts, who in 1707 made his last voyage and settled on the estate named after him. The property was on the river bank at the north end of the settlement, with the Mahratta ditch just beyond it. Perrin died in 1708, when his house, compound, and 'house moveables' were sold by auction for Rs. 2,822. It belonged to the Company in 1724, being used as a garden residence by the Company's servants and as a guard-house for an outpost. In December 1752 the place 'being much out of repair and of no use to any of the Company's servants', was sold 'at Publick Outcry' to Mr. Holwell for Rs. 2,500, and Holwell sold it in 1753 to Scott. Buchanan in 1756 only sold the powder mills; the house and the rest of the ground being sold to the Council in 1759 for Rs. 2,000 arcot.

The Court, writing in February 1756 authorizing the purchase of the mills if the price were reasonable, referred to the complaints of the powder made at Calcutta, where every ingredient was to be had in plenty and perfection. They urged manufacture by contract or under the 'Inspection of Propper Supravisors', and enjoined the utmost care to see 'that strictest justice is done us in the Quality as well as Price'. They kept a strict eye on expenses, as witness a letter of March 1759: 'to prevent needless expense of powder on board their ships, new regulations have been made allowing cheers instead of guns'.

In February 1757 the Council ordered the mills at Perrin's to be repaired and 'Major Killpatrick to supravise with same gratuity as was allowed to Buchanan'. Killpatrick was ill, so Mr. J. McDonald, assistant to Captain Brohier, the Chief Engineer, was ordered to oversee the mills and manufacture gunpowder on the Company's account, to be paid Rs. 800 a year for his trouble and attendance. McDonald got into trouble the following year on account of weak and defective powder, which was ordered to be returned to him to be made over again; but evidently that was not the whole trouble, as at the same time Government resolved to fine heavily any one with salary supervising the making of gunpowder, if it could be proved that he had made any advantage over his pay. The Court wrote again in March 1758 commenting on the Council's orders of February 1757, saying that manufacture was of the greatest importance and they should be able to make sufficient not only for Bengal but elsewhere. They directed all powder to be proved by a Standing Committee of the Major, the Engineer, the Storekeeper, and the Gunner.

In March 1759 the purchase of the whole estate was effected, as it was considered necessary that the person who made the powder should reside on the spot. The mills were again repaired and Mr. Martin Costelly was appointed to their charge, being allowed Rs. 60 a month for this. He was formerly Captain of the *London* sloop, which was lost at the capture of Calcutta and for which and for other losses he was granted Rs. 4,226 as compensation. In the register of marriages he is shown as having married 'Anna, a country woman', in February 1750.

Unfortunately in May 1759 the mills and adjacent godown took fire and blew up, with the loss of 150 barrels of powder; but the mills seem to have been quickly repaired. Brohier reported in August that the powder made by 'Pistals and Mortars' was much better and in greater quantity than formerly, and said it was necessary to enlarge the ground and to enclose it. It was found that the cost of buying ground to the southward to extend the works was excessive, being Rs. 30,000 plus Rs. 10,000 for levelling, so it was in contemplation to acquire a site about a quarter of a mile beyond the Ditch. In December the Court were informed that the works had been entirely destroyed and it was intended to erect new ones on the new site which had been rented from 'Petumber Seat' for Rs. 250 a year. Costelly had pointed out the dangerous position of the existing works from their proximity to straw and other buildings. He was ordered to take possession of the new site and to remove utensils and materials to it and to put forward a list of buildings required. When the Council saw Costelly's list of buildings required, they refused to sanction what they called the immense expense, stopped the removal, and ordered the most effectual methods to be taken to make the works safe at Perrin's. In informing the Court of their action, in February 1760, they mentioned that the powder was not turning out to their expectations.

Evidently for some time the supply of powder from the mills was neither sufficient nor good, and heavy demands had been sent home, with the result that the Court wrote in April 1760 a letter dealing with the whole subject. They said it was impossible to send out the quantity required, so they would accede to the request for some person well skilled in the manufacture. They had entertained William Smith as Powder Maker at £170 a year, and Robert Smith, as his assistant, on £100 in full for wages, diet money, and all other allowances except house-rent, and they added that they had been to the expense of having William Smith instructed in burning charcoal and refining brimstone. They sent out with these men models of a horse mill, corning and dusting houses, a gunpowder press, and several other materials for the works.

The history of these works in Bagh Bazaar during the next ten years or so seems to have been most unsatisfactory. The two Smiths inspected the works on their arrival, and in November 1760 reported, 'the method that is used now by the Director of the Powder Works, in all respects seems to us so inconsistent to true Reason that we think it a meer impossibility that it can be of Perfection, either for present or future service'. The Engineer was ordered to make inquiry of ground proper for powder mills, to calculate cost and lay plans before the Board; but nothing seems to have come of this, and in March 1761 money was allowed for repairs to the bridges and to the straw buildings for making the gunpowder. Some efforts to improve matters seem to have been made, and a Mr. Edward Davis was entertained as Millwright for three years on £100 a year; but the Court in March 1763 had again to complain of the heavy demands for powder from home, and they said they had heard from Smith who reported that the works were not completed and spoke of interruption from Costelly. The Court also referred to samples sent home and tried and found to be unfit for any service. In May 1764 the Court wrote again, and said it was very difficult to find a person well versed in the manufacture of gunpowder. Mr. Walton had been for three or four years qualifying himself and had offered to proceed during the next season, when he would be fully master of the whole process. They stated that as an encouragement they would appoint him a factor on the Bengal establishment to rank after the lowest factor at the time of his arrival. Again writing in February 1765 they said they were surprised to learn that, though Smith had greatly improved manufacture, powder was still inferior, charcoal very bad, and brimstone not properly refined. They said they were sending out Mr. Walton, who was thoroughly experienced, and they ordered that a Committee, composed of the Military Storekeeper, the Chief Engineer, and the Commandant of Artillery, was to inspect the works every month.

In June 1766 the Committee reported the works to be in a very bad condition, stating that temporary repair would cost Rs. 2,000, while the estimate for works on Mr. Walton's plan would amount to from 80,000 to 100,000 rupees. The Council, of course, decided for repair. Walton died in 1768, when Smith resumed charge as Master of the Powder Works. Some improvements were made by Major du Gloss, when he was appointed Commissary of Stores in 1769; but Smith seems to have continued in immediate control till another change was made in 1774.

The Court wrote in March 1774:

'Upon consulting with Lieutenant Colonel Campbell on the means of putting the Manufacture of Gunpowder on the best footing, We have thought it necessary to recommend it to you to Appoint Mr. Robert Stewart, Assistant Engineer, to superintend your Powder Works and to give him charge of that office, now held by Mr. Smith, as soon as may be after the receipt hereof, the latter continuing as Deputy as formerly under Mr. Walton.'

Captain Stewart took over the works in December 1774, and soon represented the inconvenience and danger of their position and submitted plans and estimates for new works. The Court were informed in November of the following year that Stewart had selected a site and had been authorized to proceed with the erection of works on the plan submitted by him. The site selected was at Akra, at the bottom of Garden Reach, four miles due west of Kidderpore Docks; it was directly opposite Muniakhali Point on the other side of the river, which is presumably the reason why the works were sometimes referred to as being at Manicolly. The site is said to be now entirely under water.

Manufacture continued in the old works in Bagh Bazaar

from December 1774 under Captain Stewart, on the Company's account, with a salary as Superintendent of Rs. 300 a month; but in January 1776 Stewart was given a contract for three years, he bearing all expenses. In May he had to report that 'the Corning house blew up and as the wind was strong the barrel shed was set on fire and thence to the Pilon sheds, petre sheds and composition house, all consumed. Eight men perished in the corning house. There was no fire engine.' He ended, 'this unfortunate accident will put a total stop to the business here. I shall therefor redouble my application towards the completion of the New Works.' Stewart's contract, which would have expired in December 1778, was renewed for a further three years, in May of that year, when he took over the works at Akra at cost price, the Company binding itself to take them back at a value to be fixed by appraisers mutually chosen.

Though the Court had in April 1777 expressed their satisfaction of the 'capability and assiduity' of Stewart and of the success of the works, yet soon after the expiry of his second contract the Council took possession, and in May 1782 ordered him to hand over the works to 'Mr. Edmund Hay, the Agent appointed for carrying into execution the new plan adopted for the Manufacture of Gunpowder'. This Stewart did, under protest, in October. Mr. Hay was at the time an assistant secretary, and in 1784 was secretary in the Secret Department with a salary of Rs. 1,700 a month.

It is probable that Stewart had not supplied the full quantity of powder required, as in April 1782 Colonel Duff, the Commissary of Stores, reported that there would only be 3,494 barrels of powder in store, after the quantity ordered to Fort St. George and Bombay had been dispatched, while 8,000 barrels were considered necessary for the defence of Fort William. In October of the same year, owing to the dependence of the other Presidencies on Calcutta for powder, the Board of Ordnance were instructed to erect without delay as many new mills as they judged necessary. The

Board, however, was so dilatory over the business that Government gave the order direct to the Agent, and informed the Board that it was in contemplation to erect mills at Chunar for supply to upper stations. Nothing came of the Chunar suggestion, and the increase to the productive capacity of the works at Akra was accelerated. Hay said at the end of the year that he was erecting ten new mills with iron instead of stone cylinders, and would be able to make 6,600 barrels a year. He had then as assistant Mr. John Farquhar, who later became Superintendent of the Ishapore Powder Works.

By June 1783 the quantity in store had increased to 7,000 barrels, so it was resolved to let Admiral Sir E. Hughes have the 2,000 barrels he asked for, to be sent at the first opportunity. The Admiral had asked for the best quality and stronger than that used for other services. Hay wrote that he did not know how to make any better, and suggested that powder deteriorated in store, and mentioned that 'Lewis the fourteenth' had all his powder packed in two barrels. Hay suggested covering barrels with coarse cloth dipped in dammar and oil.

On 1st February 1785 Warren Hastings went by coach eight miles down the river to these powder mills, where he dined with Hay and a party of his friends. Hay, like Warren Hastings and William Hickey, was an old Westminster boy. From here Warren Hastings went on board his budgerow (country boat) at 4 o'clock and left India for the last time.

From the Annual Statement for the year 1786–7 we learn that powder manufacture was suspended, as stock was in excess, also that the Agent's charges, delivered on honour, for the twelve months to the end of April 1787 were Rs. 95,636 sonat, for about 3,379 barrels, cost of each being about Rs. 30–8. By the terms of the Agency the Agent obtained as profit or reward half of the saving on the former contract price of Rs. 44–8, which gave Hay a claim on the Company for Rs. 21,103, quite a nice addition to his salary as Secretary.

In August 1787 the Court were informed that Hay had resigned the Agency at the particular desire of Lord Cornwallis, who did not think a Secretary to Government should have any charge that could interfere with his attention to his department. Government added: 'We have appointed Mr. John Farquhar, formerly a Lieutenant on the Bombay Establishment and who had assisted Mr. Hay in performing the duties of the Agency to the charge of the Works.' They also informed the Court that 'the Powder Works being in a very ruinous state and the manufacture of powder being stopped in consequence of the large quantity in store, we have directed Mr. Farquhar to look for a proper Place to erect new works and to propose a plan for them, which may be executed by contract after advertising for proposals'. In a further letter, in February 1788, the Court were told that as far back as May 1783 a survey of the works at Manicolly showed them in such a ruinous condition that 'we imagine nothing but the lowness of the Treasury prevented improvements and heavy repairs'. This is a very curious statement, as Stewart can only have completed the works at Akra at the end of 1776 or early 1777, so they were in a ruinous state after six years' work. A further survey was made in 1787, and it was reported that the mills and machinery were in a very bad state, while the site was low and unhealthy and the water bad. Farquhar recommended a site at Ishapore in the neighbourhood of Pulta.

John Farquhar was born at Crimond in Aberdeenshire in 1751 and went to Bombay, where he was commissioned as ensign on 27th September 1770 and as lieutenant on 10th January 1775. It is said that he was incapacitated by a dangerous wound in the hip, which caused him to resign and go to Bengal as a free merchant, and that he studied chemistry. His efforts to establish the manufacture of iron cannon at Beerbhoom will be referred to in a subsequent chapter; but apparently he gave up the attempt when he went to Akra about 1782 as assistant to Hay in the powder works there.

He was a man of great character and ability; but his parsimony was so great that he has been called 'the prince of Indian misers, who contracted with the solitary servant of his house to supply his table for two annas a day'. When he left India in 1814 he is said to have had a fortune of half a million sterling and to have been so dirty and disreputable in appearance that, on his arrival from Tilbury at the office of his banker, Mr. Hoare, the clerks refused him admission. One account says he walked from Tilbury to save coach-hire. There is no evidence that any of his fortune was obtained illicitly, and it is said that he had other business in Calcutta connected with a monopoly of pigs and bacon. At home he became a principal partner in a brewery and in a firm of East India Agents. He bought Fonthill Abbey with most of its contents for £330,000, and when he died in July 1826 is said to have been worth a million and a half. The description of Farquhar on the main gate of the present rifle factory at Ishapore as Assistant Surgeon cannot be correct. In no official record nor in any of the printed lists is he so described.

The site proposed by Farquhar has been called by many names. Actually it was at Bankibazaar, near the modern Palta, about three miles above Barrackpore. The name has disappeared from the map, and after a time the place became known as Ishapore, which name it has retained. Bankibazaar was originally the settlement of the Ostend Company, formed under a charter granted in 1722 by the Emperor of Austria, whose flag was flown there. It met with bitter opposition from the British and Dutch and was abandoned in 1733, when the Faujdar of Hugli besieged the place. There were powder magazines and possibly a powder mill in the settlement, some of the buildings of which still remain.

In April 1788 Farquhar put forward his plans for the new works in which he proposed a mill with a sluice to be worked by the tide at a cost of Rs. 23,230, to produce 960 lb. a day, equal to 16 bullock mills producing each 60 lb. a day and costing Rs. 3,000 apiece. Colonel J. D. Pearse, Commandant of Artillery, was ordered by Lord Cornwallis to inspect the site and to examine Farquhar's plans. He reported that 'the place chosen was better than where the mills now are. Below the Fort they were liable to be destroyed by an armed boat passing up the river. The only objection to the new site was the vicinity of the foreign settlements. The mills should make powder more equable in force than the present rolling mills, though such mills were capable of improvement till superior to pestles or pilons. He saw no impediment to the proposal.' He also said that the powder made since Mr. Stewart's time was stronger than the English powder; but was not so good 'in point of equality in force'. He expected that Farquhar would have stiff whitish-blue clay of 17½ feet thick for his foundations. Government approved the plans and authorized the completion of one mill up to a cost of Rs. 23,230. The land and buildings at Manicolly were advertised for sale by auction and were sold on 31st May 1790 for Rs. 3,000.

Farquhar was the Company's Agent for the Manufacture of Gunpowder at Calcutta from 1st June 1787 till 1st March 1814, of which period of nearly 27 years all but the first two were spent at Ishapore. He was given a salary of Rs. 500 a month while in charge of the Akra works; but at Ishapore he was allowed Rs. 5 per barrel, with a minimum of Rs. 18,000 a year, later changed to a fixed salary of Rs. 1,500 a month. The new works, though not completed till 1791–2, were soon in production. Unfortunately there is a gap in the records and it cannot be said whether or not Farquhar's plan for a tide-worked mill was ever carried out, or, if it was, whether it was a success; but it is not mentioned by any of his successors. Captain Parlby, in his introduction to Colonel Anderson's *Sketch of the Mode of Manufacturing Gunpowder at Ishapore*, published in 1862, goes so far as to state that 'Farquhar's powder was made in the native mode by foot mills under mat houses and sifted in leather sieves'. But certainly Parlby is incorrect; both rolling and pilon mills were part of the machinery installed by Farquhar. In 1794 he was complaining of the non-receipt of the iron cylinders ordered from home for grinding saltpetre and 'asked to be allowed to cast two more zinc cylinders, as those in use for pulverizing charcoal and sulphur ran true and were very good'. He added that if the iron cylinders came they could be used and the others converted into excellent powder mills which would not be subject to explosion; the cost of the two zinc cylinders would be Rs. 2,810, and Government approved. Moreover, 222 cattle were allowed for working the mills, which rather tends to show that the tide-worked plan came to nothing. It is true that, after an explosion in 1795, Farquhar had to put hand pilons and mortars into use to cope with the output required till repairs could be effected. Captain J. H. Pearson, of the Engineers, who was repairing the mills at this time, made the curious suggestion that 'prisoners from the Jails should work the mills instead of cattle, thus saving cattle and drivers, and it would be only a moderate punishment'. Economical as the idea was, it was not adopted. It is true, as Parlby wrote, that many of the buildings were mat or straw sheds, but this construction was considered suitable for all kinds of workshops, not only at that time, but for many years after; moreover, light construction had many advantages for powder work.

In 1794 an assistant was authorized, the first being Lieutenant Joseph Taylor, of the Artillery, who had just completed a contract for the manufacture of gun-carriages. The salary was Rs. 250 a month, plus regimental pay and allowances, and he was to reside at the works, to make himself acquainted with all materials and methods, to attend the weighing and mixing, to assist in keeping the books and accounts, and 'to benefit by the Talents and long Experience' of Farquhar. The Chief Engineer recommended house-rent allowance for Taylor, saying that the existing quarters were no more than sufficient for the Agent, as they consisted of four rooms, one being the laboratory, so an allowance of

Rs. 144 sonat a month was granted. The establishment in 1799 consisted of 6 Europeans—2 sergeants and 2 privates for guard, 1 cooper, and 1 sergeant for cattle overseeing—with 653 Indians, the total cost of this being Rs. 2,903 a month. Farquhar said he obtained his labour from Chittagong and Berhampore, and asked that certain skilled men might be retained and not discharged in the monsoon. This was approved. In 1800 Captain Taylor was appointed to the new Gunpowder Agency at Allahabad, and Mr. Brice, a civilian but not a covenanted servant, was appointed assistant to Farquhar on Rs. 500 sicca a month, including allowance for house-rent.

Accounts were frequently a trouble to Farquhar and were usually much delayed. He was allowed a European clerk, but this man was in the office of the Military Auditor-General in Calcutta, and Farquhar complained that he had to go into Calcutta whenever he had business with the man. The Military Auditor-General agreed with Farquhar in September 1803 that the confusion and delay in his accounts had been due to 'Separating the Responsibility of the Accounts from the Executive duty of the Agency', but then, as for more than a century after, accounts were considered to be an end in themselves rather than as means to help the Executive. There may have been suspicions of the integrity of some of the Agents of supply, as in 1810 Government issued an order to the effect that 'All persons entrusted with the expenditure of public money in Military Departments were to verify on oath'. The following were twice a year to make oath before the nearest magistrate that the sums charged in their accounts for the six months preceding had been expended for the purposes set forth: Commissary of Stores at Fort William, Agents for Manufacture of Gun-carriages and of Gunpowder; and various others. This procedure can hardly have affected any one intent on corrupt practices, nor would the next step, which was to order, later in the same year, that Agents were to swear on a form which ended thus: 'I do further solemnly swear that neither directly nor indirectly have I derived, nor will I derive, any profit or emolument whatever from my situation as . . . beyond the regular salary allowed me by Government.'

Explosions were not infrequent. There was one in 1795 due to neglect of orders and the badness of the floors, when Farquhar referred to the low rate of wages which prevented good men engaging. An increase was approved, as also was his estimate of Rs. 4,674 for repairs. Another explosion occurred in April 1796, when two men were killed and no cause was discovered. Farquhar reported that 'many of the people absconded as is usual on such occasions, but are returning to work'. The worst was one in May 1799, when 24,456 lb. of powder were destroyed, 7 men killed, 5 more died of their injuries, and 6 were disabled. There were others: one in 1800 killing 5 men; 2 in 1802; and again 2 in 1809 killing 3 men, one being due to a thunder-storm. Complaints of the quality of the powder were few, but there was serious trouble in this respect in 1800, when a deficiency in strength was noted and an inquiry was ordered by the Governor-General. The Military Board gave various reasons and proposed certain remedies, which were adopted, no blame being placed on Farquhar. In 1802, however, he got into more serious trouble and was actually suspended for some six months. In the Military Consultations of April 1802 there are several reports regarding Farquhar's conduct: his failure to supply his accounts for two years with the necessary vouchers; his excessive wastage of saltpetre; and the high cost of his gunpowder, the latter said to be Rs. 40 a barrel, against Rs. 26 and 22 formerly. Farquhar said the saltpetre supplied to him from the Company's stores was bad, so Dr. Fleming was directed to test the saltpetre and Farquhar to submit further explanations. In their consultations the Board referred to Farquhar's wide discretion, which they were unable to control; they said they thought it wise to wink at suspected abuses and to defer investigation during the pressure of a difficult and most extensive war. From later consultations in February and March 1803 it appears that Dr. Fleming agreed that the saltpetre was bad, and that the Board had received the accounts for 1800–1 and 1801–2 with explanations from Farquhar, who had pointed out errors in the Board's calculations and had insisted that the powder cost only Rs. 21–3–8 per barrel. He also stated that he had always made good powder when allowed the materials from which, from long experience, he knew good powder could be made. The Board admitted the errors in calculation and said they could not express any opinion on the number of men employed, nor on other technical matters; in fact they threw up their case, and the Governor-General ordered Farquhar to resume the duties of Agent without forfeiture of salary. In 1809 Government were informed that the average yearly output for the past five years had been 4,580 barrels.

The establishment authorized in 1801 consisted of:

Sirdars—1 at Rs. 12, 4 at Rs. 8, 2 at Rs. 6.
Mistries—Carpenter, smith, cooper, and coppersmith, each Rs. 12.
1 Jemadar at Rs. 6, 10 Peons at Rs. 4, 2 boat serangs at Rs. 10.
1 Head Sircar (clerk) at Rs. 50, 2 Sircars at Rs. 25.
6 men keeping the ground clean at Rs. 3.
4 Ghurie wallahs (watermen) at Rs. 4.
Extra people according to amount of powder to be made.

When Farquhar resigned in March 1814 his assistant was Surgeon A. Haig, who had been appointed as such in October 1810, but curiously enough a junior, Surgeon J. Hare, was appointed to act as Agent, Haig remaining as assistant. These medical officers remained in the Manufactory for not quite two years, as the Court had decided that superintendents of all factories should be military officers, with preference to the Artillery, but not medical officers. It seems evident that little progress had been made during the latter part of Farquhar's agency, and methods at home were well in advance of those in India. As has been stated in the chapter on the Madras gunpowder manufactory, Captain Fraser's visit to instruct the other Presidency Agents in the home methods never came off. However, Captain Galloway, of the 14th Native Infantry, Agent for Gunpowder at Allahabad, visited Madras on his return from leave to the Cape in 1815, and submitted a report on Fraser's proposals, which he condemned as excessively costly, and made suggestions of his own. Government decided that Galloway should take charge at Ishapore till the arrival of Captain Macleod, of the Engineers. There ensued a curious struggle between the Court, backing Galloway, and the Governor-General, supporting his choice, Captain Macleod. It had been definitely decided to carry out improvements at Ishapore, the chief being the substitution of cylinder mills of greatly increased power for the small cylinder mills and other out-of-date plant, and also alterations in the processes for refining, mixing, and drying. The Court directed that Galloway should be appointed on account of his experience and science; but Macleod had already been selected by Government, who considered him to be in no way inferior to Galloway. It was eventually decided that all reforms should be turned over to Macleod, who had arrived on 18th March 1817 as Agent, while Galloway was to have exclusive charge of the preparation and setting up of the new mills, the cylinders for which were to be cast in the foundry of Fort William. A new furnace was to be set up in the foundry, and Mr. Menaud, who was employed as brassfounder at the Madras powder works, was engaged to assist in the casting of the cylinders. Macleod was to have an allowance of Rs. 1,500 a month as Agent at Ishapore, Galloway to receive Rs. 1,000 as Agent of Allahabad plus Rs. 500 while engaged at Calcutta, while Captain Dundas was to have Rs. 500 for acting at Allahabad.

This dual control at Ishapore ended in October 1820, when Macleod was relieved and was granted a special reward for his work in the erection of the new buildings, which included the Agent's house, which is still in use. Galloway then became Agent at Ishapore and remained so till, in July 1829, the manufacture of powder was suspended as a measure of economy, when his services were placed at the disposal of the Commander-in-Chief. He was promoted lieutenant-colonel in 1826, became a Director of the Company in 1840, and Chairman in 1849, dying in the following year.

The works remained closed till September 1832, when Major R. Powney, Artillery, was appointed Agent. In October of the following year he was directed by the Governor-General to undertake the firework celebration of the renewal of the Company's charter; he had carried out a similar celebration in 1826 for the capture of Bhurtpore. In April 1837 the staff salary was reduced to Rs. 1,000 a month, when Captain T. Timbrell, Artillery, became Agent. The next Agent was Major W. Anderson, who served as such for eleven years from January 1843. He was the author of the pamphlet already referred to, from which we learn a good deal about the methods, plant, and output of Ishapore, though some statements cannot be reconciled with the Bengal Government records. He wrote: 'If any person would but implicitly follow the rules established by Colonel Galloway, he could not fail of fabricating excellent powder'; and he mentions the labour and ingenuity which first established the works at Ishapore. He further mentioned the excellent construction of the old Dutch buildings and of those erected by Macleod and Galloway.

Now, as regards the output of Ishapore: up to 1836 there were four mills in work, five to 1846, six to 1847, and in 1853 there were seven, and it was said that, with eight mills and some improvements, the output could reach 15,000 barrels in the season of eight months. In the eight years 1836 to 1843, 64,277 barrels were made with three explosions, in the five years 1844 to 1848, 52,397 with six explosions. In the season 1852–3, 10,000 barrels were made at Rs. 17–12–7 per barrel. There were two explosions in January 1854, killing 6 men. The mills were still worked by bullocks, about 200 being allowed.

In 1851 the Court were informed that the amount of powder in store was equal to four years' consumption and more than the magazines could conveniently hold. As the buildings at Ishapore required extensive repairs, Government had sanctioned suspension of manufacture for a year. They had deputed the Agent to Allahabad or even farther north to inquire into the question of removing powder manufacture to the old works at Papamhow or some other more eligible locality. Colonel Anderson, in his report in 1853, pointed out that the buildings at Papamhow were quite unsuitable for modern methods of manufacture, and he recommended the retention of Ishapore with perhaps another manufactory at Lahore. Anderson's arguments seem to have been sufficient to stop any further action.

Several distinguished officers of the Bengal Artillery had charge of Ishapore, and the factory continued to make progress and to supply the army with excellent gunpowder after it ceased to belong to the East India Company. In 1903 manufacture of powder there finally ceased, and since that date the site and some of the buildings have been utilized partly for the Rolling Mills Branch of the gun and shell factory and partly for the rifle factory.

There was a tragic event in May 1850, which shows how stores were taken up country from Calcutta and indicates once more the extraordinary carelessness in dealing with gunpowder which runs through the history of the Ordnance Department under the Company. A fleet of 34 native boats, covered with thatch and manned by some 500 dandies (i.e. boatmen), was dispatched from Calcutta soon after Christmas 1849. Of the 34 boats, 21 carried 3,000 barrels of gunpowder, and in charge of the flotilla was one sub-conductor of the Ordnance Department with some magazine men and a guard of a Jemadar and 12 sepoys. The boats remained at Baloo Ghat outside Fort William for three days. No special instructions or orders were given regarding anchoring during the voyage, and it was about four months before it anchored off Raj Ghat at Benares, within a few paces of the bank. A pinnace was allowed to anchor within a few feet of one of the powder boats, and a spark from this pinnace caused the explosion of all the powder, with the result that 348 people were killed or injured and the damage to property in the city amounted to about £17,000.

Bengal had for a time a second gunpowder manufactory situated at Allahabad, and its establishment was due to a letter which General R. Stuart wrote at the end of 1799 to the Military Board, expressing his grave doubts regarding the strength of the powder in store at Futty Ghur. It appeared later, on a proof being made, that the mean range was only about half the standard. An investigation was made at the works in Ishapore as already mentioned; but no inquiry seems to have been made to ascertain how the powder came to be passed for service. However, the Board suggested the desirability of a manufactory at Allahabad to supply the magazines at that place, at Cawnpore, and at Futty Ghur, with the result that the Court were informed in July 1800 that the Governor-General in Council had approved of the suggestion and had appointed Captain Joseph Taylor, who had been assistant to the Agent at Ishapore since 1794, to superintend the new works. It was decided to transfer three zinc cylinder mills from Ishapore to the new works and to sanction the buildings and plant necessary at a cost of Rs. 83,674, the work to be carried out by Taylor. Taylor was also authorized to entertain in Calcutta a millwright on Rs. 100 a month, a European cooper on Rs. 20, six native coopers at Rs. 7 each, and a sircar on Rs. 25.

The site, selected by Lieutenant-Colonel Kyd, approved by Taylor and sanctioned by the Governor-General, was on the banks of the Ganges, extending from the King's garden opposite the village of Papamow about 1,200 yards along the bank of the river. It was said to be the most elevated and driest site and to consist of about 630 biggahs, about five miles from the fort. The Vizier had ordered the delivery of the ground and had granted the use of the King's garden for temporary storage purposes. The estimate of Rs. 83,674, which included a house for Taylor costing Rs. 7,689, provided for six pilon mills with an annual output of 3,000 barrels of powder. The bills actually amounted to Rs. 94,241, but the explanations were accepted, though it was pointed out that Government had ceased to provide houses for officers, a hardship which was carried down to much later times. Taylor's salary was Rs. 1,000 sicca a month, plus pay, full batta, and gratuity of his rank, and his designation was changed from Superintendent to Agent.

Work commenced, apparently, in October 1801, the establishment allowed costing Rs. 2,077 a month. An explosion, attributed to lightning, occurred in June 1802, killing a man and destroying the sifting houses. There seem to have been several explosions, the worst being in March 1805, when the mixing and weighing house containing composition sufficient for about 80 barrels of powder was blown up, killing 43 men. Not unnaturally the Board considered that the house contained too many men and too much material. So much powder had been supplied to Ceylon and Madras from Bengal that early in 1804, besides the rebuilding of a press house at a cost of Rs. 1,293, three other buildings were sanctioned at a cost of Rs. 4,343.

In April 1808 Taylor applied for leave to go to the Presidency, and in June he was permitted to proceed to Europe, and Captain Matthew Stewart, Royal Engineers, was appointed Agent. Stewart seems to have started in the Royal Engineers, and was A.D.C. to the Governor-General in July 1807; in 1810 he was first in the 19th Foot, and later in the 22nd Foot, after which he transferred to the 3rd Ceylon and finally to the 4th Ceylon Regiment. In a letter written by

Stewart in July 1808, the cause of some explosions is revealed. He mentions a trough in a pilon mill in which the beams had, at some time, been brought up to size by facing with planks, and which, on the machinery being stripped for repairs, was found to have dry composition between the beams and the planking. In August 1810 Stewart was allowed to go on service with his regiment leaving for Mauritius, said to be the 22nd Foot, and Captain F. Andree, 4th Native Infantry, acted during his absence. We hear again of failure of powder, that made in the season 1811–12. Stewart explained that it was due to doing the work without European overseers, 'a measure which has become necessary from the utter impossibility of keeping them sober, the last having literally drunk himself to death'. He gave some further explanations, which were accepted, and the powder was ordered to be stored and remade the following season. Stewart resigned towards the end of 1812, as the General Officer Commanding in Ceylon refused to allow him to remain any longer away from his regiment.

Lieutenant A. Galloway, 14th Native Infantry, was appointed Agent, and the works were handed over to him in September. The Marquess of Hastings, the Governor-General, records in his private journal under date 23rd September, 1814, 'proceded to examine the powder works. They were little worth inspection'. Galloway went on leave in October 1814, when Captain J. F. Dundas, Artillery, was appointed to act, but Galloway never returned to Allahabad. During 1819 it was discovered that the whole of the powder made at Allahabad in the season 1816–17 was bad, involving a loss of about Rs. 1,50,000, and it had to be sent back to Allahabad to have the saltpetre extracted. The Board were afraid that the powder made in 1817–18 might also be bad, though in July 1817 the Court had been informed that the work done at Allahabad was a great credit to Dundas and a benefit to the service. In reporting the matter of the bad powder to the Court, Government said the deterioration arose from the manufacture of a greater quantity of powder than the mills were really capable of, owing to the exigencies of the service. The period of milling was reduced, based on the practice of a French chemist, and this was not reported by Dundas. The Court censured Dundas and asked what inquiry had been made into his qualifications before his appointment. He was relieved in October 1819 and Captain C. Graham acted for a year, Captain A. Lindsay becoming Agent in 1820. Lindsay vacated on promotion to lieutenant-colonel in May 1824, when Captain S. Parlby became the last Agent. Parlby had been engaged at Dum Dum in 1823 in the experimental manufacture of Congreve rockets, and his appointment at Allahabad was as Agent for Gunpowder and War Rockets; but the manufacture of rockets ceased in 1828. In April 1824, just before Parlby took over charge, a dreadful explosion occurred, with the destruction of a considerable part of the works, 40 men blown up, and 850 barrels of powder destroyed. The cause was doubtful but was ascribed by the Sirdars to the dropping of a barrel, and they said such a thing had happened some years before. The Agent said a great quantity of powder was in the drying and other houses, owing to the lack of magazine accommodation.

The Governor-General approved the provision of additional magazine accommodation and the immediate repair of the works, but the works were shut down in November 1829 and Parlby's appointment terminated. There were no complaints regarding the powder during Parlby's Agency, and in 1828 Government stated that they were unable to decide whether Ishapore or Allahabad powder was the better; both were unexceptionable.

Soon after Lord William Bentinck became Governor-General he decided as a measure of economy to suspend the manufacture of gunpowder at both Ishapore and Allahabad. In January 1832 the disposal of the land and buildings at Allahabad was considered, but all that was done then was to direct the Collector of the District to take charge of them.

In 1853 there was the inquiry into the capacity and advantages of Ishapore, and the suggestion was made that the works at Allahabad might be reopened; but Colonel Anderson, the Agent at Ishapore, reported that they were antiquated and ill adapted to modern requirements, so the idea was dropped. One of the buildings was granted temporarily to Major Lawrence, afterwards Sir Henry Lawrence, who resided there with his young wife, till in 1838 the outbreak of the Afghan War took him to the work of a political officer. It is said that one at least of the buildings was in use at the time of the Mutiny as powder magazine for the fort, but some time later the buildings were sold to Captain F. C. Chapman of Allahabad.

# XII

## THE MANUFACTURE OF ORDNANCE IN INDIA

THE history of Artillery in India really begins in 1526, when Baber invaded northern India from Kabul and defeated Ibrahim, the Sultan of Delhi, at Paniput. Baber alone had cannon, which he called his 'Feringhi pieces', thus indicating their far western origin, and to these weapons, till then unknown in inland India, his victory was mainly due. In his Memoirs he describes the casting of a large cannon, probably the first to be made in India, the metal flowing from eight 'forges' into the one mould. The melting-furnaces had bellows to provide the blast and were called 'forges'. In 1549 a gun, said to have been the largest piece of brass ordnance in the world, was cast at Ahmednagar; it was 4 feet 8 inches in diameter at the muzzle, with a bore of 28 inches. Hedges, in his Diary, says he saw five large brass guns at Lahar, all taken from the Portuguese at Ormuz, weighing from 31 to 44 cwt. apiece, one having a bore of 9¼ inches, some having been made at Goa in 1618.

The art of gun-casting, however, was neither widely nor properly known for many years after Paniput, not, in fact, till Europeans were available to provide the necessary skill. It is difficult to take Richard Bell's account of his gun-making for Aurangzeb, the Great Mogul, seriously. In his travels, 1654–70, he says his furnace contained 'two hundred and fifty tunns of mettle', and he cast from it eight whole cannon and four mortars; the guns 'did carrie every one a shell of one hundred and sixty pounds of poother, weight of shell being four hundred and fifty pounds English, ye thickness nine inches threw'. He made the carriages in four days. Elephants butted the cannon on to the field, and as the Emperor's fifteen gunners knew nothing about gunnery, Bell loaded with 50 lb. of powder and fired at the elephants, 600 paces away, when, to the annoyance of the Emperor, one was killed at the first shot. Bell says that at first he had refused to make guns, as he had sworn an oath not to teach any one outside the trade, but he changed his mind when the Emperor promised to show him 'how to hoist himself in the air without visible support'.

Bernier says that Aurangzeb had 70 pieces of heavy ordnance, mostly brass, each drawn by 20 yoke of oxen, with elephants to assist, 50 to 60 small brass pieces each drawn by two fine horses, and some 200 to 300 camels each carrying a swivel gun about the size of a double musket. He also states that the Indians were little skilled in artillery, which was mainly manned by Europeans, who were liberally paid. Tavernier records that the gunners were usually English or Dutch, and tells of a Dutch gunner in the service of the Great Mogul, who only obtained his discharge, after sixteen years' service, by showing a general how to mount guns on some hills commanding a rebel fort. There is also a story of an English gunner in the service of Akbar who had an extraordinary reputation for skill at gunnery and also for drinking. Once, when he found himself in a Muhammadan country with no drink provided, he told the Emperor he could not shoot as his sight was weakened by the absence of drink. As soon as arrack was forthcoming, he shot with the greatest accuracy. There is also a record in 1664 of the Subahdar of Bengal forcing the British factors at Hugli to supply him with a party of European gunners for his war with Arracan by the threat of stopping their trade in saltpetre. In 1669 Aurangzeb requested the Council at Surat to ask the Court to send out five gunfounders for him, but Surat offered to sell him several large brass guns besides mortars and shell, while the Court sent an evasive answer to the request.

Most of the guns in the early Indian armies were obtained from European traders. In 1658 the East India Company sent to Madras 15 iron guns, 2 mortars, and 800 shells to be sold 'to our most proffitt', as they thought that the wars in India would create a great demand for such things. There is an entry in the Fort St. George records, dated in August 1679, noting that three iron guns had been sold at 15 pagodas per candy, and offers accepted for four more at the same rate, and the carriages at 12 pagodas apiece, 'which is more than they cost'. Even Cromwell seems to have had some interest in this trade, as he gave a licence to a relation, one Thomas Rolt, to export 3 mortars and 2,000 shells to a Colonel Rainsford, who had been allowed to go to Surat on his own account in 1656. However, the Company ordered the Council at Surat to seize the goods and to sell them, as the licence was an infringement of their charter. Guns were sometimes presented to the Princes, and in 1647 the Madras Council gave Mir Jumlah a brass gun, in lieu of the interest due on a loan of 10,000 pagodas. They were very pleased with themselves, as the interest at the current rate of 1½ per cent. a month amounted to 2,350 pagodas, while the cost of the gun was only 641 pagodas.

The cannon used in the defence of the early settlements of the Company were mostly naval and were served by men drawn from the Company's ships, but when substantial fortifications were constructed proper armaments were sent out. In 1675, for example, 111 pieces of ordnance were sent to Madras, weighing 940 cwt. in all, costing about £1 a cwt. In 1704 the Council at Fort William agreed 'that there being an opportunity to dispose of some guns, the Storekeeper to dispose of as many as he can, not under nine rupees a cwt.' Broome, in his *History of the Bengal Army*, states that 200 guns were sent out in 1685 for works at Chittagong, but the ships having found their way into the Hugli, Job Charnock used the guns for his new settlement at Calcutta. A similar statement appears in Stubbs's *History of the Bengal Artillery*. But Charnock was not established at Chatanuttee (Calcutta) till 1690, and it was not till January 1697 that the people there reported that 'they were employed in fortifying themselves but wanted proper guns for the points' and desired Madras to send at least ten guns for present use. In 1699 the Court ordered a substantial fort to be erected, to be called Fort William, but this was not completed till 1717, and in 1707 fifty pieces of brass ordnance were asked for from England. From the plan of the fort and other evidence it is clear that there were four bastions each mounting ten guns, the main east gate had five, while on the bank of the river there was a wall of solid masonry with embrasures for heavy cannon, on which the number of guns could hardly have much exceeded forty. Chittagong did not belong to the Company till 1760, and though two expeditions were sent against it from England in 1685 and 1689 nothing was effected, and it is said that the Court did not even know where Chittagong was, nor that it was strongly held. The ships under Admiral Nicholson which reached Hugli in 1685 had about 200 guns in their armament, so perhaps this is the foundation for the story. In 1753 the Court did send out 50 pieces of ordnance, chiefly 18- and 24-pounders, but three years later, when Suraj-ud-Dowlah invested the fort, these guns lay neglected under the walls. When Captain J. L. Jones, of the Artillery Company, protested on 4th August 1755 about the defenceless condition of Calcutta, the Council voted his letter 'irregular, improper and unnecessary', but a little more than ten months after this censure was passed the fort was captured and the tragedy of the Black Hole occurred.

As early as 1709 there was an attempt at gun-making at Madras, when the Council entertained a German, Leopold Furstemburgh, in the gunner's crew at 8 pagodas a month. He was said 'to perfectly well understand casting of mortars and guns of any size as also how to play 'em'. Within three years this German, 'appearing to be a person of no judgement, by the splitting of two brass guns made by him when they came to proof', was ordered to be discharged or reduced to gunner's mate's pay. He deserted to the service of the Mogul soon after.

All accounts agree that the early Indian-made guns were very crude, mostly of iron bars bound by iron rings or of iron cylinders with brass cast round them. They were clumsy and inefficient, and Orme says that even in the eighteenth century the natives thought it good if they fired a piece once in fifteen minutes. He also mentions that at Plassey in 1757 many of their guns were mounted on a huge stage.

It was natural to use iron, though the art of casting it had not been mastered, for it was found and worked in many parts of the country. According to Bowrey, the Dutch had iron-works in their factories on the Coromandel Coast, where they made ironwork for their ships. At Narsapore, adjoining the then flourishing ship-building town of Madapollum, the Dutch Factory contained a large enclosed quadrangle in which there were forges for 300 smiths, so Bowrey states. Buchanan says that iron was worked from black sand found in the rivers in the hilly parts of Mysore and from ore at Ghettipura near Magudi. It was smelted in clay furnaces with bellows of buffalo hide, and was bought at about nine shillings a hundredweight by Tippoo, who had it hammered into shot. Bengal asked for an ironfounder from home for casting shot and shell, an object, they said, of great importance. The Court sent out a man, but Bengal had to report in September 1765 that he had died on the voyage, and no further effort to obtain an expert seems to have been made. The first attempt to use local iron in the Company's manufactories was probably that made by Captain J. G. Scott, Madras Artillery, whose proposal to smelt iron ore in the Mysore forests and to use it in the Gun-carriage Agency at Seringapatam was approved in January 1805.

An attempt to establish iron-casting was made in 1778, when Warren Hastings desired the Provincial Council of Burdwan to let the 'Iron Mines of Beerbhoom on Farm for the rent at which they are at present estimated' to Mr. John Farquhar. After some dispute the 'Iron Mehal' was let to Farquhar for Rs. 566 a year. In the middle of the following year Farquhar wrote to the Governor-General, saying that he had not intended to ask for financial aid, but the expense of cutting down jungle, erecting a dwelling and the necessary buildings, forming a dam, and cutting part of a canal to supply the bellows wheel was so great that he could not go on. He estimated that only Rs. 15,000 were required to finish the work and to erect a furnace capable of casting a 12-pounder gun. He proposed to supply shot and shell at 15 per cent. under present cost, but could not enter into any engagement, as the cannon proposition might not succeed. An advance of Rs. 15,000 was made, but it is clear that the enterprise was not a success, as twenty years later, when Farquhar was at the Ishapore Powder Mills, he was called upon to repay the advance. He protested that it had been made specifically for the manufacture of shot and shell, that he had actually cast a thousand grape-shot, and that he had had to give up the work when his services were required for the manufacture of gunpowder; but the Council refused to abandon their claim. There is a gap in the records in the India Office, unfortunately, and the reason for the abandonment of the experiment has not been discovered.

The casting of brass cannon seems to have been well established in many parts of India about the middle of the eighteenth century. The Zamzama gun at Lahore, 14 feet 4½ inches long, with a bore of 9½ inches, was cast with another of the same size at Lahore in 1757, and was used at Paniput by Ahmed Shah in 1761. Copper and brass for the purpose were obtained by a capitation tax on all Hindu inhabitants, it is said. The State of Travancore is reported to have been the first to establish a regular brass-cannon foundry. A Dutchman was appointed its Commander-in-Chief in 1757 and an arsenal was established at Udayagiri, where cannon, mortars, arms, powder, and shot were manufactured. At Monghyr, also, cannon and arms were made, and Mir Cassim had seventeen guns there in 1763.

By the end of the eighteenth century the great Indian

States had numbers of brass guns made in their own foundries, but iron guns were rare. When Seringapatam was taken in 1799 only six of Tippoo's guns were iron cast in his own foundry, though 202 of the brass pieces were of local manufacture. At Delhi in 1803 the iron guns were European, while the brass ones were Indian made from French models. Even in 1849 the brass cannon of Runjeet Singh (he had 552, mostly 6-pounders) had been made for him by General Court from French models. All progress in the manufacture and use of artillery was undoubtedly due to European supervision, though progress was not always encouraged. Buchanan says that Tippoo had a Frenchman in his employ who devised an engine driven by water power for boring cannon, but Tippoo had the water-wheel removed and used bullocks instead.

The East India Company did what they could to discourage the spread of knowledge of this subject and in 1770 informed Bombay 'that the natives must be kept as ignorant as possible both of the theory and practise of artillery'. Obviously no such advice could be of any use, as the rich and powerful Indian States could always obtain as many European experts as they cared to pay for. Buckle says that it was the policy of the Government to keep the native powers dependent on us for ordnance and to keep them in ignorance of the methods of manufacture. He does not say how this could be done, so long as the French remained in India. It is true that many of the States were content to purchase our old guns, and Lord Cornwallis after the siege of Seringapatam gave half a dozen pieces both to the Nizam and to the Peishwar; they were not the best in his artillery park, but the gifts were much appreciated.

It is curious that the Company took no steps to make guns themselves till late in the eighteenth century and no adequate steps till well on in the nineteenth. The reason for this neglect may be found, perhaps, in a letter addressed by the Court to Bengal in December 1763, in which they say:

'Your indent for brass and iron guns and ordnance stores is so great that it is a further confirmation of our before-mentioned remarks of last season upon the inattention in framing your indents. We cannot therefore by no means think of complying with it fully, more especially when we consider what large quantities have been taken from the French in the different parts of India.' The British forces in India in those days of simple armaments seem to have been expected to supply themselves from their enemies, and many of those enemies were far better equipped. At Buxar in 1764, for example, 133 pieces of ordnance were captured, though the British had 20 field-guns only. When Seringapatam was taken in 1799 over 900 guns were found in the fortress, and there were 11 armouries with workshops, 2 cannon foundries, 3 gun workshops, and 4 large arsenals. Hyderabad had 3 gun foundries and 3 arsenals belonging to the French Corps, and the guns made there were as good and as well finished as any of ours. The only source of supply for the Company's forces up to practically the last quarter of the eighteenth century for any sort of ordnance was the home manufacturer.

## XIII

## THE COMPANY'S GUN FOUNDRY

THE idea of establishing a gun foundry at Calcutta seems to have occurred almost simultaneously to the Court at home and to the Council in Calcutta. Reports had been received of the activity of Shuja-ud-Dowlah, the Nawab Wazir of Oudh, stating that 'he had made great progress . . . had established a foundry which had already supplied him with a great quantity of cannon for field service', and he was also employing French officers. The Court's letter was dated in November 1768, and referred to letters from Colonel Smith and Sir R. Barker on the subject and recommended the Council to consider the establishment of a 'Foundary' at Calcutta. The Council's first letter was dated in September 1769; it says: 'General Smith proposed to attach two 3-pounder guns to each Sepoy battalion and to cast them and they had approved. Captain du Gloss established a temporary Foundry at Patna and succeeded in casting them, so they had ordered him to the Presidency and proposed erecting a Foundry in the new Fort.' They wrote again in January 1770 that du Gloss had succeeded 'equal to the General's most sanguine expectations, not only in casting field pieces but mortars also'; and 'as we have a large quantity of old and damaged guns . . . and are much in want of mortars . . . we are determined to establish a foundry at the Presidency under the inspection of Major du Gloss and have directed the Collector General and Chief Engineer to look out for a proper spot for this purpose'.

The Council reported in December 1770 that du Gloss had cast seven brass 3-pounders and two 10-inch mortars in the new foundry, and all had passed proof, except one mortar. This Major Luis, or Lewis du Gloss, who first made ordnance for the Company, and to whose knowledge and skill was due the establishment of a gun foundry, was a Pole sent out by the Court to Bombay, where he was commissioned as first lieutenant of Artillery or Infantry on 20th August 1753. He was given a commission as engineer in 1759 and he volunteered to go to Bengal, where he was commissioned as engineer and captain in February 1764. He took charge of the Dinapore Cantonment in July 1768, and it was there that he cast ordnance and made carriages for General Smith. He was promoted brevet major in 1770, and in December of that year he wrote an account of his services to Warren Hastings asking for leave to retire and for the rank of lieutenant-colonel, pointing out that as a major, with a personal estate of rather more than £2,500, he was not entitled to a pension or a donation from Lord Clive's fund. Besides being in charge of the foundry, he was Commissary of Stores at the arsenal. He was made brevet lieutenant-colonel in January and retired in February 1773, when he was Commissary-General.

This brass gun foundry, which started work in 1770, was a branch of the arsenal in Fort William. In a plan it is shown in the North Demi-Bastion, adjoining the arsenal on the up-river side. Its output must have been fairly considerable, as in March 1779 Major Green, the Commissary, was ordered to cast 100 field-pieces with the utmost expedition, 30 to be 12-pounders and the rest 6-pounders. But it must have been a primitive affair, as two years later Lieutenant-Colonel Duff, the then Commissary, proposed the erection of two furnaces for melting metal sufficient for casting a light 18- or a 12-pounder, 'it appearing to me to be impossible to cast a Gun properly when the metal is melted in many different crucibles'. The Military Board authorized the work at a cost of about Rs. 9,000 sicca. The sanctioned establishment was small: in 1784 it consisted of 1 European master at Rs. 50 a month, 1 sircar at Rs. 15, 1 mistry at Rs. 25 with a mate on Rs. 10, 2 carvers at Rs. 18 each, 2 bricklayers at Rs. 5, and 10 other workmen at Rs. 5 apiece, and in addition there was a carpenter mistry on Rs. 15 with 4 carpenters at Rs. 7 each. The workshops were simple sheds, and all machining was done in the arsenal shops, while the material used was entirely drawn from old ordnance. The establishment was revised in 1788 and became—1 overseer Rs. 30, 1 sirdar Rs. 18, 10 founders Rs. 6, 2 engravers Rs. 12, and 2 bricklayers at Rs. 5.

As was the custom in those days, the officer in charge of the foundry drew a commission on the work done. Major C. Deare, Artillery, Commissary of Stores, received Rs. 2,434 as commission for the year 1786–7, and in 1794 Lieutenant W. Golding, Engineers, who was then Commissary, drew about Rs. 3,000 for casting guns. The basis of this remuneration is not shown, but his successor, Captain T. Anbury, Engineers, was allowed 10 per cent. on the money expended. Captain J. B. Sherwood, Artillery, who followed Anbury, complained that his total commission was only half that of Anbury, as he was allowed 10 per cent. only on the cost of guns which passed proof, and, moreover, he had reduced the cost from Rs. 132 a cwt. to Rs. 91. Sherwood stated that in 1813–14 he had produced 97 serviceable pieces with only one failure, and this included 8-inch mortars, howitzers, and 12-pounder guns. Government then fixed a rate for each nature of piece, varying from Rs. 165 for a 12-pounder heavy gun of 18 cwt. to Rs. 8 for a mortar weighing 98 lb., but they soon reverted to the 10 per cent. on the cost of serviceable pieces.

The efficiency of this foundry was questioned several times during its history and its existence threatened. In 1809 the Military Board reported its 'highly objectionable state', the 'unfitness of its present situation', and the danger of fire in the arsenal store-rooms from their proximity to the two furnaces. They recommended its removal to the southward of the fort, with new buildings, at a cost of Rs. 27,313. The Governor-General considered it inexpedient to authorize so large an expense, however desirable such a move might be, and thought past experience showed that, with care, there was little danger of fire. The Court were most dissatisfied with the foundry, and wrote in October 1811:

> 'Your report regarding the Ordnance cast in Bengal holds out but little encouragement for forwarding an expensive assortment of Boring implements. . . . You say "The Europe guns being found very superior to those made in India, we request the balance due may be sent out". Since when, you state that the whole number of howitzers cast in Bengal were found so inaccurate as to induce you to condemn those of 8-inch . . . and to restrict the Foundry from Casting more of that calibre and again, you indent for a number of 5½-inch howitzers.'

They noted the high cost and expressed the opinion that the mixing and casting required the experience and practice of a lifetime, whereas the persons in charge at the arsenal must be frequently changing. They ended, 'We see little hope that the establishment will ever succeed. We accordingly direct the Foundry be relinquished and all supplies be indented for from home as in other Presidencies.' The reply to this was not considered to be satisfactory, so the Court wrote in August 1813, 'It clearly appears that ordnance cast in Fort William is very inferior to that cast in Europe, a political evil certainly of the greatest magnitude, and cost was Rs. 1,159 sicca, or £134–4, against £55–1–3 for a 6-pounder cast in England of superior quality lodged in your Arsenal.' They referred to the condemnation of the greater part, if not the whole, of the chambered ordnance cast in Bengal, and observed, 'no sooner have their orders to abolish the Foundry been received than the Military Board report that all the evils have been removed and cannon equal to the best and at a price even less than Europe have been made; but said nothing to show how these great improvements had been made'. The Court also expressed their fears at disseminating a knowledge of casting ordnance among the natives, and ended by adhering positively to their former decision to close the foundry. Bengal's reply in December 1814 pointed out the state of efficiency to which the arsenal foundry had been brought under 'the superintendence and scientific management of this able, zealous and indefatigable officer', Major Sherwood, Artillery, Commissary of Stores; and considered that no further arguments were necessary to justify the suspension of the Court's order to close it.

In 1816 the question of casting cylinders for the powder mills was considered, and it was found that the existing furnaces 'were not capacious enough', so it was decided to erect a new one in the fort. Mr. A. Menaud was appointed founder at a salary of Rs. 313–8–3 sicca a month; he came from the Madras powder works, as has already been stated, and the new brass foundry was completed in 1818 under the superintendence of Captain Galloway, the Agent for Gunpowder.

The Court still maintained their objections to the continuance of the foundry, but in July 1817 they were informed that ordnance cast in it were cheaper and better than those imported, that India needed special patterns on account of the climate, nature of carriage materials, and draught requirements, and it was thought wrong to follow other countries.[1] They were informed further that 50 light 6-pounders had been cast, as none had been received from home and none remained in store. In October the arguments against the abolition of what was described as 'the excellent brass foundry at Fort William' were repeated and the Court informed that 20 howitzers had been cast owing to failure to supply them from home. The Court were at last convinced, and wrote in December 1818 'that in view of the arguments by the Commander-in-Chief and the Military Board, added to the excellence of the specimens sent home, they directed the reestablishment of the Foundry'. Lord Hastings had ordered several pieces of Indian-made ordnance to be sent to Woolwich, where they were examined by a committee of artillery officers, who, it is said, pronounced the workmanship and finish to be superior to those of the Royal Arsenal.

[1] In this connexion see Chapter I, p. 7.

The Court did more: they suggested the manufacture of the whole of the ordnance required in India at Fort William, thus saving expense. They thought the cost had been over-estimated, but directed that four-fifths of old metal to one of new should be used to reduce cost still further, and they mentioned that proof in India was more severe than at Woolwich.

However, according to Stubbs, the appliances and means for making guns at Fort William were very imperfect. From an order published in March 1810 we get one item of information on the methods; it directs that the 16 bullocks maintained for the boring machine were in future to be supplied and fed and their drivers paid by the Commissariat and not by the officer under whom they were employed. Still, Woolwich was not very different, for it is stated that in the Royal Arsenal the gun-shop erected in Dial Square after 1719 contained 'the famous gun-boring mill worked by horses, an archaic machine which survived till 1842'.

In 1822 Government decided that a radical change in the management of the foundry was necessary, as the proof reports showed that a far greater number of 'blemished guns' had been put forward than ever before. By an order dated 12th October, Captain G. Hutchinson of the Bengal Engineers was appointed 'Superintendent and Director of the Foundry at Fort William'. In their letter to the Court, besides quoting the bad proof reports, they said that the duties of Principal Commissary of the Arsenal and of Superintendent of the Foundry were incompatible and incongruous. They considered the arsenal duties, attendant on the extension of territory, amply sufficient to occupy the undivided attention of the ordnance officers, while the foundry work had also been greatly augmented, as it had to supply all the Presidencies. They had therefore appointed Captain Hutchinson, 'an officer of skill and of a reputation for active not less than scientific services', to the charge of the foundry. He was to have his regimental pay and allowances plus the percentage already sanctioned, with quarters in the fort. The arsenal officers protested, Major H. Faithfull, the Principal Commissary, submitting a Memorial on behalf of himself and of his deputy against the effect on their emoluments by the separation. Government declined to support them and expressed dissatisfaction with the state of the arsenal and foundry during Major Faithfull's tenure of office.

The establishment allowed was now considerable: in 1822–3 it included a conductor and a sergeant for the boring machine and two sergeants for casting, with 109 Indian mistries and workmen. All gun-work had been concentrated in the foundry workshops, and a good deal of miscellaneous work was done.

The inefficiency of the foundry was once more noticed by the Military Board, but Hutchinson in a letter dated in July 1824 refused to admit that any inefficiency existed; he said that after the Governor-General had appointed him, quite unsolicited by him, he was first engaged in setting up the new steam-engine and mill-work attached to the new boring lathe, also in making a tunnel, 200 feet long, through the ramparts to a well. He also stated he had then no European assistant and had to make a new description of ordnance worked out by the Select Committee. There had always been a stock of spare moulds, but he had to make new ones, and the order for these guns came at the beginning of the rainy season. Judging by the tone of the correspondence, there seems to have been a private feud between Hutchinson and Major Craigie, the Secretary to the Military Board, and the alleged inefficiency does not appear to have had much foundation. Madras in 1829 reported that some 9-pounders received from England in 1827–8 made by the Inspector of Artillery at the Royal Foundry were inferior to guns cast in Bengal; but the Court would not agree that there was any difference of importance.

In 1826 it was proposed to move the foundry from Fort William, and certain land at Cossipore was suggested; but it was found that the owner could not show a good title, so the matter was dropped. No doubt it was also thought to be wiser to defer consideration of any move till the return of Captain Hutchinson, who had gone home on furlough on medical certificate in February, when Captain T. Timbrell, Artillery, was appointed to act. It had become evident that the foundry was inadequate for the output required, so Hutchinson was given permission to study methods in European foundries, with the promise that his post would be kept open for him. The Court, however, strongly objected to duty being combined with leave on medical certificate and would only consider him as being on ordinary leave, and declined to let him return as Superintendent, but they ultimately gave way on this point. Hutchinson toured the Continent, visiting foundries, and in his report dated in May 1828 said he was employed in purchasing plant. The Court again refused to recognize his presence as being on public duty, but eventually allowed him £300 for his services, an amount which he stated to be quite inadequate. He reached Calcutta in May 1829 and resumed charge of the foundry.

It at once became evident that the space available in Fort William was quite insufficient for the new plant ordered by Hutchinson, and it was decided to move the foundry to the site at Cossipore which the Gun-carriage Agency was vacating. The elevating screw department and the half-wrought timber yard were to remain at Cossipore. The cost of establishing the foundry at Cossipore was estimated at Rs. 66,435, and tenders for the buildings for the 'New Brass Cannon Foundry and a small Iron Foundry' were invited on the plans prepared by Hutchinson. The Superintending Engineer reported the result in January 1830, and it is interesting to note that both Burn and Jessop, who now have large engineering works in Calcutta, were among the tenderers. Hutchinson's tender was the lowest, and it was decided that he should carry out the work. Government would not grant him a salary but proposed to consider an allowance when the work was completed, and the Court were informed that, as they had sent out the plant, the Governor-General had ordered the work to proceed without waiting for further sanction, and this was approved by the Court.

The Gun-carriage Agency left in November 1829, and in the April following the remaining stores were handed over to Hutchinson, and the construction of the foundry commenced. For about twelve months from July 1831 Hutchinson was assisted by Lieutenant T. Renny, Engineers, but it was not till near the close of 1834 that the foundry was completed. Hutchinson's salary was then fixed at Rs. 800, plus pay, batta, &c., and he had one sub-conductor and three sergeants as assistants.

Hutchinson was an architect and engineer of some note. He designed the Garrison Church at Fort William, the Bishop's College, and the Meerut Church. He had also constructed a reservoir in the fort, which a Committee in 1828 condemned as useless, and he superintended the building of the La Martinière School in 1832. He got into some trouble over costs, and in 1836 the Military Board expressed their disapproval of his action in building the gateway at Cossipore without sanction. In April 1837 his salary was raised to Rs. 1,000 a month, and in 1838 he was granted a special remuneration of Rs. 5,000, about 5 per cent. on the outlay for his work in the construction of the foundry. Major Hutchinson gave up his appointment when he left India on 28th February 1839. He retired in 1841 and for a short period was Resident Director of the new College of Civil Engineers, and he was elected a Fellow of the Royal Society.

Lieutenant-Colonel D. Presgrave, 66th Native Infantry, was appointed to succeed Hutchinson and joined at Cossipore about the middle of 1839. He had been for some years in charge of the Saugor Mint and also Superintendent of the construction of iron suspension bridges there. He smelted iron in the neighbourhood of Saugor, rolled it in the Mint rollers into bars and rods, and used them for a suspension bridge near Saugor. He left Cossipore in September 1840 for the Cape, where he died in July of the following year.

There are curiously conflicting opinions on the work of the gun foundry during Hutchinson's term. In February 1838 the Court noted with pleasure the zeal and ability displayed by him, while nine months later Government was told of the inefficiency of the foundry for the prompt execution of work of even a common description. In 1841 the Military Board wrote of 'the defective and inefficient state of the Foundry at Cossipore as exhibited in the several years under review: viz. 1836, 1837, 1838, 1839'. The production of brass guns in the year 1839–40 was 94, of which 11 failed at proof, and to make these 94 guns no less than 191 blocks had to be cast. Yet an article in the *Calcutta Review* of December 1845 refers to the gun foundry thus: 'One of the most complete and perfect to be seen in any country, erected some years back by Colonel Hutchinson of the Engineers, after he had ransacked England and Europe for the best models.' Captain L. von Orlich, travelling in India, visited Cossipore in April 1843 and wrote to Germany: 'This cannon foundry is, in every respect, better contrived than that of Woolwich.' A description of the foundry and of its plant as established by Hutchinson will be found in Appendix A.

The foundry in Fort William had been solely a brass foundry, but the new one at Cossipore was also equipped with cupolas for casting iron. Iron cannon were still obtained from home, and were never made at Cossipore, but the manufacture of shot and shell was commenced by Hutchinson, and later cast-iron carriages for garrison guns were also made there. It is curious that India was so slow in establishing iron casting. The experiment of Mr. John Farquhar at Beerbhoom in 1778–9 has already been mentioned, but the result, the production of a thousand grapeshot, can hardly have been encouraging. In 1789 Colonel Moorhouse, Artillery, and Mr. Roebuck, Senior Merchant, proposed to the Madras Council to cast shot and shell. They referred to the large quantity 'that fell into the enemy's hands in the forts taken in the late war' and to the delay of the Court in complying with the indents for replacement, leaving a deficiency of some 8,000 tons. The Court, however, would not sanction the scheme. This deficiency probably accounted for the scarcity at Seringapatam in 1791, when a reward was offered for all shot recovered and taken to the Commissary of Ordnance. Even in 1803 the troops had to pick shot out of the walls of Ahmednagger. In 1794 Messrs. Moore and Burn asked to be allowed to buy iron scrap, stating that they had established an iron foundry in Calcutta, with the first object of casting iron weights for the bazaar; and this must have been the first commercial foundry to be set up in Calcutta. In Madras, in 1831, the gunpowder manufactory, which had a foundry, cast 494 cwt. of iron weights to complete scales in arsenals at a cost of about one rupee per cwt. In 1832 Madras employed a Mr. Heath to cast iron gun-platforms and he was allowed to buy stores from the Company for the use of his foundry, but he was unable to produce any satisfactory platforms. Again, in 1836, Colonel Monteith, Engineers, was permitted by the Madras Government to erect a blast furnace at a cost of Rs. 300, for the casting of iron shot and shell from scrap, but he was unable to make them near enough to the standard dimensions. As late as 1849 a report on the Sikh Artillery stated that their round shot were beaten not cast. The gun-carriage manufactory in Bombay seems to have been successful in casting iron even earlier than 1836, for in that year the Special Committee on equipment recommended that Bombay should continue to use iron naves for wheels, as it had a large stock of pig iron and the Manufactory had the means for casting. The gun-carriage agency at Fatehgarh did not have a cupola till 1851, and when the rebels captured the place in 1857 they could find nobody who could work it and had to make shot by forging.

Captain Hutchinson took out with him in 1829 a Mr. S. Abel to assist in the erection of the plant, but in 1835 he replaced him by Sergeant Calder on an indenture for five years at Rs. 304–2–10 per month. He also had as head founder Private W. Holloway of the 38th Foot, on Rs. 60 a month, plus pay, quarters, &c. At this time foremen, overseers, and men of similar grades were usually obtained from the British troops, though in special cases the Court sent out men from home, but these were costly and not always satisfactory, and there seems to have been little need for highly skilled men for the simple manufacturing methods then in use. It was not till 1856 that there was expressed a definite desire for expert civilians from home.

The Cossipore gun foundry may have been imposing to the visitor in 1843, but its efficiency was sometimes doubtful. In 1843, it is true, there is a note of the Court's satisfaction at the report of the casting of ordnance during the fifteen months to February 1841, and of their opinion that it was 'favourable to the management of the Superintendent, Captain Archdale Wilson'. In the five years 1840–1 to 1844–5, during which Wilson was in charge, 562 brass guns were made from 659 blocks cast, and only 11 failed at proof. In 1852, however, Government was informed that the output for 1848–9 was very small and defects excessive: out of 98 blocks cast, only 45 guns were made, and of these 5 failed at proof. In the next two years production was equally poor, but from 1851–2 a great improvement began, and the output in 1853–4 of 158 guns was considered to be very creditable to Captain Broome.

Accounts caused a good deal of trouble. In January 1852 the Military Board informed Government that they had just examined the annual material accounts of the foundry for 1847–8 and recommended that they be passed, though they were not wholly satisfactory and there were numerous errors. When they recommended the passing of the accounts for 1848–9, however, they said they had been prepared on an improved system introduced by Broome, and on a later occasion they commented on the clearness and completeness of the accounts. One reason for delay and error was obviously the division of accounting between Cossipore and Calcutta. The initial accounting was under the Superintendent, while compilation was done by a Clerk specially allocated for the purpose in the Accounts Department office in Calcutta. Broome, like the officers in other factories, complained of the difficulties this caused and of the time he had to spend in visits to Calcutta.

It is of some interest to read that in 1853 Government ordered the instruction of young artillery officers 'in the scientific operations of the Foundry'. Broome asked for some scientific books and periodicals to help him in this and in his ordinary work. The members of the Military Board differed on the subject, but the majority thought it a quite unnecessary expense and presumed that Superintendents usually bought those they desired at their own expense. The Governor-General did not consider it necessary 'at present' to subscribe for any professional periodicals, but directed that any scientific works available in other offices might be supplied. The cost of the publications asked for was probably less than the value of the time of the many high officials who wrote lengthy minutes on the subject, but doubtless a dangerous precedent was avoided!

One writer has stated that 92 iron guns passed proof in 1853, but there is no record of iron guns ever having been made at Cossipore. All references are to brass ordnance, and the quantity of iron castings produced was small. Iron garrison carriages and mortar beds were cast as well as projectiles, but no guns. All guns received from England in those days were subjected to proof on arrival in India.

The outbreak of the Mutiny caused an inquiry into the possible output of guns. In the year 1856–7 the output was 415 pieces of ordnance, of which only 6 failed at proof, but in September 1857 Broome was asked what his maximum production was and if it could be increased. He stated that he could make 15 guns a month, which might be doubled by working day and night, but there would be heavy expense for lamps and oil and for extra supervision and labour, and he could not guarantee good work at night. The Inspector-General of Ordnance reported that he had not ordered night work as he was sure it would be unsatisfactory. Broome had earlier pointed out various defects in his plant for work other than guns. He stated that he had a new brass foundry under completion for miscellaneous work, which would meet all demands, and he was about to erect a new large cupola for iron castings. He wanted a 6-h.p. engine with upright tubular boiler which was available, nearly new, from Jessop and Company for Rs. 1,500. He also needed a steam hammer, not less than 10 cwt., a Ryders patent forge, a Whitworth universal shaping machine, and two new boilers—these were all sanctioned. Broome asked also for a good practical moulder and founder with good casting experience, as Corporal McDougall, then acting, had little practical experience, and wasters had increased since Mr. Vialls left.

The Company's artillery in the Mutiny fought with smooth-bore bronze and cast-iron muzzle-loading ordnance; but already, in Europe, inventors and manufacturers were busy in the production of breech-loading as well as muzzle-loading guns constructed of wrought iron or steel with rifled barrels. The Armstrong gun had been designed in 1855 and under the designation of R.B.L. had been introduced into the home army; these guns necessitated methods of manufacture beyond the plant, knowledge, and skill possessed by Cossipore at that time. Under Broome, however, from 1859 to 1861, efforts were made to rifle existing ordnance for use till the Armstrong guns could be supplied in sufficient quantities from home. It was found that the bronze was too soft to stand the high pressures resulting from the use of rifled projectiles, so the efforts, which had involved the purchase of expensive plant, ceased. Another endeavour to obtain the benefits of rifling was then made by the use of the system introduced by Sir William Palliser, which consisted in enlarging the bore of cast-iron guns and inserting a rifled barrel of wrought iron, but this was soon abandoned. By 1864 England was reverting to muzzle-loading guns, but these, being built up of wrought iron or steel coils or hoops shrunk over tubes, could not be made at Cossipore. In 1880 England had definitely adopted the breech-loading system, and steel was rapidly becoming the only possible material.

As was inevitable, the continuance of the Cossipore gun foundry came under discussion. In 1864 the Inspector-General of Ordnance reported that it was making only a few brass guns, which were very expensive, a small number of shells, a few mortar beds, and some miscellaneous work. It also had a bullet factory which had been completed in 1858–9. The Commission of Inquiry into Indian Accounts suggested the removal of the bullet factory to Dum Dum and the rest of the work to the Kidderpore Dockyard. The Governor-General favoured its immediate abolition, but many arguments were raised against this and suggestions made for adding to its usefulness. It was finally decided to retain it and to take steps to enable it to make projectiles for rifled ordnance. More land was obtained and further buildings erected, and in 1872 its name was changed from 'The Gun Foundry' to 'The Foundry and Shell Factory'. Further extensions were completed by 1878 to enable it to meet demands from all India for projectiles.

The problem of making modern breech-loading guns of steel in India was one of great difficulty. It would not be enough to install plant for making the gun only, for not only did the modern gun have complicated fittings which would require replacement and repair, but it also required metal cartridge cases, primers, vent-sealing tubes, and elaborate fuses. Moreover, the provision of the material from which these must be made had to be studied, if India was to be made self-supporting to the fullest extent possible. Steel forgings, castings, and bars were required, also brass, copper, and cupro-nickel strip, and these should be manufactured in India from local materials if at all practicable. Not only would many new buildings and much expensive plant be required, together with a highly skilled staff from England, but time was necessary for the training of the Indian workmen. Such a programme required many years for completion, and it was not till 1905 that Cossipore was once more manufacturing ordnance and became 'The Gun and Shell Factory'. Thus for some forty years India was again dependent on England for the supply of ordnance.

It was in 1887 that the long series of additions began which was to make the factory at Cossipore, with its branch at Ishapore, the largest of India's munition works and the one with the greatest range of production. Progress was continuous, and the little brass cannon foundry which started in sheds in a bastion of Fort William in 1770, with an establishment of one European overseer and 15 Indian workmen, became eventually the 'Gun and Shell Factory' which in 1918, at the close of the Great War, had a staff of 196, with 179 clerks and 13,700 workmen on its rolls.

From the time that Colonel Presgrave left Cossipore, in 1840, until a year or two ago the officers in charge were all drawn from the Artillery, first from the Bengal and then from the Royal Artillery. One curious fact should be mentioned: while the work and responsibility of the Superintendent increased from time to time, his remuneration actually decreased. Captain Hutchinson was given a staff salary of Rs. 800 a month, increased in 1837 to Rs. 1,000, the Superintendent in the Great War was on a scale of Rs. 600 rising in ten years to Rs. 800, while the value of the rupee had very greatly diminished and the cost of living very much increased.

While complaints of the inefficiency of the gun foundry were not infrequent, criticisms of the 'Gun and Shell Factory' have been neither numerous nor serious. As in all Government establishments, economy has often been the enemy of progress, and the division of the factory into two parts[1] separated by some twelve miles of road rendered efficient supervision somewhat difficult. No doubt the organization and system of management, as well as the plant, sometimes failed to keep pace with modern ideas, but the climate and the distance from England do not help the man who may desire to keep his knowledge up to date, and he has few contacts with men engaged in similar work. Still, the eulogy on Major Sherwood's work conveyed to the Court by the Government of Bengal in December 1814, in the words 'the superintendence and scientific management of this able, zealous and indefatigable officer', might well have been expressed by the Government of India on the work of most of the Royal Artillery officers employed at Cossipore since 1887. The value of such an establishment as that at Cossipore to the commercial manufacturing industry of India can hardly be overestimated. The training which the Indian worker gets there in accurate mechanical processes and in modern scientific methods is of the highest value, and there is a constant drift to commercial firms of skilled men attracted by a rather higher standard of wages.

[1] This has been altered, the two parts being now distinct factories.

## XIV

## THE SUPPLY OF GUN-CARRIAGES

THE first gun-carriage manufactory to be established by the Company was one in Bengal, at Cossipore, in 1801; the next was the Madras one at Seringapatam in 1802; the third was at Bombay in 1810, and the last was at Fatehgarh in 1816. Before dealing with the institution of these manufactories and giving sketches of their histories, it is necessary to give some account of the methods adopted to provide gun-carriages and allied stores prior to the beginning of the nineteenth century.

Fort St. George at Madras was commenced soon after the acquisition of the site by the Company in 1640, the fortification of Bombay began not long after the Island was taken over from the Crown in 1668, while old Fort William was commenced about 1699. For all these defences guns were necessary and were at first supplied complete with carriages and stores from the ships, but it was very soon found possible and economical to make the carriages locally, importing from home only such ironwork as was necessary.

At Madras in April 1672 the Council noted that timber was required for from 40 to 50 carriages, and it is known that at each Presidency the Storekeeper had smiths' and carpenters' yards under him, with a number of artificers, and that he undertook at first the limited amount of manufacture and repair required. At a consultation in January 1668 it was noted by the Madras Council that all carriages received from the King's ships, of European wood, were decayed and useless, and that the continued supplies to out-stations had taken all the new ones and there were very few left in store. It was ordered that the carpenters and smiths must be kept employed all the year or until an ample supply had been made for the fortifications of Fort St. George. It was ordered, also, that the master carpenter and the master bricklayer were not to engage in any private work, but they might advise any gentleman how to erect any building. It was further ordered that the Under-Paymaster might be allowed to have 15 carpenters, 2 sawyers, and 2 smiths to make cots, chairs, tables, &c., for officers and others newly arrived in the country, owing to the difficulty experienced in obtaining the necessary furniture. Strikes were not unknown: there was one of painters at Madras in October 1680, accompanied by threats to other workmen if they did not join. It was not settled till December, when the Company's peons seized the ringleaders and committed them to prison. People were sometimes forced to work, especially in the powder mills, but this was usually after an explosion had frightened the workpeople away. Still, it is certain that in the early part of the eighteenth century, at least, impressment of the inhabitants of the fortified settlements for various purposes was permissible though not encouraged.

Calcutta was captured in 1756 by Suraj-ud-Dowlah largely by reason of the neglect of the defences. Captain J. L. Jones of the Artillery wrote in August 1755 that there were no carriages for the new guns, nor any gun mounted fit for service, but the Council did nothing. Mr. Holwell, in his report after the capture, stated that there was hardly a carriage that would bear a gun. At Madras in September 1744 Mr. Joseph Smith, the Gunner and Engineer, reported that all guns were mounted on ships' carriages, which were very inconvenient, and some required ten to twelve men to work them, while the establishment of the garrison only provided one man per gun. He recommended the provision of field-carriages, but as there was no timber in the town suitable he asked for a supply from the Malabar Coast. The Council agreed and ordered timber from Tellicherry.

When, in 1748, the Court decided to have a regular company of artillery at each Presidency, they ordered that as many as possible of the men should have been bred in the occupations of smiths, carpenters, or other trades of use in the artillery. Such men would, of course, be useful in maintaining the equipment in repair, but obviously could be of little use in providing the large amount of equipment required for the growing fortifications, and for the use of the field armies. The field carriages of the time were very weak and often broke down, as Clive found when he attacked the Nawab outside Calcutta in February 1757; he had only six 9-pounder guns and two of the carriages broke down. There were no ammunition vehicles, the ammunition being carried on lascars' heads, guarded by sailors.

In Madras, in 1756, gun-carriages were being made under the superintendence of Captain Brohier, the Chief Engineer, in the public workshops. Brohier reported in August that the carpenters' work for 50 carriages had been completed, but 'the smiths were very tedious in completing the iron work'. He said there were 29 boxes of ironwork on board ships for Bengal, so the Council ordered them to be landed. They observed that ironwork for 255 carriages was due from England. In Bombay, in 1756, gun-carriages were made and repaired by the Military Storekeeper, who had charge of the public workshops.

Throughout the eighteenth century military stores were almost entirely supplied under some system of contract, from which the contractors, who were often civilian officials or military officers, derived considerable profits, licit or illicit. Even when the contractors were private merchants, they were often connected in some way with the Company's servants. Broome, referring to 1770, said 'carriages, ammunition and stores generally were of exceedingly inferior quality, supplied by contractors who, having interest to obtain the contracts, had also sufficient influence to force their wretched produce into the service and to cover themselves from loss or exposure, by getting all power of choice or rejection taken from the hands of the Artillery Officers'. He omits to mention, however, that artillery officers were sometimes themselves contractors.

The rate of commission varied from 10 per cent. to as much as 30 per cent., but 10 per cent. was the more usual, though the basis on which the commission was charged was often remarkable. In 1782 Mr. Thomas Powney had a contract for gun-carriages at Calcutta, and he was allowed a commission of 15 per cent. on the whole of his disbursements, certified by him 'on honour'. Unfortunately for him, it was discovered that he had charged for sheds, tools, and other articles not actually expended, so his bill was cut down. The stipulation that a declaration must be made on oath that the expenses charged were actually incurred was often included in the contract. The method of fixing prices on which commission could be charged, which was another system, varied: sometimes they were the lowest previously paid, and sometimes they were based on an estimate furnished by the Storekeeper or the Commissary of Stores. There were other systems: for example, in 1794 supply was transferred to the Commissary of Stores at Fort William arsenal, and he was allowed any amount which he saved on the fixed prices. Sometimes the saving was shared fifty-fifty between the Company and the Commissary or Agent.

If we go back to 1771 we get some idea of the scale of these contracts. Early in that year Mr. A. Hathaway was contractor for field gun-carriages and he employed on an average 90 carpenters, 220 smiths, 14 sawyers, and 6 painters. He died later in the year, and the remainder of his contract was given in December to Mr. J. Anderson, who was contractor for garrison carriages, the contract specifying that he must buy materials from the Company and must make, if required, 86 garrison and not less than 9 field carriages every three months, in a place set apart in new Fort William. The contractor was to be under the Military Storekeeper, who, it must be remembered, had a commission on everything supplied by or through him.

The establishment of the grand arsenals at the Presidencies made the position of Commissary of Stores, who held charge of the arsenal and of its workshops, one of considerable importance. Fort William had its arsenal in 1769, the one in Fort St. George was finished in 1772, and that in the Castle at Bombay was completed in 1794. The Commissary of Stores at Fort William in 1778 was Major Green, Artillery, with a seat on the Board of Ordnance. There is a letter from the Court, dated in December of that year, strongly disapproving of the commission of 15 per cent. on the prime cost of gun-carriages granted to the Commissary of Stores in opposition to the Commander-in-Chief. The proposal was made at the Board by the Commissary himself, and was carried by the casting vote of the Governor-General, Warren Hastings. The Court ended their remarks, 'We order no member to have any contract or to receive any benefit or emolument from stores to be furnished or work to be performed in consequence of any resolution or recommendation of the said Board.' If this letter had any effect at all, it did not last long, for when Mr. Powney, the contractor for garrison carriages, died in November 1782, his executors were allowed to make over the agency to Lieutenant-Colonel P. Duff, Commissary of Stores; and when Duff was ordered up country he made over the contract to his successor, Major C. R. Deare.

In Bengal, up to about 1800, the system seems to have changed many times, sometimes contract with or without advertisement, then agency on honour or based on fixed prices. We get a fairly clear idea of the business in the Consultations of the Military Board in September and October 1794 and in October 1800. From these we learn that in 1786 the rate of commission was reduced from 15 to 10 per cent., and that in consequence of this Major Deare proposed a fixed agency, including commission, instead of one on honour, i.e. that the prices should be fixed and the commission paid on these. Deare's proposal was accepted, but in 1791 it was decided to advertise for tenders, and a three years' contract was given to Lieutenant Fireworker J. Taylor of the Artillery. When this contract expired the Board asked that it should be given to the Commissary of Stores, saying that though he was allowed Rs. 750 a month as Commissary plus regimental pay and allowances and got about Rs. 3,000 a year from the casting of guns, yet the position was one of great responsibility, involving exposure to the climate and great bodily exertion. The Board went on to remark that formerly, except for the short period when Mr. Powney had the contract for garrison carriages, the situation of Commissary 'was made very eligible by the agencies for field and garrison carriages'. They recommended rates to be fixed at the lowest hitherto obtained, and at the end of the season the Commissary to render a bona fide account upon honour of the actual expense and to be allowed half the difference between the cost and the standard rates for his trouble. This was approved by Government, but as the Commissary was in charge of stores and artificers in the arsenal, it was ordered that carriages were not to be made in the arsenal, but in workshops to be provided by him not more than two miles from the fort. Moreover, his bills were to be attested on oath, that no part of the Company's stores or tools or any artificers had been employed.

It was not long before it was considered to be desirable to separate the duties of the Commissary of Stores from that of a contractor for the manufacture of gun-carriages, and in 1800 the Governor-General ordered manufacture to be under an Agent on a fixed salary. The Court remarked, when approving this action, 'As you have at length seen reason to concur with us in opinion that the duties of the Agency for the provision of gun carriages were incompatible with those of the Commissary of Stores . . . and as the Commissary of Stores is a check on the quality of the stores delivered into the Arsenal, we approve.'

Both in Bombay and Madras the supply of gun-carriages rested with the Military Storekeeper until late in the eighteenth century, and it does not appear that the Commissaries of Stores at the grand arsenals in those Presidencies were ever given contracts for either field or garrison gun-carriages. In fact, when in 1799 the Commissary of Stores at Bombay, with his deputy, put in tenders for the contract which had been advertised, the Board stated such action to be quite contrary to regulations, and most improper. The Military Storekeeper at Bombay was allowed a commission of 25 per cent. on the cost of all stores he supplied, while the same official in Madras had 15 per cent. reduced to 10 in 1791.

Bombay invited tenders in February 1794 for the supply of 400 gun-carriages and 58 tumbrils, to be made under the immediate inspection of the Commandant of Artillery. Tenders were received from five Indians, one artillery officer, and two civilian officials, one being a senior merchant. The tender of Bazan Manockjee, amounting to Rs. 1,24,564, was accepted. Madras started a system of contracts with European firms in 1791.

Besides the use of inferior or unseasoned timber, the lack of skill in the workmen was a not infrequent cause of trouble. In 1776 a report was submitted by Ensign H. Witman to the Bombay Council, in which he stated that one European was equal to six Indian workmen, that each carpenter required a bigari[1] to move his timber, and that the smiths burnt the iron so that each piece had to be made larger than was necessary. He also reported that the foundry which the Company possessed in Bombay did not deserve the name, and said that no one knew enough of turning to make brass screws for the repair of the fire-engines, and finally that the gun-carriages made were extremely clumsy.

It is probably not very far from the truth to say that little progress in artillery equipment was made up to the time of the Mutiny; certainly little could be expected under the conditions which obtained in India during the eighteenth century. Improvements did come when gun-carriage manufactories were established by each Presidency and placed

[1] Labourer.

under the management of experienced artillery officers, with a permanent nucleus of trained artificers. Committees were appointed from time to time to consider equipment questions and the possibilities of improvements. In 1836 a Committee of artillery officers from all three Presidencies was convened at Calcutta for the purpose of assimilating the ordnance equipment throughout India, but without complete success, and many differences persisted up to the time of the Mutiny. Generally speaking, improvements were mainly in material and workmanship, and a good deal was done to lighten vehicles without loss of strength. Axle-trees were first of wood, then of wood strengthened by an iron bar, and finally wholly of iron. Iron axles first appeared on the ledgers of the Fort William arsenal in 1782, but there were only two, so they were probably experimental. Sir Arthur Wellesley had some carriages with iron axle-trees in 1803, but said they broke after a limited amount of firing. This may have been due to the use of old iron, or perhaps of country iron, for they were undoubtedly country made. He asked for iron from home to go out as ballast and be landed at Cannanore for the gun-carriage manufactory at Seringapatam. Sir Jasper Nicoll, however, asserted that teak axles, if well seasoned, were the best. Probably the greatest improvements were in the vehicles for the carriage of ammunition and in the provision of proper means for elevating the gun.

# XV

# THE BENGAL GUN-CARRIAGE MANUFACTORIES

## A. COSSIPORE

IN November 1800 the Court were informed that the Governor-General had determined that 'such Mortar Beds, Gun Carriages, Ammunition Carts, Tumbrels and other carriages for Military purposes, as might be required for the term of three years, should be provided by an Agent allowed a fixed salary . . . subject to the Controul and direction of the Military Board', and also that Major Andrew Glass, of the Artillery, had been appointed Agent for providing ordnance carriages, &c., and barrels for the use of the gunpowder manufactory. Major Glass was to receive a salary of Rs. 1,200 sicca a month, plus pay, gratuity, half batta, and house-rent. It was agreed in May 1801 to purchase for Rs. 40,730 all the materials and tools belonging to Captain Anbury, the Commissary of Stores, who had taken over the affairs of the late Captain Golding, including his gun-carriage contract, workshops, &c. All materials, tools, &c., to be handed over to Major Glass.

It was proposed, at first, to purchase also the ground and buildings occupied by Captain Anbury's workshops at Kidderpore, in Watson's dockyard, for Rs. 12,000 for the new Agency, but the Governor-General suggested it might be rented. Further consideration showed that the site was not really suitable and was insufficient in area, while the cost and even the rent, Rs. 150 to 200 a month, were thought to be excessive. The next recommendation was the purchase of land and houses at Cossipore from Mr. Cuthbert Thornhill for Rs. 20,000, but the Governor-General regarded this as too costly and suggested another piece of ground at Cossipore which was much cheaper. The first piece was between the river to the west and the rice-fields to the east, and between the garden to the south and Mr. Touchet's estate to the north. The second plot also belonged to Thornhill and was to the south of the other, also on the river, and it consisted of approximately 20 bigahs, priced at Rs. 250 per bigah. The purchase of this latter plot was approved, as also was the erection of essential buildings to cost Rs. 21,688. In December 1801 Glass received the land from Thornhill, who was given a Treasury Bill for Rs. 4,757–12 sicca in payment.

The buildings were completed by March 1802 and a survey gives the following details: Yard surrounded by a wall, 1,435 feet long, 8½ feet high above the foundations. In the centre, a 'tyled' shed, 80 by 40 feet and 20 feet high, for sawyers; adjoining the wall 'tyled' sheds 30 feet wide, 16 feet high, those on the south and west sides as far as the river entrance, 494 feet in length, for carpenters, coopers, &c., those on east and west sides, 630 feet long, containing 40 'puckha' forges. From the river entrance to the north wall, five godowns for various uses. The interior of the yard was levelled and the floors of sheds and godowns were raised with earth one foot, well rammed. The rafters and posts were made of saul timber. Not a very imposing factory according to modern ideas, but very typical of a good many buildings in the ordnance factories, existing even down to the present century. On this survey report, Government authorized the removal of everything from the Kidderpore workshops, which had been in use temporarily, and the relinquishment of that ground. The erection of two bungalows for the European artificer and for the overseer at a cost of Rs. 2,489 was also sanctioned. Such were the very modest beginnings of the Cossipore Factory.

Major Glass was allowed to resign and to proceed to Europe on account of ill health in December 1803, when Captain Sherwood was appointed to act as Agent. In a report on the results of the agency from its commencement till the middle of June 1803, it was stated that carriages and powder barrels were rather more expensive than formerly. Glass gave as reasons for this: cost of the temporary buildings used till those at Cossipore were ready, cost of the removal, high price of materials from the Company's stores, and the bad quality of iron supplied. It was agreed that the quality of the carriages made was high.

The resources of the agency yard at Cossipore were found to be quite inadequate to meet the demand for carriages, and eleven tumbrils were even ordered from a European artificer in Calcutta, so Sherwood was authorized to construct two extra sheds for 20 more forges and to engage more labour. It is interesting to note the rates of wages for workmen then current in Calcutta: sawyers—annas 2–10 a day; smiths, first class—annas 5–4; hammermen—annas 2–6; bellows-men—annas 1–6; carpenters, first class—annas 5–4; turners—annas 4. The Second Mahratta War was on at this time, and it was found necessary also to establish a temporary manufactory at Kidderpore at the end of 1804, under Captain Grace of the Artillery. It was hoped that by the efforts of both establishments 235 carriages would be completed by the end of March 1805, and, moreover, that 2,000 powder barrels would be finished in 30 days. The temporary manufactory was not closed till the end of June 1805; it was located in sheds rented from Mr. Waddles for Rs. 200 a month and from Ramkissen at Rs. 80.

Captain T. Green, Artillery, had been appointed Agent at Cossipore in November 1804, and he got into trouble when taking over the stock of timber from Sherwood because he did not report 'the state of those materials, which he soon after returned under the head—Unserviceable'. Green referred to the survey made by the Military Board itself and on which he signed the usual receipt on transfer. He stated that the President asked him if he was satisfied with the numbers, and he replied that he was, but was guided as to condition by the Board's survey. The Governor-General thought the Board ought to take exceptional measures on such occasions to obtain a proper survey, but the Board explained that there were huge piles of timber and they could not possibly examine their contents, but they did ask Green if he had done so. The Military Board had to attend at the transfer of a manufactory from one officer to another and to hold a survey of the buildings, stock, &c. The Board consisted of the Commander-in-Chief, the senior officer at Calcutta, the senior officer of Artillery, the Chief Engineer, the Adjutant-General, the Quartermaster-General, and the Military Auditor-General. The attendance of these highly placed officers can hardly have been of the slightest use, and they could not possibly know what portion of a number of huge piles of timber consisted of serviceable pieces. Some members of the Board did realize the absurdity of such surveys, and, when in October 1806 it was reported that the temporary buildings, erected when the Agency was first established at Cossipore, were in a ruinous state and it was proposed that the Board should inspect them, the Chief Engineer said it was improper to have the whole of the Staff of the Bengal Army running out to look at tiled sheds and old timbers, and he would not attend unless positively ordered to do so. The fondness of India for Committees of all kinds continued, however, into the present century, as witness the assembly of three officers to investigate the circumstances under which a pair of boots had not lasted the prescribed period, or, worse still, a huge standing barrack committee, composed of representatives of all corps and various civilian officials, to decide on the site for a barrack cook-house. There is a story of one of these standing barrack committees assembling to decide on the site of a cook-house that had already been built, but owing to the neglect to have such a committee the cook-house did not officially exist!

Further sheds had been added to Cossipore in 1805 at a cost of Rs. 23,732, but, as already stated, the original sheds were found in October 1806 to be in a very ruinous condition, so the Board recommended rebuilding at a cost of

Rs. 43,624. Towards the end of 1807 Lieutenant-Colonel Green was permitted to go to England on account of ill health, and Captain-Lieutenant J. Young, Artillery, was directed to attend from and after 1st October, 'to take a careful survey and minute Inventory of the whole of the Public Stock of Timber, Ordnance Carriage Materials, Tools, &c. at the Yard, satisfying himself in the fullest manner of the condition . . . as well as their numbers and description'. The Board proposed to attend on 1st November to witness the transfer and to make a general inspection. The 1st being found to be Sunday and the 2nd the day for the General Muster of troops, the Board attended on the 3rd.

At this time the manufactory at Cossipore was known officially as the Gun-carriage Agency Yard and the officer in charge was entitled the Agent for Gun-carriages and Powder Barrels. The permanent establishment, which was fixed in 1800, included the following: *Europeans*: an overseer on Rs. 100 a month, a carpenter and wheelwright at Rs. 60, a smith and a cooper at Rs. 35 each, in addition to army pay and allowances. *Indians*: a mistry carpenter at Rs. 14 with a mate at Rs. 12, a mistry smith and a mistry brazier at Rs. 12 each, with a mate each at Rs. 10, a mistry cooper at Rs. 14 with a mate at Rs. 12, also two sircars at Rs. 20 each. An allowance of Rs. 60 a month was also given for a writer and stationery.

Captain Young wrote in 1810 that the allowance of Rs. 60 for office and stationery was quite inadequate and mentioned that a number of new forms and books had been introduced. The Military Accountant-General considered the allowance to be ample, especially as the two sircars kept rough daily accounts, and he actually wrote that, if the Agent wished to save himself the trouble of attending to his own accounts, then he thought it fit that he should pay for it, and the Military Board agreed with him! Fortunately the Governor-General took a more sensible view, evidently thinking that the chief duty of the Agent was the production of good carriages, and ordered that the Agent was to be allowed to charge his actual expenses, to be verified on oath.

Captain Young also wrote in the same year about the inadequacy of his house-rent allowance of Rs. 90 a month, as Captain Green had likewise done in 1806, but an increase was refused on the ground that the salary allowed for this. In 1814, however, it was found that the Agent was still drawing a commission from a contract for half-wrought iron-work, though all such contracts had been abolished. Young asked for compensation for the withdrawal of this, but was refused, and in lieu was allowed full batta and was granted Rs. 250 a month for house-rent actually paid from July 1814 till he obtained accommodation at a more moderate rent. A year later Young became A.D.C. to the Governor-General and ceased to be Agent at Cossipore. As an instance of the difficulty in keeping any close watch over the details of expenditure, it is interesting to note that the Court wrote on 26th August 1818 approving the accounts of the Agency for the year 1811–12, and considered them to be a credit to Captain Young.

In 1814 steps were taken which led eventually to the establishment of the gun-carriage agency at Fatehgarh, which will be dealt with later, but the effect on Cossipore was to diminish its importance and to stop any increase in its resources. There were only two permanent Agents between 1815 and 1830, Major H. Faithfull till 1821, when Captain C. H. Campbell succeeded, though several officers acted for short periods. There was also a half-wrought timber yard adjoining the manufactory, but the supply of timber will be dealt with separately. The permanent establishment in 1825 consisted of a conductor at Rs. 70, five European overseers-carpenter at Rs. 50, wheelwright at Rs. 25, blacksmith Rs. 40, founder Rs. 25, for charge of coolies Rs. 25, and there were three smiths at Rs. 25 each, all these Europeans having army pay in addition. The Indians were: four mistries-carpenter at Rs. 25 with mate at Rs. 20, smith at Rs. 25, brazier at Rs. 16, cooper at Rs. 12; a head sircar at Rs. 72, three at Rs. 10 and one at Rs. 8; two lascars at Rs. 5 each; one durwan at Rs. 6; two sweepers at Rs. 4 each and one moordah at Rs. 4 per month. A moordah was a gentleman employed to push off dead bodies which grounded on the river bank in front of the yard; the poorer classes often disposed of their dead economically by consigning them to the river. Towards the end of 1829, as a part of the economy measures instituted by Lord William Bentinck, it was decided that one gun-carriage agency would be sufficient for Bengal. So the Agency at Cossipore was combined with the one at Fatehgarh, and the Cossipore land and buildings were handed over for the new foundry in 1830.

### B. FATEHGARH

In June 1814 the Court were informed that in August 1813 a large stock of half-wrought materials for the maintenance of artillery equipments had been authorized by Government for the field, and the Military Board had proposed to distribute it among the several magazines in the field. The Commander-in-Chief, however, was strongly against this: he stated that the ordnance officers in the field had quite enough to do as it was, and he pointed out that the existing gun-carriage agency at Cossipore was removed from the field of action by a difficult and uncertain navigation of several months, and he considered it necessary to have close to the frontier an establishment of expert and ready trained artificers under a skilled and experienced officer, by which all contiguous depots might be kept complete and the losses of war made good. He further observed that the Presidency agency had ample work to make good the deficiencies of the garrisons and added that the whole of the carriages in Fort William required renewal. The Military Board agreed and said they would have put it forward before but for the expense, and they mentioned that the fort at Allygurh would require a complete set of carriages. They thought that carriages would be more durable when made in the climate in which they would be used, and referred to the repairs which carriages made at Cossipore had to undergo from shrinking on the way up country. Allahabad was considered to be the best situation, as it was not too far forward, was on the Jumna and the Ganges on which all the field magazines were located, while it was secure and near the Saul and Sissoo forests. On this Government, so the Court was informed, had sanctioned a second Agency at Allahabad with Brevet Major Clement Brown, Artillery, as Agent, salary to be Rs. 1,254–1 sonat a month, plus pay, full batta, gratuity, and house-rent if quarters were not provided.

In July 1814 Major Brown was directed to proceed at once to Allahabad, to consider the situation in the fort and the use of public buildings, and to submit a report to the Commander-in-Chief when the latter arrived there. An establishment was sanctioned, including two European artificers, five mistries, four sircars, with an office allowance of Rs. 250 a month. In December, however, the Board directed the establishment to be discharged, the two Europeans, being soldiers, to be employed temporarily in the Allahabad magazine, and the office allowance discontinued, till the state of the agency rendered the preparation of accounts necessary; and the discharges were effected at the end of January 1815.

The fact is the agency was never established at Allahabad, for the simple reason that Brown never obtained any accommodation for it. The Commander-in-Chief did not want it in the fort, though there had been an idea of using the east and south ranges of the European barracks, which, at the time, were mostly unoccupied. A site at Papamhow was found to be unsuitable, and moreover the Court had ordered that no new magazines or similar buildings were to be erected without their express command. So a whole year was occupied in the search for suitable buildings and in correspondence between the various people concerned. Eventually the

Board proposed to locate the agency in the magazine at Fatehgarh, and, the Commander-in-Chief not objecting to the removal of the magazine from Fatehgarh, the Governor-General approved the proposal in December 1815. Only a part of the magazine was appropriated, at first, for the use of the agency, the ordnance and stores being transferred to the magazine at Cawnpore.

Thus the gun-carriage agency was established at Fatehgarh early in 1816, but it was some years before the whole of the magazine was vacated and taken over by the agency. The original idea of moving the magazine to Allygurh was abandoned, as a depot was not needed there, but it was not till 1822 that the matter was settled. Much discussion took place in 1819, when it was considered that the troops along the Jumna and in the Upper Doab were well enough provided for by the extensive magazines at Allahabad, Agra, and Delhi, with the depot at 'Kinnaul', while those in the Lower Doab, part of Bundlekhand, and Oude were supplied from Cawnpore. It was the troops in Rohilkhand and Kumaon which needed a magazine for which a small fort was being constructed at Bareilly.

Fatehgarh had become an important military cantonment in 1777, when the temporary brigade was formed there, but after the Second Mahratta War it lost its importance and by 1815 it had only one regular battalion of infantry as its garrison. The fort, which was built of mud in 1720, was in a very ruinous state in 1777, but was used by the artillery as well as for a magazine. From 1790 it was used as a magazine and depot only, the artillery having moved their lines outside. When it was decided in 1815 to establish the gun-carriage agency there, the Marquess of Hastings, the Governor-General, who was also Commander-in-Chief, had personal knowledge of the fort and its magazine, as he had himself inspected them in March of that year, during his five months' stay at Fatehgarh during the Nepal War, and he had the fort put in a better state of repair.

It is obvious that one of the chief reasons for the selection of the Fatehgarh fort for the new gun-carriage agency was the existence of buildings which could be utilized at no great expense, needing only a few additional sheds and a bungalow, bought for Rs. 700, for the two European artificers, while the city of Farrukhabad and the district round would provide, it was no doubt assumed, plenty of good workmen. Farrukhabad was, at this time, a great trading centre, but neither it nor its surrounding district was industrial in the true sense. Tents were made in large quantities and there was some manufacture of metal utensils, while it was noted for excellent swords, but there was unlikely to be much of a surplus of workers for a new industry. It does not always follow that even a populous city and district will provide workmen willing to be, and capable of being, trained in a class of work strange to them. This was found to be the case at Fatehgarh and was so also at Jubbulpore when the gun-carriage factory was established there in 1901.

Certainly all did not go smoothly with the Fatehgarh agency, for it was not till 1822 that the Military Board received the first accounts, those from its creation till the end of April 1818, when it was seen that the work done was more expensive than similar work produced at Cossipore, while there were many errors in the accounts. Major Brown explained that he had only untrained workmen, that he had experienced many difficulties in starting work, and moreover the accounts were the first of the kind that he had prepared. When Captain R. B. Fulton was appointed Agent in 1824 on Brown's promotion to lieutenant-colonel, Government wrote that 'he must obtain the fullest results from the low rates of wages in the Upper Provinces'. There were curious 'side-lines' for officers in those days. Major Brown, for example, was appointed in 1821 by the Board of Trade, with the sanction of Government, Agent for the sale of the Honourable Company's wines at Fatehgarh, but the emoluments of the post are not known.

In a letter to the Court dated in January 1830 Government wrote: 'A Minute by the Governor General having demonstrated that one Gun Carriage Agency, when in full operation, would be sufficient to answer all the demands of this Presidency, it has been resolved to abolish the Agency at Cossipore, transferring the Senior Agent, Major C. H. Campbell to Futty Ghur.' Actually the move took place in November 1829, when Campbell went to Fatehgarh and took over from Fulton. Most of the Cossipore permanent establishment went with Campbell, together with some of the plant and much of the materials, especially of the half-wrought timber. Lord William Bentinck, when considering the matter, noted that each permanent establishment cost about Rs. 600 a month, that the buildings at Cossipore had cost about a lakh of rupees, and that the Agents had each Rs. 1,254 as salary, besides pay, batta, and residence. He considered the salaries to be extravagant, as also was the Rs. 1,400 allowed in Madras, and remarked that the Agent at Bombay received Rs. 600. Gun-carriages made at Fatehgarh, he was assured, were superior to those from Cossipore, the great dryness of the climate making the seasoning of the timber more perfect. As showing the great interest he took in economy, it may be mentioned that Campbell was ordered to proceed by Dawk (carriage). Travelling by Dawk would be much more expensive than by river, but would be so much shorter in point of time that there would be probably a saving of at least two months' salary of one Agent. No alteration was made in the rate of salary till April 1837, when it was reduced to Rs. 1,000 a month.

Major Campbell had been commended in 1827 for his management at Cossipore, and in 1832 was noted as a diligent, methodical, and economical manager. He died at Fatehgarh on 19 May 1832 and was buried in the fort cemetery, but the inscription tablet was destroyed in the Mutiny, when the Rebels removed many of the tablets for use as curry stones. His expenses for the repair of the

Agency buildings were considered to be excessive, so Government directed that all buildings were to be handed over to the care of the Executive Engineer. The Governor-General had intended appointing Campbell to be Agent for Gunpowder at Ishapore had he lived.

Captain T. Lumsden became Agent till at the end of 1842 he was succeeded by Brevet Major A. Abbott, who had commanded the artillery of the 'illustrious garrison' of Jellalabad in 1841–2. Lord Ellenborough, in a letter to him dated in September 1842, offering him the appointment, wrote thus: 'Your practical knowledge of the service of Artillery in the field under the most difficult circumstances, renders you eminently fit for this appointment.' He also made Abbott an Honorary A.D.C., which honour was continued by the next three Governors-General. Abbott became Principal Commissary of Ordnance in 1848, the first Inspector-General of Ordnance and Magazines in 1855, and in 1858 was Commandant of the Bengal Artillery, but he had to go home on account of ill health and died at Cheltenham in February 1867.

From time to time new buildings were erected; for example, in October 1835 a range of tiled sheds for the storage of half-wrought timber and for the painters was sanctioned at a cost of Rs. 12,368. But real progress only came when, in 1847, Government sanctioned an expenditure of Rs. 10,000 on the introduction of steam power into the agency. In March 1848 the Military Board reported that they had purchased a new 6-h.p. high-pressure steam-engine from Messrs. Teel & Company for Rs. 1,800, and had had it completed at the Mint, while a fan blast and speed gear had been constructed at the Iron Bridge Yard. They had engaged a competent Engineer, Mr. W. R. P. Roberts, on Rs. 200 a month with quarters, and he had arrived at Fatehgarh in October 1847. In August 1849 the Board were able to report that the engine with fan blast had been completed in May 1848, and a new lathe room had been erected and furnished with drilling and other machines, and they had extended the work of the agency by giving it a quantity of miscellaneous work for the field magazines. They said the plant gave air to fifty forges and could give more, and it worked, also, an effective drilling-machine, two lathes, two grindstones, and a circular saw. They reported that they had only expended Rs. 9,939, but wanted sanction for a spare boiler. They instanced, as one saving, that there had been eighty bellows in use valued at Rs. 8,258, half being worn out and the remainder would not last more than three years, and now no replacement would be necessary. In fact the Military Board were almost hysterical over their wonderful achievement. However, both Government and the Court were gratified at the success and commended Lieutenant-Colonel J. Alexander, the Agent, and Mr. Roberts, the engineer and foreman.

Roberts was a man of ideas. He proposed in 1849 to construct a steamer to work across the Ganges in place of the bridge of boats, but Government turned the proposal down, pointing out that there would only be water enough in the river during four months in the year. He fell ill in 1851, and, his quarters in the fort being pronounced to be unhealthy, the Agent was directed to arrange for other accommodation; but Roberts died in June, aged only 34, and was buried in the fort cemetery, a memorial stone being set up in his memory by Isan Chander Deb, the head clerk of the agency. Another subordinate worthy of mention was Conductor W. Hine, who in November 1826 was ordered from Cossipore to Fatehgarh, as the medical officer declared the climate of the Lower Provinces to be 'enimical' to his health. He was pensioned as an invalid in 1832, made his home in Fatehgarh, became first a merchant and then got a job as Superintendent of Road Making. However, he was dismissed from the last job, as his accounts were found to be in disorder, but he lived until February 1855, when he was aged 66.

Alexander had become Agent in January 1848 and was

succeeded in May 1853 by Brevet Lieutenant-Colonel J. Fordyce, and in September 1856 Brevet Major A. Robertson was appointed to act as Agent. Robertson was granted a Brevet for his services in the Punjab with effect from March 1853, and he also served in Pegu in the same year.

Government wrote to the Court in May 1851 that the erection of a cupola had been sanctioned for casting iron as a measure of convenience and economy as regards both the Ordnance Department and the Public Works Department in the Upper Provinces. There would be a charge of 5 per cent. annually on the production to cover the cost of setting up, as was done in the case of buildings and machinery of the steam-engine.

Objections to Fatehgarh as the location of a gun-carriage agency had been raised from time to time. The first seems to have been in 1825, when the advantages of Cawnpore were suggested and the disadvantage urged of having timber stored in the half-wrought yard at Cawnpore while it was used at Fatehgarh; moreover, it was said that there were never enough artillery officers at Fatehgarh to form a committee of survey on new carriages. However, expense decided the matter, and the timber was ordered to be transferred to Fatehgarh. Then in 1834 the Board discussed a proposal to move the agency to Allahabad, on account of the difficulties in the supply of trained labour and the high cost of production, but it was decided that such a step was not expedient. Then in 1854–5 there was much writing on a suggestion that the manufactory should be moved to Calcutta. A Committee of Investigation had found great losses in half-wrought timber at Fatehgarh, varying from 30 to 90 per cent. of most valuable material, due it was said to splits in seasoning and not from poor quality, and this was presumed to be the result of the hot dry winds. It was stated that this was not apparent at first, as, when the manufactory moved from Cossipore, there was a large stock of good material, from which there was little loss. It was remarked, however, that the godowns were very crowded and were not ventilated. The Committee also referred to the excessive cost of obtaining timber from the forests and to the difficulty in purchasing at the border markets, as the merchants were holding back for railway buyers. The Military Board in their letter dated in March 1854 said that experience showed the superiority of timber seasoned in Calcutta, also that it was easy to obtain there, while saul fit for carriages was not obtainable at Fatehgarh, and they recommended the removal of the manufactory to the left bank of the river at Calcutta. One member of the Board went so far as to assert that the climate of Calcutta was the best in the world for seasoning timber, being equable and subject to no extremes, while that of Fatehgarh was the worst; being the Military Accountant-General he was no doubt an expert on the subject! The Governor-General, in May, expressed his doubts, feared the expense, and asked for more information and opinions. He then found that the Select Committee on Artillery Equipment and the Committee of Investigation did not recommend the removal, and stated quite definitely that carriages made at Cossipore had proved to be inferior to those made at Fatehgarh. In October he minuted that Lord William Bentinck, in 1829, decided to close Cossipore and had recorded that the Military Board had referred to the superiority of the carriages made at Fatehgarh over the Cossipore ones, many of which had failed. He observed that all evidence was against the Cossipore carriages and wheels for use in the Upper Provinces, and the Select Committee and all the artillery officers on the Board were against the restoration of Cossipore. He then quoted Sir John Horsford, who wrote, 'the Wheels of the gun carriages received from Fort William are not, nor cannot be, fit for service in this climate, make them up in Calcutta with what art and care soever, they always prove ricketty after the first day's march in Hindustan'. The Governor-General would not agree to the removal of the agency from Fatehgarh, but decided to establish a timber depot at Balloo Ghat in Calcutta, and he sanctioned the writing off of the loss in seasoning timber to the amount of Rs. 63,248. It is curious, however, that no steps seem to have been taken then to remove the obvious cause of the heavy loss, by constructing adequate and properly ventilated store-rooms for the stock of valuable timber. Later experience showed clearly that saul and sissoo timber of the finest quality were obtainable from the forests on the borders of Nepal, and its preservation depended entirely on proper storage conditions.

In 1857 Fatehgarh and its gun-carriage agency were deeply involved in the Mutiny. The Agent, Major Robertson, of the Bengal Artillery, was living in the Agent's bungalow within the fort with his wife and child and a sister-in-law. The European establishment consisted of: Conductor M. Ions, the engineer and foreman, with wife and four children; Sub-Conductor P. Hammond, assistant engineer, with wife; Conductor M. Rohan, the carpenter foreman, with wife and nine children; also Mr. Lows, blacksmith foreman, with wife and two children. The fort was very dilapidated and of no real strength; it was 1,500 yards in circumference, of which 450 overlooked the river with no defences. There were ten bastions in bad repair, overlooked from many places, and the mud walls were sloping and easy of ascent. It contained, besides the Agent's house, some quarters for the staff, a walled cemetery, and the workshops and godowns of the agency. The main timber yard was outside the fort, south-east of the gate and abutting on the fort rampart, with low walls surrounding it. Much of the foregoing description and of what follows is extracted from a very interesting book by Colonel Cosens and Mr. Wallace, *Fatehgarh and the Mutiny*.

Soon after the Mutiny broke out, the district round Fatehgarh became very disturbed, and the civilian authorities had cause to distrust the regiment, the 10th N.I., in garrison at Fatehgarh, but little was done to prepare for any rising.

As the situation steadily deteriorated, the civil authorities decided to leave and seek refuge elsewhere, but the Colonel of the regiment refused to agree to this course. However, a number of the residents left by boats on the night of 3rd June. Included in this exodus were Conductor Hammond and Mr. Lows with their families: they did not go to Dharampur to seek refuge with Hardeo Baksh Singh but remained on the boats which went on down the river to Cawnpore, where they were all killed on 12th June. The remainder of the agency staff stayed in Fatehgarh and were in the fort when the siege began on 27th June.

There were two guns attached to the troops in garrison, but they had not been secured, so the fort could only be armed with the muster guns of the agency. These consisted of a 3-pounder, a 6-pounder, a 9-pounder, a 12-pounder, an 18-pounder, with a 24-pounder howitzer and a small brass mortar. There was little or no ammunition for these guns, as they were only used for fitting the new carriages as they were made; actually only about 30 round shot could be found, and powder was obtained by breaking up blank cartridges. Hammer-heads, bolts, and nuts were sewn up in canvas bags by the women to serve as grape-shot. There were about 300 muskets, for which Mallu, the fort gatekeeper, and Sheoparshard, the agency Jemadar, managed to steal some five to six thousand cartridges from the 10th N.I., and got them into the fort; these two men with Isan Chander Deb, the head clerk, were also instrumental in getting provisions, but the supply was inadequate. In some places the heavy half-wrought gun-wheel naves were used to heighten the parapet, and when an assault was made they were rolled off on to the scaling-ladders with great effect.

There were only 35 able-bodied defenders among the 110 refugees in the fort. There were lots of gun-carriages, and many were used with dummy guns—blackboard shields with a hole cut in the centre—to deceive the rebels. The defence continued till two breaches had been made in the walls and a mine had been driven underneath: the men were exhausted, three had been killed and several others disabled, so it was decided to evacuate the fort. The survivors left at 2 a.m. on 3rd July in three overcrowded boats, one of which had soon to be abandoned. On the 4th one boat went aground at Manpur Katri and its occupants were all killed, drowned, or captured, with the exception of a very few, who managed to reach the other boat, and of Major Robertson, who, although wounded, managed to reach land and eventually a place of safety, assisted by Mr. D. Churcher, an indigo planter. Robertson died of wounds and exposure on 27th September and was buried at Baramau. Robertson's family were all drowned or killed on 4th July, as also was Conductor Ions with his family, except one daughter who was captured and afterwards killed on the parade ground at Fatehgarh on 23rd July. Conductor Rohan, with his family, was in the other boat which went on down the river: he was killed on the journey, but his family were among those who were massacred at Cawnpore on 15th July. There was another European on the staff of the agency in 1857, this was Lieutenant Moses Sheels of the Veteran Establishment, who was the Timber Agent; he was a sub-conductor there as far back as 1837. His fate is uncertain, though he is shown in the Army List for 1859, under the heading of Casualties, as 'killed by Mutineers, Futtehgurh, 1857'. In the book already referred to there is mentioned a Mr. Shiels, with wife and two children, who went in the first exodus and who were all killed at Cawnpore on 12 June; he was said to be the schoolmaster, and his name was also spelt Sheels. Mr. Wallace in another book, *Fatehgarh Camp*, writes: 'It cannot be said exactly whether he [Moses Sheels] became a schoolmaster himself, or was a relation of the schoolmaster.' In my opinion it is unlikely that the Timber Agent was this schoolmaster, and more probable that he was out in the forests or the district selecting timber, and it seems impossible to say how Lieutenant Moses Sheels met his death, nor where, nor when. Thus the whole of the Fatehgarh gun-carriage agency's European staff with their families perished in the Mutiny.

Fatehgarh was reoccupied by Sir Colin Campbell on 3rd January 1858, when it was found that the gun-carriage factory was in no way damaged. The rebels had established a gun and shell factory on the premises, which, when abandoned by them, contained a number of brass guns half turned on the lathes, many more just cast, and a quantity of materials for the manufacture of powder and shot. They managed to cast brass guns but could not cast iron shot, but instead hammered them out on the smith's forges. On the 12th Sir Colin ordered the repair of the fort and put Major Nicholson in charge of the work. The village of Hussainpore which extended right up to the fort was cleared, elephants being used to push down the houses, while much was done to the fort itself, crowds of coolies being employed at two annas a day. Major Le Geyt Bruce, Bengal Artillery, was appointed to act as Agent, and much useful work was quickly done for the army, including mounting captured 18-pounder guns on 24-pounder carriages, altering other carriages for the naval 8-inch guns which did good service at the capture of Lucknow. A new permanent staff was quickly found from the European regiments, and Captain F. Turner, Bengal Artillery, became Agent.

After the events of 1857 there were doubts as to the wisdom of having so important a manufactory in such an isolated and unprotected place as Fatehgarh, necessitating the employment of a considerable body of troops as garrison. In 1863 the matter was further considered on a suggestion that Allahabad should become a third-class fortress and the gun-carriage agency be moved there. The matter was dropped till 1875, when the Special Ordnance Commission reopened it with the recommendation that the move should take place, and both the Fatehgarh and Bombay factories be closed, but again nothing was done. But there had always, since the Mutiny, been advocates for the concentration of gun-carriage manufacture in one central factory. Lieutenant-Colonel Adye, R.A., in his report on Artillery Material in India in 1860, advocated the concentration of all three factories at Allahabad, but Sir Patrick Grant, the Commander-in-Chief, considered it too great a risk to have all in one place. The question was taken up again in 1894, and a site at Chinsurah, on the Hughli above Calcutta, was seriously proposed as being a good labour centre with cheap water transport. However, after much discussion, Jubbulpore in the Central Provinces was selected, and the work of building the Central Gun-Carriage Factory was commenced in 1901.

Some description of the Fatehgarh factory as it was towards the end of last century may be of interest. It occupied the greater part of the fort, which was well kept and not unimposing in its way; the earth ramparts were high, covered with grass, with gun emplacements and musketry banquettes, and it was surrounded by a dry ditch. It could, however, be climbed into with little difficulty almost anywhere, and its extent was hopelessly out of proportion to any immediately available garrison. The Superintendent's house had been burnt down in 1892, but its plinth showed its extent. There were a few quarters for some of the European and Indian staff and there was a guard-room, a magazine, and a stable for the two elephants used in timber and forest work. The factory proper formed an enclosure within the fort, but the main timber godowns, well built and well ventilated, were between the factory wall and the river bank. The workshops were mostly of the tiled-shed type, many dating from early days, but fairly suitable for the class of work then required and the nature of the machinery. Some of the sheds were almost uninhabitable on a typical June day, with a hot wind blowing, and the workmen had sometimes to be sent home, but actually the factory was quite an efficient one up to the time of the introduction of quick-firing equipments. It possessed both an iron and a brass foundry, and a fair equipment of machinery; it had also a furnace, a heavy hammer, and a small rolling-mill, by means of which it worked up wrought-iron scrap into axle-trees for transport and similar vehicles. The usual number of workmen was in the region of 800, but in its later years it suffered from the superior attractions of Cawnpore, whose growing industries tended to draw the younger men away. The factory had a superintendent with an assistant, both officers of the Royal Artillery, but the staff salary was no longer Rs. 1,000, and had come down to Rs. 600 a month. The European staff was still mainly drawn from the Army, there being only two civilians, an engineer and foreman, and a head blacksmith. The Fatehgarh gun-carriage factory was finally closed in June 1905 after a useful life of ninety years.

# XVI

## TIMBER SUPPLY IN BENGAL

THE supply of good timber has always been a matter of great importance to a gun-carriage factory, but it was vital to the gun-carriage manufactories of the East India Company, when all gun-carriages and vehicles were constructed almost entirely of wood, with the exception of purely garrison carriages, which after 1825 were increasingly made of cast iron. In the contract made with Mr. J. Anderson in 1771 it was stipulated that he must buy all materials from the Company, and as he had to make, if required, 86 garrison and not less than 9 field-carriages every three months, the amount of timber necessary would be considerable and would be obtained by the Military Storekeeper. Then in 1775 it was ordered that all gun-carriages and vehicles were to be made at the Presidency under the Commissary of Stores, and in 1781 Colonel Duff, the Commissary of Stores, was permitted to transport naves and felloes on boats, returning from Cawnpore and the Upper Provinces, provided there was no extra expense to the Company. But the system for the supply of timber, if there was any system at all, is by no means clear; it seems evident, however, that the Commissaries of Stores at the arsenal had some responsibility in the matter. For carriage bodies teak was the usual timber, and there was difficulty in 1796 in obtaining it large enough for the cheeks. There was certainly a depot at Chitpore in 1798 where timber was stored and seasoned, and obviously this furnished timber for some at least of the manufacturing needs. In 1800 the gun-carriage agency was established, and the Agent became responsible for the provision of timber under the control of the Military Board. He was authorized in 1803, for example, to purchase sissoo timber from Mr. Binny in Calcutta, this timber having been in use for some years for wheels, and in 1802 it having been decided to make the cheeks of gun-carriages of two pieces of sissoo.

It has already been described how Captain Green in 1805 had trouble in connexion with the taking over of the huge piles of timber from the acting Agent. This stock was evidently stored at Chitpore on ground for which a monthly rent of Rs. 53–10 was paid. But the Commissary-General also had control of timber buying and storing. In 1810 Mr. Assistant Surgeon Rutherford was Agent for the supply of half-wrought sissoo and saul for the use of the magazines at Allahabad, Cawnpore, Fatehgarh, Agra, and Delhi; he was under the control and orders of the Commissary-General, and had a personal salary of Rs. 500 sonat a month, plus bona fide expenses. In 1813 the half-wrought timber yard at Cossipore was extended and secured from fire by the removal of some houses at an extra monthly rental of Rs. 75, and was made a separate charge. Captain H. Faithful, Artillery, was appointed Superintendent of the yard, under the Commissary-General, with a salary of Rs. 300, plus pay and allowances, and he had to attest on oath half-yearly that he derived no advantage, directly or indirectly, beyond the salary. In 1816 complaints were made of the lack of progress and success of Mr. Rutherford in the supply of timber for the Ordnance Department, and it was decided that all timber required for military purposes should be furnished by the Commissariat Department, the Commissary-General becoming the sole Agent for the provision of timber at the Presidency. It appears, however, from a Military Consultation of January 1817, that Mr. Rutherford was still Agent for the supply of timber in the Upper Provinces, and that he had been appointed an Extra Assistant Commissary-General on Rs. 1,000 a month for his services in Nepal.

The Military Board proposed the erection of a saw-mill in the timber yard at Cossipore, and Government thought a saw of 4 h.p. would answer, and asked the Court in October 1817 to send one out with full instructions. The

Court in their reply, dated in September 1819, did not approve, and wrote, 'We are of opinion that it is advisable to continue the present system of manual labour. We shall not therefor comply with your indent for a Saw Mill.'

There was also a Government timber yard at Cawnpore in 1820, as in that year Deputy Assistant Commissary of Ordnance C. Feldwick was appointed its Superintendent, and in 1824 Sub-Conductor I. Fuller of the Army Commissariat was appointed its overseer, 'under the general supervision of the Commissariat Officer who may be nominated to the charge of the Yard, at Rs. 100 plus military allowances'.

The system under which the Agents for the manufacture of so important an article as a gun-carriage were entirely divorced from the selection and storage of timber, the main material from which it was constructed, was of course a bad one, but it was some years before it was altered. In November 1823 Government directed that,

'from the 1st of December, the Commissariat half-wrought material depot and establishment at Cossipore shall be annexed to and re-united with the Gun Carriage Agency there. The Agent for Gun Carriages will keep the accounts separate. Captain R. B. Fulton, Superintendent of the Cossipore half-wrought yard is appointed from that date and till further orders, Assistant to the Agent with his present military allowances and staff salary.'

This transfer resulted in considerable economy, amounting to between four and five thousand rupees a year, and the Military Board, in November 1825, expressed the opinion that Fatehgarh would never be able to compete with Cossipore in efficiency and economy till a similar step was taken there. So Government ordered that from 1st December 1825 the Commissariat half-wrought material depot and establishment at Cawnpore was to be transferred to Fatehgarh.

It must be understood that the conditions at Cossipore in this matter of timber supply were very similar to those at Bombay and Madras: all these three gun-garriage manufactories were situated at big ports, which were also great commercial centres, and it was possible to obtain timber with comparative ease from many places by both private and public agencies. Fatehgarh, on the other hand, was far from any port and from any really great commercial centre, and it had to build up its own system of timber supply from sources as near as possible. The obvious source was the forest on the borders of Nepal, where sissoo and saul were to be found in plenty, but it is evident that it was many years before any satisfactory arrangements were made to exploit this source economically and satisfactorily. In 1827 Fatehgarh had a timber depot at Byram Ghat near the Nepalese border, but it was withdrawn the following year owing to the expense and the unsatisfactory nature of the timber obtained. Still the agency depended in large measure on the forests, and it cannot have been long before operations were recommenced. In 1837 Sub-Conductor M. Sheels, one of the staff of the manufactory, was employed in purchasing timber from the local market or direct from the forests; later he was designated Timber Agent and was still so employed as late as 1857, when he was a lieutenant on the Veteran Establishment.

The Commissariat timber agencies did not cease with the removal of the Cossipore and Cawnpore half-wrought material yards to the charge of the Gun-carriage Agents. There was one at Nautpore in the Purnea district in 1827, with Captain G. W. Moseley, 38th N.I., as Agent and Lieutenant A. Knyvett, 64th N.I., as his Assistant, which is said to have supplied fine timber to the Commissariat timber depot at Balloo Ghat, Calcutta. In 1829, however, the Nautpore Agency was found to have been subject to much mismanagement and was closed, while the timber at Balloo Ghat was transferred to Cossipore. Teak was obtained from Tenasserim, where there was a Conservator who was also Agent for supply; in 1840 Captain G. B. Tremenheere, Engineers, held the appointment.

As has already been stated, the timber depot at Balloo Ghat was re-established by order of the Governor-General in October 1854, and it remained till 1864, when it was abolished and other work found for Mr. W. Clifford, who was the Commissariat Timber Agent. It had then been decided that stores were no longer to be supplied to the Ordnance Department through Commissariat agency, and moreover it was considered that the cost of this timber agency was excessive. From this time Fatehgarh depended mainly on forest operations conducted by an officer of the Ordnance Department as Timber Agent. In 1879 the operations were placed entirely under the Superintendent of the gun-carriage factory and were carried out by his own establishment. Trees were selected in the Nepal forests under a contract with the Nepalese Government and felled by the Nepalese, who conveyed them to the factory depot on the border, where they were measured and paid for. The logs were then cut up, stored for a time, and then transported to Fatehgarh. Excellent saul and sissoo logs were obtained in this way.

## XVII

## THE MADRAS GUN-CARRIAGE MANUFACTORY

THE experience of the Madras Government with contractors for the supply of gun-carriages was not a happy one. In 1791 the proposals of Messrs. Topping & Parry were accepted, and a contract given them for five years, but there was grave delay on their part in carrying out the contract. Further proposals were invited at the end of 1797, and in January of the following year tenders were opened from a number of contractors and the contract was given to Messrs. Goldingham & Lys. The contract included a large number of articles besides gun-carriages and iron axles. There were serious complaints about the carriages which these contractors supplied, and a Committee of Inspection, reporting in June 1801 on bad carriages at Hyderabad, recommended that the Company appoint its own Agent for the supply of carriages and vehicles, the Agent to be an officer of the Army, and they further suggested Seringapatam, Trichinopoly, Masulipatam, or Fort St. George as suitable locations for the Agency. The Military Board appointed a Committee of the Board to investigate this 'alarming failure of gun carriages of every description supplied by the contractors within the last two years'. In the report of this Committee, dated in June 1802, the failure was attributed to bad teak from Pegu, and they recommended that all ordnance carriages should be made from timber to be supplied by Government, and, if possible, from forests in the Peninsula. They also recommended that they should be made by Government artificers under the supervision of a public officer. They observed further that they believed the contract prices to be exorbitant and said the contractors were allowed to charge for the slightest deviation from the original pattern—'on honour', with an additional percentage to them. They remarked that carriages sent from Madras to Gooty in January, painted, with no guns on them, arrived unfit for service. They appointed a further Committee to examine the materials and construction, which reported in January 1803, confirming the badness of the timber from Pegu, but they exonerated the contractors!

In August 1801 Sir Arthur Wellesley wrote a memorandum on Seringapatam, stating that it possessed means for equipping an army which no other place in the Company's territories had except Madras; it also was the most convenient depot for service in Malabar and Canara and even in Mahratta territory. He admitted that it was unhealthy, but put this down to bad buildings, and thought it no worse than other places. He pointed out its proximity to the Mysore forests, the abundance of old iron, the numerous and extensive buildings, and the security of such a fortress. Moreover, there was, he stated, no difficulty in obtaining good workmen from among those who had been employed by Tippoo in his numerous workshops.

On 26th October 1802 it was decided that 'all carriages, &c., made by contractors, were in future to be made in a Manufactory to be established at Seringapatam under the Military Board, and directly under an Agent, who shall have a salary and expense for writers and stationery'. The manufactory is said to have occupied the site of the ancient palace of the Mysore Rajahs. The following regular establishment was sanctioned: *Europeans*: 1 overseer at 25 pagodas; 2 smiths at 15 and 12; 2 carpenters at 15 and 10; 1 brass founder at 10; 1 cooper at 8; 1 wheelwright at 15 and 3 at 10. *Indians*: 1 carpenter and 1 smith mistry at 8; 6 carpenters, 6 smiths, 1 brass smith, 1 sawyer, 1 turner, and 1 filer each at 6 pagodas; 12 sawyers at 3½; 4 turners, 6 filers, 30 carpenters, 30 smiths all at 4 pagodas; 30 hammer-men at 2, and 30 bellows boys at 1 pagoda a month. Extra men on daily pay to be engaged as necessary. This was by far the largest permanent establishment sanctioned for any of the gun-carriage manufactories, and the rates of pay were higher in several trades. Timber was to be obtained by contract under the Military Board, the contractor to cut, but a conductor with a party of lascars and sepoys to superintend the cutting and to remain in charge of the timber while it was in the forest. The contractor was to square the logs and collect and pile them in suitable spots. When the piles were in some degree seasoned, the conductor was to inform the Agent for Gun-carriages who would then indent for transport. The Board recommended that the terms of contract lately entered into by 'the Honorable Colonel A. Wellesley' be adopted and also that his instructions to the conductor in the forest be approved.

Captain J. G. Scott of the Artillery was appointed Agent. He was then Commissary of Stores at Seringapatam, an appointment he owed to Sir Arthur Wellesley, when he discovered the scandal in the Stores Department which has already been described. Scott was given, at first, a salary of 500 pagodas which was to cover all expenses for writers, stationery, and the establishment of his office; in addition he drew pay at pagodas 43–31(fanams)–40(cash), batta 28–5–20, gratuity 11–10–40, and tent allowance 18. His salary was altered in 1808 to 400 pagodas without liability for the expenses of his office. He had a certain amount of building work to do for the accommodation of stores, but the cost was small, being only Rs. 3,662.

The Court approved of the establishment of the agency, but were alarmed at the reports of the failure of the contract-made carriages and directed that all relevant papers should be laid before the Company's Attorneys. The Madras Council had to admit that action against the contractors was not likely to be successful, as unfortunately the Advocate-General expressed the opinion that the Military Board had sole responsibility for the goodness of the timber. The Court, writing in September 1808, sadly ended the matter with the remark, 'it would seem that the failure of the articles was due to the want of proper attention of the Board'.

The work done at the agency under Captain Scott received praise on many occasions. Bombay wrote in December 1804 that the carriages received from Seringapatam were superior in workmanship to anything they had seen of the kind. In July 1805 the Military Board reported that the progressive improvement of the gun-carriage manufactory had enabled them to extend its work and to obtain further economy in supplies. In April 1809 the Court wrote that they were highly pleased that the agency had saved the public 28,575 pagodas in 1805–6. Scott had to resign from ill health and proceed to England in October 1809, but the Court wished him to resume as Agent when he returned in 1813, but he was appointed to the command of Seringapatam instead.

The demand for equipment consequent on the operations against the Mahrattas was so great that a temporary gun-carriage yard was established at the Presidency in 1803, and Lieutenant J. C. Franke, Artillery, was placed in charge on a salary of 200 pagodas a month, which the Court thought was too high. Franke was originally a deputy commissary, but was appointed the junior Lieutenant Fireworker of Artillery in September 1798 for 'merits and long service'. A number of the workmen formerly employed by the contractors were engaged for this yard and materials and tools were purchased from them, both for the agency and the temporary yard. This temporary factory was not very successful, as Franke only managed to make fifty carriages annually, though the quality was said to be excellent. It was closed at the end of April 1808, when Franke became Commissary of Ordnance at Trichinopoly.

Captain-Lieutenant J. Moorhouse, Artillery, succeeded to the post of Agent in 1810 and held it till he died at Mysore at the end of May 1823, and when he was appointed, the manufacture of powder barrels was added to the work of the manufactory. In 1811 three companies of store lascars, each consisting of a syrang, two tindals, and fifty lascars, were allotted to the agency. In February 1818 the Court wrote to Madras approving the Council's action in refusing the application from the lascars at the manufactory to be exempted from work on Sundays, such work not interfering with the performance of their religious duties. In 1818 salaries were fixed in rupees instead of in pagodas, and the Agent for Gun-carriages was allowed, in lieu of 400 pagodas a month, Rs. 1,400, the highest salary granted to any Agent for Manufacture in India.

Captain W. Cullen, Artillery, became Superintendent of the manufactory by General Order dated 2nd July 1824. He had been employed with a small party of artificers from 1819 in preparing and fixing blocks and tangent scales to the brass ordnance throughout the Presidency. He moved with the manufactory from Seringapatam to Madras in June 1830, and the Military Board reported in 1831 that Lieutenant-Colonel Cullen had saved Rs. 1,41,517 in five years in the business of felling and removing trees from the Mysore forests. It is rather curious that in 1827 a demand was made on the Company's Agent at the Cape of Good Hope, for timber 'to be applied to the manufacture of wheels for field carriages', recommended by Lieutenant-Colonel Morrison, the Commissary-General of Stores.

The circumstances in which the removal of the manufactory from Seringapatam was decided upon are interesting. Already in 1811 many of the troops had been moved to Bangalore owing to fever and general unhealthiness. Seringapatam was described as a 'sink of nastiness' when it was occupied though not then considered to be unhealthy; this, however, does not agree with the comment of Sir A. Wellesley already quoted. Colonel James Welsh in his *Military Reminiscences* says that in 1812 his Corps was ordered to Seringapatam, 'that grave of thousands', and mentions that out of a Brigade of nearly 3,000 men only 834 were present at a field-day in March of that year. In 1827 Government informed the Court that it had been decided to remove the manufactory to the vicinity of Fort St. George, and gave as reasons that the climate caused great waste of life and loss of health so that a large portion of the establishment was always ineffective. Scott lost his wife and daughters at Seringapatam,[1] and his successor in the Gun-carriage Agency, Captain Moorhouse, died from the effects of the climate. Government also stated that the Mysore forests no longer supplied the necessary timber, that the buildings were falling into disrepair, and that the importance of the place was disappearing. They considered that it would be better to have the manufactory near the sea-coast as timber could be easily landed from Malabar, Penang, and Amherst, while the manufactured stores could be more readily distributed; moreover, supervision by higher authority would be facilitated. It was proposed that the more valuable stores should be kept in the arsenal and all new buildings would be tiled sheds only. The Court approved but awaited further details which were still under the consideration of the Military Board.

In June 1828 the piece of ground originally selected for the new manufactory was found to be too expensive; this ground seems to have been at Trivatoor in the Chingleput district. The land was acquired by Government but was never paid for, so when it was definitely decided not to use it the collector was directed to pay compensation to the owners for the three years during which they had no benefit from it. It is said that another site was also proposed, but in October 1828 the President of the Council, Mr. Lushington, respond-

[1] The tragedy which befell Colonel Scott is the subject of a poem, 'The Deserted Bungalow', in the *Lays of Ind*, by Aliph Cheem. It is true that he lost his wife, in childbed, on 19th April 1817, and two daughters from cholera, but he did not disappear as legend states. Scott left the bungalow as it then stood and went on leave, and after two months obtained furlough to England on medical grounds. He became a major-general in 1821 and died in London on 1st January 1833. It is true that the bungalow remained untenanted and practically untouched, and it was seen as late as 1906, cleaned but otherwise much as Scott left it in 1817.

ing to the call for economy which went to India with Lord William Bentinck, made some remarkable suggestions. He proposed that, to avoid the expense of making a new gun-carriage factory at the Presidency, estimated at about 3 lakhs of rupees, the Artillery Depot should prepare the models, plans, and sections for all carriages, that gun-carriages and limbers should be made at the arsenal by artificers of the establishment, and that all wagons, carts, and common work be made by contract, timber being stored by Government and furnished to the contractors. He hoped to save in this way Rs. 72,000 a month on establishment. He did not explain how the artificers of the establishment could do their normal arsenal work while engaged on making gun-carriages, nor in what way contract work would be cheaper. Had he consulted the records he would have seen that the gun-carriage agency not only made more serviceable articles, but did so at a cost much less than that of the contractors.

However, in June 1830 Government wrote to the Court that the Military Board had made substantial objections to the President's proposals, and they had therefore resolved, rather than erect new buildings, to appropriate the premises occupied by the collector of Madras for the gun-carriage manufactory, as it might be conducted there under the supervision of Lieutenant-Colonel Cullen without any additional buildings. They had resolved to purchase a building known as the Pantheon for Rs. 28,000 for the collector's establishment, the cost of the necessary repairs and alterations being Rs. 17,067. Some reduction in the establishment of the manufactory at Seringapatam had been ordered, but could only be partially effected, owing to the amount of wood and ironwork which was done for public buildings in the Neilgherries. The collector was ordered in August 1830 to remove the remainder of his establishment and to hand the buildings over to Cullen.

The collector's cutcherry, which was handed over for use as the gun-carriage manufactory, was the old Naval Hospital on the Poonamallee Road; it had been purchased in April 1797 by Admiral Rainer from Doctor Lucas, or perhaps from his executors, in order to separate naval from military sick and to provide more accommodation. The repairs to the buildings were carried out by Cullen and his establishment at a cost of only Rs. 2,000.

Soon after the move of the gun-carriage manufactory to Madras a saving was effected by combining the appointments of Principal Commissary of Ordnance at the arsenal and superintendent of the gun-carriage manufactory. By a General Order dated 28th January 1831, Colonel Cullen was appointed to both posts without increase of salary, Rs. 1,400, and out of the Rs. 1,050 saved by the combination, Rs. 700 was allowed as staff salary to Captain C. Taylor, Artillery, who was appointed Deputy Superintendent. In October 1832 a further change was made, Taylor becoming also Deputy Principal Commissary of Ordnance, so that he could be used for all departments; also reductions were made in the establishment of the manufactory which was to be based on an out-turn of only sixty carriages of all descriptions a year. The Deputy had to reside in the factory, in the quarters which remained the Superintendent's house till they were required for additional factory purposes early in the present century. In 1840 the stables were taken over as store sheds and new stables were built for the Superintendent.

Captain Taylor was transferred to the gunpowder manufactory in 1839, the staff salary being higher, and Captain J. Maitland became the Deputy, but in September 1840 the Court were informed that it had been decided to separate the manufactory from the arsenal, making a separate charge, the Deputy becoming Superintendent, but there would be no change in the allowances. The Military Board were directed to transfer artificers from the arsenal to the manufactory, which was to undertake all manufacture, the arsenal to be the depot to which all equipments were to go for examination and issue. This latter order was modified in

December 1845, when the manufactory was restricted to the particular work for which it had been established, and the arsenal was to carry out such other work as the Military Board considered properly to belong to it. The permanent establishment of the manufactory was then fixed at—1 conductor, 1 sub-conductor, 1 store sergeant, 12 mistries, 210 artificers, and 103 coolies, with an office allowance of Rs. 300 a month.

From the establishment of the gun-carriage manufactory in Seringapatam in 1802, boys from the Orphan Asylum had been taken as apprentices, and in 1813 there were 13 of these lads, rated as Europeans and allowed 5 pagodas each per month. There was a draughtsman on the staff at 15 pagodas a month as schoolmaster, and some asylum boys were still shown on the rolls up to 1834.

In June 1821, however, a much more important scheme was started, when the Governor in Council authorized the formation of a corps of Carnatic Ordnance Artificers, to be recruited from the sons of Europeans born in India and to be enlisted as European soldiers. The reasons given for this step were two: the difficulties experienced in procuring artisans to accompany troops on service and the desirability of providing suitable employment for a portion of the half-caste population. The corps was to be commanded by an officer of the non-effective establishment, not of the rank of field officer, and to be under the direction of the Principal Commissary of Ordnance under the general control of the Military Board. The establishment was to consist of a sergeant-major on Rs. 35 a month, plus Rs. 14 staff allowance, 10 sergeant-instructors at Rs. 35, and 100 artificers. The men were to receive provisions and necessaries, and quarters, with Rs. 2 a month till rated as qualified workmen, then Rs. 12, after five years Rs. 18, and after ten years Rs. 25. They were to wear ordnance uniform and to have certain pensionary rights. They were to come from the Orphan Asylum, the fort school, and from other charitable institutions.

The first Commandant was Lieutenant P. Bready, of the Carnatic European Veteran Battalion, who was granted early in 1823 the pay and allowances of a Deputy Commissary of Ordnance. Soon after Bready's death in September 1824, Mr. John Braddock was appointed to be Superintendent of the Corps, with the rank, pay, and allowances of a Deputy Assistant Commissary of Ordnance, plus a staff salary of Rs. 155, or 352 in all. Curiously enough the Court were not informed of this action of the Madras Government till June 1826, when they were asked for two technical magazines for the use of the Corps. The Court, ever economical in such matters, thought the matter in one publication would find its way into the other so would only send one, but while approving of the formation of the Corps, expressed their surprise and displeasure that the matter had not been brought to their notice before.

In 1833 the buildings occupied by the corps were desired for the improvement of the General Hospital and it was decided to disband the corps, which then consisted of 103 artificers and 84 pupils, of whom 39 were qualified to be rated as artificers. The artificers were to be distributed among the various departments, while pupils from the public charities would still be instructed in many trades in the arsenal and the gun-carriage manufactory. The actual effect of the disbandment seems to have been the disappearance of the superintendent and the sergeant-major and the gradual reduction of the instructors: in fact, there was no longer a corps, but the Carnatic Ordnance Artificers remained.

In September 1841 the Military Board wrote that the objects for which these artificers had been enlisted had been fully realized; they would have liked to, but did not, ask for an increase of establishment, which was 156. They stated, however, that the rates of pay, i.e. Rs. 21 a month after ten years, with Rs. 5 extra if a foreman, were not adequate for good workmen and they recommended 4 first-class foremen on Rs. 20 extra, 8 second-class on Rs. 10 extra, and 10 third-class on Rs. 5 extra. They also advocated the formation of the artificers into a Company, the Superintendent of the gun-carriage manufactory being placed in command, to avoid having all questions submitted to the Board from the numerous departments to which the men were attached. The Government of India sanctioned all the proposals, but ordered the reduction of the establishment to 146 to cover the increased cost. Some years later the question of discharge was raised and the Advocate-General stated that discharge could not be claimed. The Military Board then reported that the cost of training an artificer was Rs. 640, and recommended that a man wishing to leave before the completion of ten years' service should pay Rs. 640 for his discharge, a reduction of Rs. 100 being made for each further year of service, and this was approved.

On 17th July 1840 Captain J. Maitland, Madras Artillery, was appointed Superintendent of the gun-carriage manufactory, by then a distinct charge. Maitland held the post for 25 years, and as Superintendent also commanded the Company of Carnatic Ordnance Artificers. He had on his establishment at the outset also 30 pupils with 2 sergeant-instructors and 8 native bellows boys. Maitland took a very keen interest in the artificers; when he joined he found that many could neither read nor write, that intemperance and dissipation were rife, so much so that they were often a nuisance to the neighbourhood, and few were more than common workmen. Maitland at once started a school with the object of reclaiming them and turning them into skilful and scientific workmen. The school lasted from 7.30 to 9 each morning, with lectures and readings on three evenings a week, and all the men and boys were either teachers or pupils. The teachers were voluntary and the school was maintained at Maitland's expense. News of this institution reached Government and it was inspected and praised by the Education authorities, and in 1855, after a report on it had been considered by the Government of India, it was definitely adopted as a Government Institution. In the Administration Report for 1859–60 it was noted with satisfaction that the school had 113 pupils. With the opening of other avenues of employment for the Eurasian population, in the railways, post office, public works, &c., the Company of Carnatic Artificers was allowed to fade away, aided unfortunately by neglect on the part of the Ordnance Department to recognize its possibilities in providing skilled supervision, at any rate in the lower grades, in the rapidly expanding ordnance factories. There were still two or three of these artificers remaining in the factories as late as 1907.

Like the other gun-carriage factories at Fatehgarh and Bombay, the factory at Madras was, at the beginning of the twentieth century, an establishment which had a history of good service to the Army in India, but it could not be modernized to deal with the complicated artillery equipments then coming into use. The establishment of the Central Gun-carriage Factory at Jubbulpore rendered its continuance unnecessary, and the Madras factory was closed, after rather more than a hundred years' existence.

## XVIII

## THE BOMBAY GUN-CARRIAGE MANUFACTORY

A PLAN of Bombay dated 1750 shows a 'Foundery' and a smith's shop outside the Castle, and in 1767 a Committee was appointed to find a proper spot for a smith's shop and a carpenter's yard. The Committee reported that the only site within the town walls was between the Castle and the Bunder warehouse, the present Custom House, and this site with the house on it was bought for Rs. 5,510. In 1794 it was decided that the workshops, which up till then had been under the Military Storekeeper, were in future to be under the Commissary of Stores at the grand arsenal, which had just been established. It was decided at the same time to invite tenders for the supply of gun-carriages, and this introduced the system of depending on contractors for the supply of artillery vehicles, though repairs and even some manufacture were still carried on in the public workshops.

Sir Arthur Wellesley, when he was in Poona in 1803 and 1804, found the resources of Bombay to keep him supplied with gun-carriages and other artillery equipment quite inadequate. The Bombay Government had made a contract with one Shamjee Bhicajee in 1803 for some 279 carriages, but he asked for an extension of time in 1805, and even in 1806 the contract was still in progress. Sir Arthur had to form an establishment at Poona early in 1803 for the construction and repair of ordnance vehicles which he placed under Captain-Lieutenant J. D. Brown of the Madras Artillery. In 1804 he sent General Stuart a list of new carriages and stores required for his division, which he said could not be procured from Bombay and must be made at the Madras gun-carriage agency at Seringapatam.

In 1805 Bombay proposed to the Court that they should make their own carriages and such carriages as would be required for His Majesty's ships then building in Bombay, and referred to the failure of contract-made carriages constructed in an emergency from unseasoned timber. The Court would not agree to the expense, estimated at Rs. 20,000, pointing out that, in the same circumstances, a Government factory would have had to use unseasoned timber. Bombay wrote again in 1806 on the subject, but without success. In March 1810 Government agreed to the request of the Agent for Supplies for space near the Bazaar Gate on which to erect temporary sheds for the manufacture of gun-carriages for His Majesty's ship *Minden*, but ordered that all further carriages were to be made in the arsenal.

The Court had again been addressed regarding the establishment of a Government factory and had been given figures showing the economy obtained at Madras from the building of carriages at the agency in Seringapatam. As a result, the following General Order was published on 8th October 1810: 'The Honourable Court of Directors, having authorized the establishment of a Gun Carriage Manufactory at the Presidency, and having directed that an officer of Artillery be appointed to the charge thereof, Lieutenant L. Russell to be Agent in that Department.' The Bombay Government had wished to place it under the Commissary of Stores, but this the Court would not approve. The manufactory occupied the sheds which had been erected by the Agent for Supplies for the *Minden* carriages, the site being that now occupied by St. George's Hospital. The carriages for the *Minden* were finished by the Agent for Gun-carriages, who reported in January 1811 that twenty-one 18-pounder carriages would be ready within a month. The Court were asked to send out three foremen for the manufactory, a blacksmith, a carpenter, and a wheelwright.

It was laid down by Government that the manufactory was established to make carriages for His Majesty's Navy, the Company's Military and Marine Departments, barrack furniture, and powder barrels. It was to be under the general supervision of the Military Board, but under the immediate control of the Officer Commanding the Artillery for the ordnance part, and under the Quartermaster-General for the barrack part. Materials were to be obtained from the Agent for Supplies, or, if in store, from the Commissary of Stores or the Storekeeper. It seems to have been a somewhat cumbrous arrangement and must have required great tact on the part of the Agent. Even in 1834 all demands and correspondence from the Agent had to be submitted through the Commandant of Artillery.

Early in 1813 the Military Board reported that the temporary sheds constituting the manufactory were completely decayed, but Government deferred consideration of the matter. However, in December of the following year, Government thought the site could be used to better advantage for European barracks and asked the Board to report the cost of moving the manufactory to Moody's Bay, near the Castle. The cost being estimated at Rs. 56,226, the proposal was abandoned, but the Court were informed that the site occupied by the agency was the most suitable for a European Hospital. Nothing was done till December 1817, when the Court were informed that it was definitely proposed to erect the European hospital on the site and to move the manufactory to the barracks lately occupied by the Artillery on Old Woman's Island. Bombay said the cost for the move would be Rs. 30,765, only Rs. 643 more than would be the cost of repairing the buildings then in use by the Agent. They mentioned also that the timber yards and wharves were situated at the proposed site and that it would be a convenient place from which to fit out His Majesty's ships.

It was not till May 1819 that the Court approved of the move, so the temporary sheds erected in 1810 had done good service, but they were expensive, the monthly rent being Rs. 1,185. The Agent's salary was fixed at Rs. 500 a month plus pay and allowances, and he was given Rs. 200 a month as office allowance. His permanent establishment had been fixed by a Minute of Council, dated in October 1810, and consisted of: 1 head carpenter mistry at Rs. 20, 2 under-mistries at Rs. 15, and 10 carpenters at Rs. 10; 1 head mistry smith at Rs. 20, 2 under-mistries at Rs. 15, 15 smiths at Rs. 9–1; 15 hammermen at Rs. 5–1; 15 bellows boys at Rs. 3; 2 drillers at Rs. 15; 12 sawyers at Rs. 8–3; 2 turners at Rs. 10. Also 1 tindal at Rs. 10–2 and 30 lascars at Rs. 7–1. By 1816, however, Captain R. MacIntosh, who had succeeded Russell, had also a principal overseer on Rs. 200 a month, 1 conductor on Rs. 70 plus 10 tent allowance, 3 sub-conductors on Rs. 30 plus 10, and 3 storekeepers on Rs. 30 plus 10. This principal overseer was a Mr. Armstrong, who had been in the service of the 'King of Persia', but he returned to Persia at the end of 1816 and was replaced by Mr. Kemp on Rs. 150, who had been sent out for the Rocket Establishment as master artificer.

The situation of the manufactory on Old Woman's Island, or Colaba as it is now called, was no doubt convenient in some ways, but it had communication with Bombay in those days by road only at low water, otherwise a ferry had to be used. In 1823 the Agent, Captain Thew, complained of the smallness of his permanent establishment, the low rates of wages allowed, the insufficiency of his office allowance, and the difficulty in obtaining seasoned timber. This led to a visit from the Commander-in-Chief accompanied by the Quartermaster-General and the Commandant of Artillery. The Commander-in-Chief, in a minute written in April, said that he had not visited the factory for some time and referred to it as a great establishment, more important than generally considered, which had not met with the assistance and support to which it was entitled. He thought the work and supervision was good, but wondered whether steam machinery was not necessary, owing to the lack of good workmen, though not generally desirable 'owing to such myriads of half-employed people in India'. He drew attention to various offensive nuisances in the vicinity of the works. It was noted that the establishment consisted of 1 overseer, 1 conductor, 4 sub-conductors, 190 permanent Indians, including 75 lascars, with 790 extra workmen. The following were on the order book: 2,681 powder barrels, 9 mortar beds, 84 gun-carriages with limbers, 110 carts, 40 gun-platforms, 95 wagons, 9 tumbrils, and a lot of barrack furniture and other stores.

Government had recommended that the salary of the appointment should be raised to Rs. 600 a month, and the Court approved of this in a letter dated in June 1823. But the Commander-in-Chief and the Military Board, after the inspection of the manufactory, considered the amount to be inadequate and pointed out that the same office in Bengal and Madras carried far higher salaries. The Bombay Government then decided in November to allow Rs. 10,000 a year and they informed the Court and hoped they would consider it justified. Thew's complaints and the visit of the Commander-in-Chief also led to the office allowance being increased from Rs. 200 to Rs. 369 per month, while the rates of pay of the workmen were raised. The average monthly cost of the extra workmen rose from Rs. 5,559 in 1822–3 to Rs. 10,333 in 1825–6. There was a decision in 1823 that the permanent artificers were not to have Sunday liberty as the extra workmen did not have it.

In 1827 came one of the calls for economy from the Court, and, in Bombay, in the case of the gun-carriage agency, it led to the suggestion by the Military Board that the extra workmen in the manufactory should be dispensed with and all barrack furniture, powder barrels, ammunition boxes, wheelbarrows, handspikes, and many other stores be obtained by contract. Apparently gun-carriages were to be made by the few permanent artificers, and of course the overhead charges of the manufacture would remain. They showed a large saving by the discharge of the workmen, but did not attempt to show in what way supplies would be cheaper, and evidently nothing came of their suggestion. The salary of the Agent was reduced, however, to Rs. 600 a month by an order dated in December 1827.

The manufactory possessed a foundry which in 1833 made the chandeliers for the Scotch Church; it was used mainly for iron naves for wheels, though it also made castings for private firms. On the establishment in 1836 there was a master founder, a bombardier on Rs. 52–5–6, with a founder at Rs. 31–1–5.

In 1836 the then Agent, Captain Foy, wrote that he had asked for a grant of the land on which his house stood, but was refused, as all land in Colaba was reserved for public purposes, so he asked that his house might be bought by Government. Government decided that his successor must buy it at a valuation, not exceeding Rs. 6,000, and any locum tenens would have to pay rent at Rs. 75 a month. Agents had been granted a house-rent allowance at Rs. 50 for a captain and Rs. 80 for a major, but later it was increased, and in 1841 had risen to Rs. 135 for all Agents whatever might be their rank.

Models were largely used in the early days of these factories as a help in manufacture; they were made to scale and of the correct materials. 'Muster' or pattern vehicles were also kept, especially to show the details of packing, &c. Even at the beginning of the present century there were very few Indian workmen capable of understanding and following working drawings. In 1822 a number of models were made in the Bombay gun-carriage manufactory, some of which were in the Fatehgarh factory in 1900; they were beautifully made and bore the name of the Bombay Agent (Captain Thew), the date, the scale, and the description. There was one which showed very clearly how impossible it was to prevent shrinkage of wood in India; its wheels were 13 inches in diameter with iron tires not secured in any way; in the dry season the tires could be removed with ease, while during the monsoon they could not be shifted even with a hammer. Yet the wheels were well varnished and the wood was at least eighty years old.

Timber, the most important material, was not at first purchased by the Agent. In 1811 the Conservator of Forests in Malabar was ordered by Government to send a consignment of logs fit for gun-carriages, and in 1815 superior planks were to be obtained by public tender. In 1834, however, the Agent was authorized to procure his supplies wherever he liked, instead of through the Commissariat Department. In 1840 Commander Williams of the Indian Navy was Government Agent for the purchase of timber in Malabar. In 1844 babool logs were supplied through the agency of the Government of Scinde. In later years timber was bought by the Superintendent of the factory, under the orders of the Inspector-General of Ordnance, teak and rosewood from the Conservators of Forests in Malabar and Coorg, paddowk from the Andamans or Burma, while babool was obtained from contractors in Scinde. In the year 1825–6 the monthly average cost of timber amounted to Rs. 19,412.

In 1841 the cooperage work for the Military and Marine Departments was transferred from the Commissariat to the gun-carriage factory. The Commandant of Artillery objected to this, stating that the factory was already overburdened, that it could not and had not carried out its proper duties, and that it had 250 carriages to construct. Government reported to the Court that the Agent had supplied 423 carriages in three years against 298 made in the previous seven, that they considered the Agent, Captain Stanton, to be able and zealous, and they observed that he had obtained a new class of coopers and thus had broken down the monopoly of the Parsees. The Court agreed that Colonel Griffith's opposition was not warranted and was based on unsound grounds. Later, Colonel Griffith was removed from his seat on the Military Board for continued opposition to the opinions of the Board, as expressed on the annual accounts of the factory for the year 1843–4. Captain Stanton received the warm thanks of Government for his work, and his savings from the use of coke in place of charcoal were specially noted.[1] Cooperage work formed a separate branch of the factory under, in 1859, the superintendence of Mr. Harrington on Rs. 120 a month, with an assistant on Rs. 60. Such work ceased in 1864, when the new gunpowder factory at Kirkee was established with modern machinery for the manufacture of barrels.

In 1858 buildings and plant were added to the factory for the manufacture of Minié bullets and also for cutting fuses and tubes. In 1859 Mr. J. Green was superintendent of this branch on Rs. 250 plus house-rent of Rs. 60, with Mr. G. Lawder as Engineer on the same rate, and a storekeeper at Rs. 120. This work was transferred to the ammunition factory at Kirkee when it was established there in 1879.

Far more so than the other gun-carriage factories, the Bombay factory did work for other departments. In 1864 it was stated that it made castings for the Mint, Marine, and Commissariat Departments, and for other public services. In 1870 it made a ten-ton iron crane for the grand arsenal wharf. In the report of the Special Ordnance Commission of 1874–5 it is stated that the factory made and repaired barrack furniture and undertook work for sixteen different departments. But its out-turn of carriages was small compared with the other gun-carriage factories, for in the ten years ending March 1874 it had made 397, against 947 at Madras and 1,032 at Fatehgarh.

In October 1864 it was proposed that the gun-carriage factory and the arsenal should both be removed to Kirkee and placed with the gunpowder factory within a fort to be

[1] He must have had better luck than I had in 1893, when I used coal briquettes in lieu of firewood at the Quetta arsenal. As the cost for a maund of the coal exceeded the cost of the same weight of firewood, I was involved in much correspondence with the Accounts Department, who would not consider the less weight of coal used, and wanted to charge me personally for the excess price. However, eventually the highest authority sanctioned the change of material, but there were no 'warm thanks'.

constructed on the site of the Kirkee village. The move of the gunpowder works had already been decided upon. It was estimated that the premises and site of the gun-carriage factory would fetch at least 20 lakhs of rupees, while the cost of the new buildings would be 9 lakhs, of the land 4 lakhs, of the water-supply 2 lakhs, while the fort would probably cost another 9 lakhs. In 1868 the removal to Kirkee was again urged by Colonel J. Worgan, the Inspector-General of Ordnance and Magazines, who referred to the humiliating failure of carriages and wheels made in the moist climate of Bombay. Lord Napier of Magdala, the Commander-in-Chief, strongly supported the proposal, and his recommendation was endorsed by the Governor in Council. In September 1869 the question was asked when the gun-carriage factory could be vacated, in connexion with the erection of the railway terminus at Colaba, but the Inspector-General could only reply that it depended entirely on the new factory being undertaken. Curiously enough nothing was ever done on the various recommendations, the factory continued under increasing difficulties, especially when a strip of land running right through the centre of the factory was handed over to the railway. This hampered the work of the factory, rendered almost impossible the safeguarding of its contents, and lessened enormously the value of the site. The complaint regarding the moist climate of Bombay was met by transferring the manufacture of wheels and other important woodwork to the workshops of the Poona arsenal, but this proved to be unsatisfactory, so in 1873 the 'artificer branch' of the Poona arsenal was handed over to, and became a branch of, the gun-carriage factory.

The Special Ordnance Commission of 1874–5 recommended that there should be two gun-carriage factories only, one at Madras and one at Allahabad, though Colonel Hatch, the Inspector-General of Ordnance, who was a member, urged the advantages of Poona, but nothing came of the proposal. Some additions were made to the buildings in

1891, and the need for quarters for the Superintendent was urged, as the old bungalow which had been built many years before by Captain Foy had long been uninhabitable. No decision on the closing of the factory, however, was taken till in 1901 it was settled that there should be one central factory located at Jubbulpore. The Bombay factory with its branch at Poona ceased working at the end of 1906, and the best of its plant and stores was transferred to Jubbulpore, with some of its staff.

The Bombay gun-carriage factory was little known outside the Ordnance Department, and very few people other than those directly concerned in its working ever entered its gates. The exterior was certainly not impressive and the place can have altered little in the ninety years or so of its life. Yet it did good work, and towards the end of the nineteenth century at least there was no trace of the inefficiency of the workmen described by Ensign Witman in 1776 as characteristic of the local workers. For nearly a century the gun-carriage factory was training the local workmen, and it had a considerable influence on the progress of industry in Bombay. It had for many years an apprenticeship system which produced men for supervisory posts, and it was unfortunate that it was allowed to die out some time before the close of the century. It was most regrettable that nothing was ever done to house the workers at a time when decent housing could have been cheaply provided. Conditions grew steadily worse as the population increased, and it was not till the awful plague epidemic swept the city that anything was done to improve the housing of the working classes of Bombay.

# XIX

# AMMUNITION MANUFACTURE UNDER THE COMPANY

THE East India Company never had an ammunition factory, but the forts in their settlements had a laboratory even in the earliest days, in which ammunition was prepared for use. In old Fort William, for example, there was a laboratory in 1718, and in 1742 there is a record of an order to the Gunner to employ 'as many people as he could to make gunpowder for service, with all kinds of ammunition necessary'. When the Court of Directors in 1748 ordered the formation of a regular company of artillery at each of the three Presidencies they sent out not only a commanding officer, but also a captain-lieutenant, who was designated the Director of the Laboratory. The instructions sent out regarding this officer specified that he was to have possession of storage and of the stores for the laboratory and was to make, and to instruct in making, all military 'fireworks'. He was also to enter in a book all receipts of composition with the manner of making. He has been referred to as the Ordnance Commissary of his time, but this is hardly a correct designation, though we can certainly regard his laboratory as the original of the ammunition factory. The Court insisted that the laboratory must be a complete mystery; they ordered that 'no Indian, black or person of mixed breed, nor any Roman Catholic of what nation soever, shall, on any pretence, be admitted to set foot in the Laboratory or any of the military magazines, either out of curiosity or to be employed in them, or to come near them so as to see what is doing or contained therein'. Moreover, in 1770 they told Bombay that 'the natives must be kept as ignorant as possible both of the theory and practice of artillery'.

It is not easy to trace the history of the laboratory till, late in the middle of the nineteenth century, it became the ammunition factory. It is clear, however, that in Bengal and Bombay the laboratory ceased to be a purely artillery institution and became, before the end of the eighteenth century, an integral part of the arsenals and magazines. In Madras it remained definitely a regimental establishment until near the middle of the nineteenth century. Even when located in the ordnance establishments, the laboratory was not for some years entirely free from the control of the commanding officer of artillery. This may have been due to an outburst by Colonel Pearse, Commandant of the Bengal Artillery, in 1772. For a short time the laboratory in Fort William seems to have been under the Military Storekeeper until the appointment of a Commissary of Stores, and Colonel Pearse said he had nothing to do with it, and complained that 'when at practice the fuzes varied 19 to 48 seconds burning, portfires went out, tubes would not burn and cartridges badly made'.

At Madras in 1775 the artillery at St. Thomas's Mount had to furnish one officer daily for duty at Fort St. George and as many men as necessary for the laboratory. It was ordered also that musket ammunition was to be made up by storekeepers at out-stations and drawn by corps. Commanding officers were to save the lead and return it to the storekeepers for recasting into bullets and use again in making up cartridges. In 1786 fresh regulations were issued for the management of the laboratory, which was to be under the superintendence and control of the officer commanding the battalion of artillery at the Presidency, assisted by an officer as Sub-Director. All officers and men were to go in small parties to be instructed in making all kinds of ammunition and later a number were to be detailed for regular duty in the laboratory with working pay. Then in 1807 the laboratory was established at St. Thomas's Mount in connexion with the magazine at that station, and it was to be under the Commissary of Ordnance at that station, but still to be under the supervision of the artillery commanding officer. In 1824 came yet another change, when the Artillery Depot was established at the Mount under a Director, who not only superintended the laboratory and the percussion-cap factory, but also carried out the proof of gunpowder, gun-carriages, and all trials and experiments. Small-arm ammunition was made up in the arsenal. The Artillery Depot seems to have been abolished about 1855, at least in that comprehensive form. Laboratory work was, of course, not confined to Fort St. George and St. Thomas's Mount; it was carried on to a smaller extent in every magazine at out-stations, but in very primitive conditions in the early days. In 1763, for example, a party of artillerymen were driving portfires in the magazine at Trichinopoly when one blew up, and, in consequence of powder being carelessly exposed in every direction, the building blew up, killing 18 men. Infantry men had to be instructed in artillery work to replace the casualties.

In 1788 the arsenal at Fort William had among its establishment, under the Commissary of Stores: 3 sergeants, 6 European soldiers, 14 sirdars, and 330 workmen for laboratory and magazine work. In 1790 it was ordered that commissaries and deputy commissaries of ordnance in charge of the various magazines were 'to perform the business of making up stores and ammunition and all laboratory work, under the direction of the Commanding Officer of Artillery at their respective stations'. It is evident, however, that this kind of work was considered to be definitely the province of the Ordnance Department in Bengal, and the control in that Presidency by the artillery soon became nominal.

In Bombay the laboratory remained under an artillery officer as Director, controlled by the commandant of artillery up to 1793, when it was incorporated in the grand arsenal and became a part of the Ordnance and Laboratory Branch, but even then the Commissary, in accordance with orders issued in 1797, had to report each morning on its work to the Commandant of Artillery. The Commissary was allowed a Deputy Commissary specially for the supervision of the laboratory and the expense magazines.

Thus the arsenals, including those out-station magazines which later were renamed arsenals or depots, were not only storage and distributing agencies, but were also manufacturing establishments, to a varying degree, of ammunition, which for a long period remained almost unaltered and required little more than was provided by the 1748 Director of the Laboratory with his book of 'receipts for military fireworks'.

The first real break-away from the arsenal laboratory was the establishment of percussion-cap manufactories. It is said that the battle of Punniar in 1843 was the last occasion of the use of flint-lock muskets by the British troops in India. Early in that year plant was received in Bombay from England for the manufacture of percussion caps, but there was delay in the provision of buildings. New ones were said to involve the expenditure of over Rs. 10,000, and would therefore require the sanction of the Court; so inquiries were made at Poona and at Ahmednugger for suitable accommodation, but eventually it was decided to place the manufacture in the gunpowder manufactory at Mazagon. This was done in 1844, the Agent expressing the opinion that there was no danger in doing so. There was another cap manufactory at St. Thomas's Mount, under the Director of the Artillery Depot, and yet another at Dum Dum, under the control of the Commissary of Ordnance at Fort William. In 1854 this manufactory at Dum Dum was found to be insufficient in capacity, and additional buildings and plant were sanctioned in the following year to bring the output up to three millions a month instead of two, and its establishment was fixed at 1 overseer in charge with 3 assistant overseers and 113 workmen.

Factories for the manufacture of Minié bullets were completed between 1857 and 1859, one in the gun foundry at Cossipore, one in Fort St. George, and one in the gun-carriage factory at Bombay, and combined with these there seem to have been plants for the cutting of fuses and tubes.

Dum Dum had been vacated by the Bengal Artillery in 1853 and gradually became the place where most of the laboratory work of the Fort William arsenal was carried on; it had an establishment for the making up of small-arm cartridges and it was there that the trouble over the 'greased cartridges' started in 1857. In Kaye's *History of the Sepoy War*, the author refers to Dum Dum as no longer the headquarters of the Bengal Artillery, and adds the rather absurd remark: 'and buildings which from their very birth had held nothing but the appliances of ordnance, were degraded into manufactories and store houses of small arm ammunition'. By 1858 the various works at Dum Dum had become the Cartridge and Percussion Cap Factory under Captain P. M. Syme, Artillery, Deputy Commissary of Ordnance. This factory steadily grew but did not receive a Superintendent till Captain A. Walker was appointed as such on 4th April 1874. But the factory proper really dates from the end of 1868, when the Secretary of State sanctioned the establishments for the new small-arm ammunition factories at Dum Dum and Kirkee. Eventually the Dum Dum factory made not only small-arm ammunition but also fuses and many other components of ammunition.

The Kirkee small-arm ammunition factory was commenced in 1869, but was not completed till 1872. Up to that time laboratory work seems to have been distributed between the arsenal at Bombay and a hired bungalow at Kirkee, with the bullet factory and the cutting of fuses still in the gun-carriage factory, while the cap factory was in the gunpowder factory. However, the Secretary of State sanctioned the new small-arm ammunition factory at the end of 1868, with Captain A. J. Wake as Inspector till in April 1874 he became its Superintendent.

# XX

# THE SUPPLY OF HARNESS, SADDLERY, AND ACCOUTREMENTS

There is nothing very definite in the early history of the British in India regarding the sources and methods of supply of military equipment of this kind. There is little doubt that most leather work was sent out from England in the early days, and that supplies in part of requirements continued from there up to well on in the nineteenth century. But it is also clear that efforts to obtain such equipment in the country were made certainly from early in the eighteenth century and continued with varying success till the establishment of the Cawnpore harness and saddlery factory had put the manufacture of leather on a sound basis.

In 1712 there were in Fort St. George various workshops, and President Harrison ordered that the Paymaster's disbursements were to be shown monthly under different heads, separate accounts being kept for work done for the Storekeeper in those shops, 'as in making gun carriages and accoutrements for the soldiers'. In 1720 it is recorded that scabbards, pouches, and cartridge boxes were made in those yards. In a report on the stores in the grand magazine at Patna, dated 1st January 1771, there are shown as in stock—1,206 belts, sword, country, described as very good, 2,206 European; also 11,650 belts with frogs for bayonets, also country made. The early establishments of the grand arsenals did not include many artificers capable of making up leather articles, and, in any case, leather was not, at that time, produced by any government manufactory. A Bengal regulation of 1790 laid down that ordnance establishments were to make any articles which could be made from the rough materials by the artificers. But it is evident from an order issued in 1797, directing that all accoutrements required by the field stations at Chunar and Dinapore were to be made by the Agent (of supplies), either at Cawnpore or Futty Ghur, as he found most convenient, and to be delivered by survey into the magazines there and sent down to Chunar, that such supplies were made under contract with local manufacturers. It is also evident that much leather work, especially articles of harness and saddlery, was obtained from England, certainly up to the early years of the nineteenth century, and whatever was obtained in India came from contract with local suppliers.

Leather had been made, of course, from very early times by the native tanners, but the methods were crude in the extreme, and the product usually most indifferent. Buchanan in his *Journey through Mysore*, referring to his visit to Bangalore in 1800, where he saw leather made by the local tanners, wrote that the ox and buffalo hide leather was very bad. The first trace of Europeans in the industry seems to be an entry in the East India Register of 1803, where Mr. J. Cook and Mr. R. Jones are shown, under the heading of persons not in the employ of the Company, as curriers, Kidderpore tannery. Again, in the list of 1827, Messrs. Tomlin and Company are shown as leather manufacturers at Kidderpore, and a European tanner is shown at Cawnpore. An article in the *East India United Service Journal*, dated in October 1833, refers to the former buff leather manufactory at Kidderpore, and states that about a dozen years previously the contractor, having to leave Calcutta on account of illness, placed it under an incompetent person, who allowed the process to deteriorate and the product only lasted half the time, so supply had to be changed to Europe. However, in 1839, the Court declined to supply buff accoutrements to Madras, and directed them to obtain them from Bengal, where, they said, manufacture was established at the Kidderpore tannery.

The Governor of Madras, Major-General Sir Thomas Munro, in a minute dated in March 1824, noted that the

Commissariat first began to tan leather in 1821 at Seringapatam, and had made great progress, and he recommended that no more leather accoutrements should be obtained from England. The Military Board had reported that the local-made accoutrements were dearer than and inferior to those from home, but the Deputy Commissary-General stated that this referred to those made at the Madras tannery and said that the Commissariat could supply such articles of superior quality at half the price. The Madras tannery, which is mentioned in the records more than once, also made boots and harness and seems to have been a private undertaking, which about 1829 belonged to Mr. Disley. The Seringapatam tannery does not seem to have had a long life; probably the unhealthiness which drove the gun-carriage manufactory from the place also caused the tannery to move. In 1832 the Madras Government reviewed the whole system of leather supplies in a letter to the Court, and reported that boots and leather appointments of different kinds, formerly supplied by contract, were being manufactured of very superior quality and at reduced rates at the Commissariat tannery in Mysore. In 1840 the Court were further informed that buff leather for accoutrements was being made by Major Watkins, Assistant Commissary-General in charge of the Commissariat tannery at Hunsoore (Hunsur). The *Imperial Gazetteer* states that Hunsur had a large tannery, blanket manufactory, and timber yard maintained by the Madras Commissariat till 1864.

Harness and saddlery were also being made in the Madras Presidency, and the Court in 1832 directed Bombay to obtain such articles from Madras, saddle-trees being supplied from home for the purpose. In 1833 Madras transferred the duty of providing, repairing, and maintaining saddles, bridles, harness, and horse appointments for artillery and cavalry to the Military Board, and abolished the system of regimental contract. The position at Bombay is not clear, but apparently they depended mainly on sources outside the

Presidency, though there was a private tannery at Bombay owned by Mr. Bates, who in 1845 had a contract for hides for accoutrements. The 14th Dragoons also had, it would seem, a tannery of their own at Kirkee, because there is a record of a request by the Bombay Military Board in 1845 that some hides cured by Mr. Bates might be tested by the officer commanding against some prepared in the regimental tannery.

It is most difficult to come to any definite conclusion as to the quality of the production of the Indian leather manufactories at this time, whether Commissariat, regimental, or privately owned. Complaints were frequent, but it is certain that ever since Indian-made leather equipment has been issued to the Army in India there have been complaints, often with no more substantial grounds than the difference in appearance when compared with the highly finished product of an English tannery. It is, however, obvious that in the days of the Company all was not well with the leather produced in public as well as in private tanneries, and it could not be so with the methods then in use. In 1832 Lieutenant-Colonel C. Hopkinson, giving evidence before a Committee, stated that 'when he was commanding the Madras Horse Artillery, he had the contract for the supply of its harness and saddlery, he had tan pits and made the leather which was of superior description. When he was Commissary, pouches, belts, &c. came from England, but after the establishment of the Commissariat it furnished country made articles of most inferior kind, which did not last nor look well'. In 1843 Bombay informed the Court that the harness supplied to the horse artillery by the contractors was very inferior, but no worse than that made in Bengal and Madras. They said that European-made articles were much more efficient and economical and they could not understand why Bengal and Madras preferred the country harness. In the *Calcutta Review* for 1848 there is an article on the Bengal Artillery, in which the author declared that 'the worst part of the equipment is harness and saddlery in which considerable improvement is required, which can never be obtained till all is supplied from England. Country harness costs nearly as much, lasts half the time, and is in every respect inferior. It is understood that the only reason is that the Court desires to improve and encourage Indian manufactures. Supply is furnished almost exclusively at one station by Commissariat agency and profits go to one or two native contractors and a few dishonest native officials.'

Sir Patrick Grant, the Commander-in-Chief in Madras, when reviewing a report on artillery material in India, by Lieutenant-Colonel J. Adye, commanding Royal Artillery in Madras, dated in 1860, remarked, 'that the harness and saddlery were vastly inferior to the English, but it was very serviceable and infinitely less expensive'. Adye had said that there were few places where good leather could be obtained, but, as will be shown later, the Commissariat tannery at Hunsur had a good reputation.

Cawnpore had been noted for leather work for many years, and Stocqueler, in his *Handbook of India*, says 'it was famous for the manufacture of saddlery, harness, and gloves, though less durable than those of English make, the cheapness and beauty of the two former articles recommend them, and the gloves are a respectable substitute for those from France'. The idea of establishing a Government leather factory at Cawnpore seems to have originated with Lieutenant-Colonel A. Abbott, when he was Principal Commissary of Ordnance. In a letter dated in December 1854 he proposed that, on the abolition of the Cawnpore magazine, a manufactory of saddlery and harness should be established there under the supervision of an officer of cavalry or artillery. He said that such an establishment was absolutely necessary to ensure a certain supply of good equipment. In August of the following year, when he was Inspector-General of Ordnance and Magazines, he reported on the inferiority of the saddlery supplied to the troops, and again urged the necessity for a Government factory. Government agreed as to the desirability, but wished for a trial, leather to be tanned and dressed under the supervision of a European currier sergeant and sets of saddlery and harness made under a European saddler sergeant; this was in September 1855. The Court were addressed on the subject at the same time, but they would not sanction the proposal to establish a manufactory at Cawnpore, as they feared it would paralyse the efforts of the Contractors, and wrote to this effect in April 1856, and their orders were communicated to the Inspector-General in June and all action ceased. Messrs. Bohlé & Co. of Meerut made some supplies but refused any contract for less than ten years.

During 1856 the Inspector-General reported large deficiencies from the contractors and much long overdue to corps on indents, and the Commander-in-Chief said it was impossible to keep cavalry and artillery efficient under the present contract system and also urged the establishment of a Government factory. Early in 1857 further complaints were made, many stating that the articles looked good when new, but after some use it became apparent that the leather was badly tanned, and the Inspector-General referred to the Government factory in the Madras Presidency. The Court were again addressed and in reply wrote in January 1857, noting the failure of the contractor, and said, 'if you shall be thoroughly satisfied that reliance can no longer be placed on private sources of supply . . . we cannot withhold a compliance with your strong recommendation in favour of the establishment of a Government Factory'.

Then came the Mutiny. At Cawnpore the magazine, which was in a fort on the banks of the Ganges, was unfortunately not held by the British when the outbreak occurred. The Assistant Commissary in charge was Lieutenant N. Reilly, who had orders to blow the magazine up at the last, but was unable to do so and perished, along with Sub-Conductor G. H. Manvill. Cawnpore was lost on 27th June and its defenders massacred, but was regained on

16th July. But nothing could be done in establishing any leather factory until stable conditions arrived.

In May 1859 the matter was reopened by the Inspector-General of Ordnance and Magazines, Lieutenant-Colonel E. W. S. Scott, and from his letters and the Proceedings of the Military Department for that year, it is clear that the intention was to form a Harness and Saddlery Depot at the Ordnance Depot in Cawnpore, from which the stores had been transferred to Allahabad, this depot to be under Lieutenant John Stewart, Bengal Artillery, Deputy Commissary of Ordnance at Cawnpore, and to be housed in temporary store rooms, altered and adapted from those existing. The articles were to be tanned and made by contract under strict supervision and inspection at every stage. An extra allowance to the officer in charge had been recommended by the Inspector-General, Rs. 150 for a Deputy Commissary, Rs. 100 if a second-class Commissary, and none if a first-class Commissary, but the Military Auditor-General disagreed and considered the duties to be no more than for any ordnance officer. Government decided that the Harness Depot should be a branch of the Ordnance Department with no extra allowance for its charge. Stewart found his duties of supervision very difficult and reported that the Cawnpore tanners could not supply hides as good as those made at the Madras tannery at Hunsur, without a greatly increased price and a complete alteration in their system of tanning, and they would not spend the money to make the proper tanning pits. It should be mentioned that in Bengal the duty of supply of harness and saddlery belonged to the Army Commissariat Department up to 1855, when it was transferred to the Ordnance Commissariat Department.

In 1860 the experiment of tanning in pits for from six to eight months instead of in bags, the usual native practice, was started. The first idea was to get the native tanners to do this by offering higher prices, but this was not successful. Stewart wrote thus about the two contractors chosen for the experiment: 'Both built their pits of bad lime, with bad bricks, with insecure foundations and with insufficient cover, in fact both did the thing as cheaply as they could, through disinclination to lay out capital. Many hides got much darkened and some got injured with the falling of the mud roofs and from muddy rain water flowing into the pits.' So in 1862 masonry pits were built by Government with temporary buildings, and in 1869 permanent buildings were erected. Actually in 1869 the factory was complete for leather work, but it was not till 1873 that it was equipped with the necessary workshops for the manufacture of the metal and wood fittings of the finished harness and saddlery. The factory was built on the site of Wyndham's entrenchment on the banks of the Ganges, and, like the other older factories, was added to piecemeal, as extensions became necessary, and it is now a curious mixture of old and new.

So once more India had to realize that the supply of equipment on which the efficiency of its Army depended could not be left safely to local contractors, and that in such a matter as the provision of serviceable leather, entailing a considerable capital expenditure, a well-equipped Government factory under skilled European management was absolutely essential. John Stewart remained at Cawnpore till he retired in 1888; and it is said that 'the tradition of Colonel Stewart riding round the bazaar on his grey pony persists to this day', and his memory is perpetuated by a mounted figure in the temple situated outside the factory walls.

Leather work was done on a considerable scale for a time both in Bombay and Madras in the arsenal workshops, hides being purchased mainly from contractors in Bombay. Then in 1893 the work at the Madras arsenal was moved to the old gunpowder factory at Perampore, which became the Perampore harness and saddlery workshops, and to which the work hitherto done in the Bombay arsenal workshops was also transferred in 1897. In 1899 the Perampore workshops became the Madras harness and saddlery factory, but it was closed in 1909, when all such work was concentrated in the Cawnpore harness and saddlery factory. The existence of this factory at Cawnpore has been threatened on occasions, the idea being that, owing to the establishment of private leather factories, especially in Cawnpore, it was unnecessary to have a Government factory. It was certainly well for India in the Great War that this idea had never come to anything, as the private factories had more work offered to them than they could well perform, and could do little to assist the Government factory. The Superintendent made many efforts to obtain satisfactory tanned hides from the smaller Indian tanneries in Cawnpore and elsewhere, but was faced with much the same difficulties as was Stewart when he tried to induce contractors to spend money in constructing proper pits and to use the best methods.

# XXI

## SMALL ARMS AND MISCELLANEOUS STORES

THE East India Company does not seem ever to have made muskets, though their grand arsenals at the Presidencies had extensive armouries for the storage and repair of small arms. Arms were mainly obtained from England, muskets entirely so unless those captured were repaired and utilized, but swords were partly obtained from local manufacturers eventually. In a Court Minute dated in January 1672, the Shipping Committee were ordered to provide 200 snaphance muskets and bandoliers and 200 swords for Bombay. Madras in 1662 asked the Court for good swords, as they said the soldiers had butchers' knives only, and in 1665 they reported the receipt of muskets. There is a curious Court Minute, dated in 1675, directing the purchase of one or two sets of armour, to be sent to Bombay for disposal there to the best advantage. There are many references in the records during the seventeenth century regarding demands for and receipt of muskets and swords. In 1687 Mr. John Cheney, Storekeeper at Fort St. George, reported the following warlike stores to be available:

| | |
|---|---|
| 150 Iron Ordnance | 70 Swords |
| 220 Blunderbusses | 3 Poleaxes |
| 30 Muskets, firelocks | 29 Pikes |
| 890 Matchlocks | 23 Suites of Armour for Horse |
| 34 Halberts | 28 Suites of Armour for Foot |

He was ordered to provide 97 more poleaxes and 500 pikes to be made with bamboos.

Small arms were not infrequently purchased in the country, but it is not stated where they were made. For example, in December 1731, Bombay directed the payment of Rs. 466 for 60 muskets and bayonets received from George Breton. In 1742 the Council at Fort William bought 120 muskets and also 500 sword-blades, the latter at 2 Madras rupees each. They also asked Madras for small arms, and, the need being great, directed the Master of Arms to purchase good small arms in the town, after proof, on the best terms possible. Again, in June 1758, they referred to the want of arms, though there were many in the town, so a notice was issued to the inhabitants to send in all, except fowling-pieces, to the Military Storekeeper, when they would be valued and paid for.

The Select Committee at Calcutta wrote to the Court in September 1765 asking for 10,000 stand of arms for the first year, and thereafter 4,000 annually. They referred to the bad quality of those received and said metal was badly tempered and locks ill finished. They suggested that arms be purchased from the same persons as furnish them to the home Government, paying 27 shillings per firelock, instead of 18 shillings as before. A year later they asked the Court to provide by every possible means against the illicit importation of small arms and said it had lately become a very profitable trade with European ships' captains, and it furnished Indians with arms.

In a survey report on the stores in the Patna Magazine in March 1771, there were shown 1,206 swords, country, described as very good, and 2,206 European, so it is evident that these weapons were being manufactured of good quality in the country. And it is a fact that muskets and swords were being made in many parts of India; Travancore was making them at Udaygiri about 1757; Mir Cossim was manufacturing firelocks at Monghyr in 1763, and these latter ones were said to be better than the best Tower-proof muskets sent to India by the Company, especially in the metal of the barrels and in the flints, which were made of agates found in the Rajmahal Hills. Shuja-ud-Dowlah was said to have made amazing improvements in the manufacture of small arms in 1768. The French made serviceable muskets at Chadarghat, a suburb of Hyderabad, while Seringapatam had eleven armouries for making, finishing, and repairing small arms. India only established a small-arms factory in 1905, when the rifle factory was erected on a part of the site of the old gunpowder factory at Ishapore, and its first rifle was completed in 1907.

At Fatehgarh, Captain A. M. Matthews of the Artillery, who had lost a leg at Delhi in 1803 and had been appointed Deputy Commissary of Ordnance at the Fatehgarh magazine in 1804, is said to have done much to stimulate the local manufacturers in the supply of military stores. Tulwars were largely obtained from Shamsabad and cost Rs. 7–4 each, but Matthews encouraged their manufacture at Farruckabad and was able to supply them at Rs. 5–8 each. Fatehgarh was also a centre for the manufacture of tents, large numbers being made there for the Army.

Though there is no record of any attempt having been made to manufacture fire-arms by the Company in India, it can safely be said that efforts were constantly being made to obtain all possible supplies of military stores from local sources. As stated in the Introduction, the author of the *History of the Army Ordnance Services* is quite wrong when he asserts that 'munitions were bought from the British Board of Ordnance'. A glance down the Account of the Military Stores exported to India in the year 1830–1 shows clearly how few were the articles of equipment obtained from England. There was £458 worth of leather articles, mainly stores not easy to make in India, such as sabretaches, buckets, bellows, powder horns, and the like. There were iron guns, carronades and mortars, which were not made at the gun foundry, and, of course, fire-arms of various descriptions. Most of the imports were materials, though there was one large item of £38,106 for soldiers' clothing. As regards the clothing of the Army, as early as December 1809 an order of the Bengal Council directed that the clothing of the

Army was to be arranged for by an Agent to be stationed at Fatehgarh, but the first Agent seems to have been appointed in 1813, Major C. S. Fagan. By the time of the Mutiny the agency must have been a considerable manufactory, having besides the Agent, Colonel Tucker, a European staff of five, all of whom lost their lives.

# APPENDIX A

## THE COSSIPORE GUN FOUNDRY

THE following description of the gun foundry at Cossipore is taken from *The Handbook of India* by J. N. Stocqueler, published in 1844:

'. . . presents a chaste and simple façade of the Tuscan order, 178 feet in length. On ascending a flight of steps the entry is into the instrument room, in which are arranged the various boring bars, bits and knives, &c., used in the process of boring and turning the ordnance. Here is also preserved a model of the old boring machinery of four lathes, wrought by bullocks, forming a striking contrast with the present extensive and beautiful steam machinery. Right and left . . . rooms for the office, model and pattern departments, &c. Adjoining and extending along the whole length . . . is a magnificent boring room, 170 feet long by 50 feet wide and 40 feet high. . . . The roof of this room has been much admired for its lightness and novelty, being formed of iron trusses covered with planks and copper sheathing. Down the east side of the room is arranged the beautiful millwork and machinery sent out by the Honourable Court, consisting of 12 boring and turning lathes for ordnance . . . worked . . . by two small steam engines in adjoining rooms. Down the west side a range of lighter lathes . . . for all the small miscellaneous work. . . . The ordnance boring and twining lathes are of an entirely novel self-acting principle, by which the piece of ordnance is turned as well as bored by the machinery itself. . . . On the north and south . . . are the rooms for the vice-men, carpenters and finishing departments. The water for the . . . steam engines is brought from a tank in another yard, at a distance of more than 200 feet, by means of a siphon of 5 inch bore made in the foundry, which is believed to be the first instance known of a siphon . . . used upon so large a scale. At a short distance . . . the casting or smelting house, furnished with cupola blast furnaces for the smelting of iron, of which a good deal is now manufactured . . . and the large reverbatory furnaces for the smelting of the gunmetal. . . . Adjoining are the moulding sheds and blacksmith's department, together with other store rooms. . . .'

A plan of the foundry, signed by Major Hutchinson, shows the following plant: 6 gun lathes, 1 10-h.p. engine, 4 mortar lathes,

1 12-h.p. engine; 5 lathes, 2 elevating screw lathes, 1 dead-head lathe, 2 boring cylinders, 1 trunnion and vent machine, circular saw, cross-cut saw, loam mill, grindstones, &c.

The main building so admired by Stocqueler, which was for many years the turning and boring room, still exists, and is used mainly as a museum.

## APPENDIX B

## OFFICERS OF THE GUN FOUNDRY

| *Dates* | *Names* | *Service* | *Remarks* |
|---|---|---|---|
| 1770–3 | Major L. du Gloss | Bengal Engineers | Commissary of Stores |
| 1775–80 | Major J. Green | Bengal Artillery | ,, ,, |
| 1781–5 | Lt.-Col. P. Duff | ,, | ,, ,, |
| 1785–91 | Major C. R. Deare | ,, | ,, ,, |
| 1790–1 | Lt. Humphries | | Acting while Deare was on service. Deare was killed in Sept. 1791 |
| 1792–6 | Lt. W. Golding | Bengal Engineers | Commissary of Stores |
| 1796–1807 | Lt. T. Anbury | ,, | ,, ,, |
| 1807–8 | Capt. T. Dowell | Artillery | ,, ,, |
| 1809–21 | Major J. B. Sherwood | ,, | ,, ,, |
| 1821–2 | Major H. Faithfull | ,, | ,, ,, |
| 1822–6 | Capt. G. Hutchinson | Bengal Engineers | Director and Superintendent |
| 1826–9 | Capt. T. Timbrell | Bengal Artillery | Officiating |
| 1829–39 | Major G. Hutchinson | Bengal Engineers | Moved to Cossipore |
| 1839–40 | Lt.-Col. D. Presgrave | 66th N.I. | |
| 1841–5 | Capt. A. Wilson | Bengal Artillery | |
| 1845–6 | Capt. G. Hart-Dyke | ,, | |
| 1846 | Lt. C. Douglas | ,, | Acting |
| 1846–64 | Capt. A. Broome | ,, | |
| 1864–74 | Lt.-Col. H. Maxwell | ,, | Acting 1863–4. Special duty 1868–70, Cols. C. V. Bowie and H. A. Carleton acted. |
| 1874–82 | Major T. Nicol | ,, | The last of the officers of the Bengal Artillery to hold charge |
| 1882–90 | Major R. Wace | Royal Artillery | |
| 1890–1 | Major E. B. Standbridge | ,, | |
| 1891–9 | Capt. R. H. Mahon | ,, | |
| 1899–1905 | Major S. M. Renny | ,, | |
| 1905–14 | Major C. T. Bell | ,, | |
| 1914–17 | Major G. S. Ogg | ,, | |
| 1917–22 | Major E. Parbury | ,, | |
| 1922–30 | Major T. C. Fraser | ,, | |

# APPENDIX C

## OFFICERS OF THE BOMBAY GUNPOWDER MANUFACTORY

| *Dates* | *Names* | *Service* | *Remarks* |
|---|---|---|---|
| | IN BOMBAY ITSELF: | | |
| 1677 | Mungi Dugi | | Powder maker |
| 1744–6 | Mr. Gregorius Meisters | Merchant | Contractor |
| 1746 | Capt. Isaac Ainsworth | The Gunner | ,, |
| 1747 | Mrs. Ainsworth and Capt. Hugh Cameron | The Gunner | ,, |
| 1748 | Mr. J. Spencer and Capt. H. Cameron | Accompt-General | ,, |
| 1748–52 | Mr. S. Le Blank | Merchant | ,, |
| 1752 | Mr. W. Delagarde | Civil | In charge |
| 1753–4 | Capt. W. Walton | | In charge. Sent out by Court |
| 1754–6 | Mr. W. Delagarde | Civil | Superintendent |
| 1756 | Mr. J. Stuart | | Superintendent, provisional |
| 1756–9 | Mr. W. Delagarde | ,, | |
| 1759 | Mr. Waters | ,, | Provisional |
| 1760 | Mr. T. Byfield | ,, | Temporary in charge |
| 1760–? | Mr. Beaumont | ,, | Asst. in charge under the Powder House Committee |
| | AT MAZAGON: | | |
| 1779–84 | Mr. B. Hollamby | ,, | ,, ,, ,, |
| 1785–7 | Mr. J. Rivett | ,, | ,, ,, ,, |
| 1788 | Mr. J. R. Smyth | ,, | ,, ,, ,, |
| | Mr. E. Galley | ,, | ,, ,, ,, |
| 1789–90 | Mr. J. Rivett | ,, | Contractor, Committee dissolved |
| 1790–4 | Rustomjee Manockjee | | Contractor, Powder maker |
| 1794–5 | Bomanjee Hirjee | | ,, ,, |
| 1796–1807 | Surgeon Helenus Scott | Medical | Agent |
| 1808–10 | Surgeon G. Keir | ,, | ,, |
| 1811–17 | Surgeon J. Inverarity | ,, | ,, |
| 1818–21 | Surgeon D. Christie | ,, | ,, |
| 1822–7 | Capt. A. Manson | Bombay Artillery | ,, |
| 1827 | Capt. J. G. Griffith | ,, | ,, |
| 1827–9 | Capt. J. Barton | ,, | ,, |
| 1829–34 | Capt. T. Stevenson | ,, | ,, |
| 1834–44 | Capt. W. Jacob | ,, | ,, |
| 1844–6 | Lt.-Col. J. Lloyd | ,, | ,, |
| 1846–8 | Brevet Major W. Coghlan | ,, | ,, |
| 1848–52 | Brevet Major M. F. Willoughby | ,, | ,, |

| *Dates* | *Names* | *Service* | *Remarks* |
|---|---|---|---|
| 1852–5 | Brevet Major E. A. Farquharson | Bombay Artillery | Agent |
| 1855–9 | Brevet Major J. B. Woosnam | ,, | ,, |
| 1859–60 | Brevet Major B. K. Finnimore | ,, | ,, |
| 1860–2 | Brevet Major E. Wray | ,, | ,, |
| 1862–3 | Lt.-Col. W. S. Hatch | ,, | Agent, five months only |
| 1863–8 | Brevet Major T. T. Haggard | ,, | Agent. Kirkee factory commenced in 1864 |
| | AT KIRKEE: | | |
| 1868–77 | Brevet Major T. T. Haggard | ,, | Superintendent from 1874 |
| 1877–81 | Brevet Col. A. A. Bayly | ,, | Superintendent |
| 1881–94 | Brevet Lt.-Col. F. J. Caldecott | ,, | ,, |

# APPENDIX D

## OFFICERS OF THE MADRAS GUNPOWDER MANUFACTORY

| *Dates* | *Names* | *Service* | *Remarks* |
|---|---|---|---|
| To 1796 | Mainly by contract under the Military Storekeeper | | |
| 1796 | Mr. B. Bishop | Commissary | Agent |
| 1797–1813 | Mr. B. Bishop | ,, | Superintendent |
| 1813–23 | Lt. F. N. Balmain | 6th Cavalry | ,, |
| 1823–34 | Major J. Napier | 15th N.I. | ,, |
| 1835–9 | Major A. L. Murray | Madras Artillery | ,, |
| 1838–9 | Lt. J. Braddock | 1st N.V. Batt. | Temporary |
| 1839–46 | Major C. Taylor | Madras Artillery | Superintendent |
| 1842 | Capt. G. Alcock | ,, | Acting |
| 1846–9 | Brevet Major P. Anstruther | ,, | Superintendent |
| 1849–54 | Capt. T. Lavie | ,, | ,, |
| 1854–6 | Brevet Lt.-Col. P. Anstruther, C.B. | ,, | ,, |
| 1854–5 | Brevet Major W. M. Gabbett | ,, | Acting |
| 1856–8 | Major G. W. Y. Simpson | ,, | Superintendent |
| 1859–72 | Lt.-Col. G. Rowlandson | ,, | ,, |
| 1870–1 | Col. P. Hammond | Invalid Est. | Acting |
| 1872–3 | Col. R. Cadell | Madras Artillery | Superintendent |
| 1873–5 | Lt.-Col. N. G. Campbell | ,, | ,, |
| 1875–80 | Lt.-Col. E. W. Childers | ,, | ,, |
| 1881–6 | Lt.-Col. I. Ketchen | ,, | ,, |
| 1886–7 | Major C. A. Empson | Royal Artillery | ,, |

# APPENDIX E

## OFFICERS OF THE BENGAL GUNPOWDER MANUFACTORIES

| *Dates* | *Names* | *Service* | *Remarks* |
|---|---|---|---|
| 1734–48 | The Gunner and Master Attendant | | Contractors |
| 1749–53 (?) | Capt. L. Witherington | Artillery | Contractor |
| | AT PERRIN'S GARDEN: | | |
| 1756 | Capt. J. Buchanan | Infantry | Overseer. Died in Black Hole, 26.6.56 |
| 1757–8 | Mr. J. McDonald | Asst. Engineer | Overseer |
| 1759–60 | Mr. Martin Costelly | Ship's Captain | In charge |
| 1760–6 | Mr. William Smith | Sent out by Court | ,, |
| 1766–8 | Mr. W. Walton | ,, ,, | ,, |
| 1768–74 | Mr. William Smith | | ,, |
| 1774–6 | Capt. R. Stewart | Asst. Engineer | Superintendent |
| | AT AKRA: | | |
| 1776–82 | Capt. R. Stewart | Asst. Engineer | Contractor |
| 1782–7 | Mr. E. Hay | Civil Service | Secretary to Government |
| 1787–9 | Mr. John Farquhar | | Agent. Had been Asst. to Hay |
| | AT ISHAPORE: | | |
| 1789–1814 | Mr. John Farquhar | | Agent |
| 1814–16 | Surgeon J. Hare | Medical | ,, |
| 1816–17 | Capt. A. Galloway | 14th N.I. | Agent. Also at Calcutta preparing plant till 1819 |
| 1817–20 | Capt. D. MacLeod | Bengal Engineers | Agent |
| 1820–9 | Capt. A. Galloway | 14th N.I. | ,, |
| 1829–32 | Works closed | | |
| 1832–5 | Major R. Powney | Bengal Artillery | ,, |
| 1836 | Major J. Tennant | ,, | ,, |
| 1837–43 | Capt. T. Timbrell | ,, | ,, |
| 1843–54 | Brevet Major W. Anderson | ,, | ,, |
| 1854–8 | Major J. Abbott | ,, | ,, |
| 1858–63 | Brevet Col. V. Eyre, C.B. | ,, | ,, |
| 1863–72 | Lt.-Col. C. E. Voyle | ,, | ,, |
| 1872–82 | Major E. Tierney | ,, | Superintendent |
| 1882–92 | Capt. C. H. Scott | Royal Artillery | ,, |
| 1892–4 | Capt. C. A. Muspratt-Williams | ,, | ,, |

| Dates | Names | Service | Remarks |
|---|---|---|---|
| | THE ALLAHABAD MANUFACTORY: | | |
| 1800–8 | Capt. J. Taylor | Artillery | Agent. Had been Asst. at Ishapore |
| 1808–10 | Capt. M. Stewart | Royal Engineers | Agent |
| 1810–11 | Capt. F. Andree | 4th N.I. | Agent. Acting, Stewart on service |
| 1811–12 | Capt. M. Stewart | | Agent. Had transferred to a Ceylon Regiment |
| 1812–14 | Lt. A. Galloway | 14th N.I. | Agent |
| 1814–19 | Capt. J. F. Dundas | Artillery | ,, |
| 1819–20 | Capt. C. Graham | ,, | ,, |
| 1820–4 | Major A. Lindsay | ,, | ,, |
| 1824–9 | Capt. S. Parlby | ,, | |

# APPENDIX F

## OFFICERS OF THE BENGAL GUN-CARRIAGE MANUFACTORIES

| Dates | Names | Service | Remarks |
|---|---|---|---|
| | AT COSSIPORE: | | |
| 1800–3 | Major A. Glass | Bengal Artillery | Temporary at Kidderpore 1800–1. Agent |
| 1804 | Capt. J. D. Sherwood | ,, | Acting Agent |
| 1804–7 | Capt. T. Green | ,, | Agent |
| 1807–15 | Capt.-Lt. J. Young | ,, | ,, |
| 1815–21 | Major H. Faithfull | ,, | ,, |
| 1821–9 | Capt. C. H. Campbell | ,, | Agent. Moved to Fatehgarh |
| | AT FATEHGARH: | | |
| 1814–15 | Brevet Major C. Brown | ,, | Agent. At Allahabad; but no work done |
| 1816–24 | Major C. Brown | ,, | Agent |
| 1824–9 | Capt. R. B. Fulton | ,, | ,, |
| 1829–32 | Major C. H. Campbell | ,, | ,, |
| 1832–42 | Capt. T. Lumsden | ,, | ,, |
| 1843–7 | Brevet Major A. Abbott | ,, | ,, |
| 1848–53 | Lt.-Col. J. Alexander | ,, | ,, |
| 1853–6 | Brevet Col. J. Fordyce | ,, | ,, |
| 1856–7 | Brevet Maj. A. Robertson | ,, | ,, |
| 1858 | Major Le Geyt Bruce | ,, | Agent, temporary |
| 1858–64 | Brevet Lt.-Col. F. Turner | ,, | Agent |
| 1864–8 | Capt. M. E. Currie | ,, | ,, |
| 1868–72 | Brevet Col. C. V. Bowie | ,, | ,, |
| 1872 | Col. H. Lewis | ,, | Agent, acting |

| *Dates* | *Names* | *Service* | *Remarks* |
|---|---|---|---|
| 1872–6 | Col. R. G. F. Henegan | Madras Artillery | Superintendent |
| 1877–86 | Capt. H. M. Mackenzie | Bengal Artillery | ,, |
| 1886–91 | Lt.-Col. H. J. F. Shea | Royal Artillery | ,, |
| 1891–8 | Major E. B. Standbridge | ,, | ,, |
| 1898–1901 | Major C. C. Townsend | ,, | The last permanent Superintendent |
| 1901–4 | Capt. H. A. Young | ,, | Officiating |
| 1904–5 | Capt. J. H. Lawrence-Archer | ,, | Assistant Superintendent in charge, closing factory |

# APPENDIX G

## OFFICERS OF THE MADRAS GUN-CARRIAGE MANUFACTORY

| *Dates* | *Names* | *Service* | *Remarks* |
|---|---|---|---|
| | AT SERINGAPATAM: | | |
| 1802–9 | Capt. J. G. Scott | Madras Artillery | Agent |
| | AT MADRAS: | | |
| 1803–8 | Capt. J. C. Franke | ,, | Temporary Agency |
| | AT SERINGAPATAM: | | |
| 1809–23 | Capt.-Lt. J. Moorhouse | ,, | Agent |
| 1824–30 | Capt. W. Cullen | ,, | ,, |
| | AT MADRAS: | | |
| 1830–3 | Major W. Cullen | ,, | Superintendent |
| 1833–9 | Lt.-Col. J. H. Frith | ,, | ,, |
| 1839–40 | Major P. Montgomerie, | ,, | ,, |
| 1840–65 | Capt. J. Maitland [C.B. | ,, | ,, |
| 1865–72 | Lt.-Col. T. H. Campbell | ,, | ,, |
| 1872 | Lt.-Col. R. G. F. Henegan | ,, | ,, |
| 1872–3 | Lt.-Col. N. G. Campbell | ,, | ,, |
| 1873–4 | Lt.-Col. T. I. M. Hog | ,, | Acting |
| 1874–5 | Lt.-Col. E. W. Childers | ,, | Superintendent |
| 1875–6 | Lt.-Col. N. G. Campbell | ,, | ,, |
| 1876–80 | Lt.-Col. W. D'O. Kerrich | ,, | ,, |
| 1880–1 | Col. S. H. E. Chamier | ,, | ,, |
| 1881–6 | Col. H. McLeod | ,, | ,, |
| 1886–93 | Major A. F. Fletcher | Royal Artillery | ,, |
| 1893–8 | Capt. C. C. Townsend | ,, | ,, |
| 1898–1902 | Capt. C. T. Bell | ,, | ,, S.P.T. |
| 1903–7 | Major C. C. Townsend | ,, | ,, |
| 1907–8 | Major H. A Young | ,, | Officiating |
| 1908–10 | Colonel S. D. G. Smith | ,, | Superintendent |

# APPENDIX H

## OFFICERS OF THE BOMBAY GUN-CARRIAGE MANUFACTORY

| *Dates* | *Names* | *Service* | *Remarks* |
|---|---|---|---|
| 1810–16 | Lt. L. Russell | Bombay Artillery | Agent |
| 1816 | Lt. D. Hogarth | ,, | Acting |
| 1816–21 | Capt. R. Macintosh | ,, | On service in Arabia, 1820–1 |
| 1820–1 | Capt. W. Miller | ,, | Acting |
| 1821–7 | Capt. R. Thew | ,, | |
| 1827–34 | Capt. A. Manson | ,, | Ceased on promotion to Lt.-Col. |
| 1834–8 | Capt. W. H. Foy | ,, | |
| 1838–9 | Major F. P. Lester | ,, | |
| 1839–41 | Brevet Major J. W. Watson | ,, | |
| 1841–8 | Capt. E. Stanton | ,, | |
| 1848–57 | Brevet Major J. Grant | ,, | Acting from Oct. 1847 |
| 1857–9 | Brevet Major J. M. Glasse | ,, | |
| 1859–63 | Brevet Major J. Worgan | ,, | |
| 1863–78 | Lt.-Col. W. S. Hatch | ,, | Designation altered from Agent to Superintendent in 1874 |
| 1878–88 | Major H. W. Stockley | ,, | |
| 1888–91 | Lt.-Col. T. Walker | ,, | |
| 1891–1906 | Capt. S. G. D. Smith | Royal Artillery | The last permanent Superintendent |
| 1906–7 | Capt. H. A. Young | ,, | S.P.T. till closing of Factory |
| 1906 | Capt. J. H. Lawrence-Archer | ,, | Acting |

# APPENDIX I

## BIBLIOGRAPHY

*Army Historical Review*.

Army Lists, Indian and English.

*Army of the Indian Moghals*; Irvine.

*Artillery in the Mutiny, History of the*; J. R. J. Jocelyn (Murray), London, 1915.

*Baber's Memoirs*; J. Leyden and W. Erskine (Longmans), 1826.

*Bare Betty, The Five Sons of*; Colonel the Hon. A. C. Murray, 1935.

*Bell, The Travels of Richard, 1654–1670*; Sir R. Temple, 1908.

*Bengal Army, Abstract of Orders and Regulations*, 1812.
—— —— *Code of Military Regulations*, 1791; Grace.
—— —— *Code of Pay Regulations*, 1810; Green.
—— —— *History of The*; A. Broome, Calcutta, 1850.
—— —— *List of Officers of the*; Hodson.
'Bengal Artillery, The'; A. Broome (*Calcutta Review*), 1848.
—— —— *History of the*; F. W. Stubbs (Allen & Co.), 1895.
—— —— *List of Officers of the*; Stubbs.
—— —— *Memoir of the*; E. Buckle and J. R. Kaye (Allen & Co.), 1852.
*Bengal, Early Annals of the English in*; C. R. Wilson.
—— *in 1756–1757*; S. C. Hill (John Murray), 1905.
—— *List of Europeans in, in 1756*; S. C. Hill.
—— *Military Repository.*
—— *Obituary*; Calcutta, 1848.
—— *Old Fort William in*; C. R. Wilson (John Murray), 1906.
—— *Past and Present*; various numbers.
*Bernier's Travels, 1656–1668*; Oxford, 1914.
*Bihar, Annals of Early English Settlements in*; N. N. Raye, Calcutta, 1927.
Biographical Dictionaries.
*Bolts, William*; Hallward.
*Bombay Artillery, List of Officers in the*; F. W. Spring, London, 1902.
—— *Compilation of Military Regulations, 1750–1801.*
—— *The Origin of*; J. G. Da Cunha.
*British Army, The History of the*; Hon. J. W. Fortescue (Macmillan).
—— *Officer, The*; Stocqueler, 1851.
*Calcutta, Echoes of Old*; H. E. Busteed (Thacker), 1908.
—— *Review*, 1845, 1852.
*Civil Service, The Indian*; L. S. S. O'Malley (John Murray), 1931.
*Clive, Life of Lord*; various authors.
*Cossipore, Brief History of the Gun and Shell Factory*; C. T. Bell, 1910.
*Countries round the Bay of Bengal*; Bowrey (Hakluyt Society), 1905.
*Dalhousie, Private Letters of Lord*; ed. J. G. A. Baird, 1910.
Dodwell and Miles, Lists of Officers.
*East India Military Calendar.*
*Encyclopaedia Britannica.*
*Fatehgarh and the Mutiny*; F. R. Cosens and C. L. Wallace, Lucknow, 1933.
—— *Camp*; C. L. Wallace, Lucknow, 1934.
*Fifty Years with John Company*; U. Low.
*Gazetteer, Bengal and Agra*, 1842.
—— *Hamilton's*, 1828.
—— *Imperial*, 1908.

*Gazetteer, Thornton's*, 1854.
Gazetteers, Various District.
*Gentleman's Magazine*, 1822.
*Gunpowder Manufacture at Ishapore*; Anderson and Parlby.
—— *Memoir on*, 1829; Braddock.
*Hastings, Private Journal of the Marquis of*; London, 1858.
—— *The Letters of Warren*; Sydney Grier, 1905.
*Hedges, Diary of William*; (Hakluyt Society), 1887–9.
*Hickey, Memoirs of William*; A. Spencer (Hurst and Blackett).
*India, The Army in, and its Evolution.*
—— *British Government in*; Lord Curzon (Cassell).
—— *Cambridge History of.*
—— *Cyclopaedia of*; E. Balfour, London, 1885.
—— *English Factories in, 1618–1669*; W. Foster, Oxford, 1906–27.
—— *Handbook of, 1844*; Stocqueler.
—— *Office Records*; F. C. Danvers, London, 1888.
—— *Office Records, Guide to the*; W. Foster, London, 1919.
—— *Rise of British Dominion in*; A. C. Lyall, 1907.
—— *Travels in, 1845*; L. von Orlich.
—— *Unpublished Records of the Government of, 1748–1767*; J. Long.
*Madras Army, History of the*; W. J. Wilson, Madras, 1882.
—— *Artillery, List of Officers of the*; Leslie.
—— *Artillery Records.*
—— *Artillery, The Services of the*; Begbie.
—— *Code of Regulations of the Gunpowder Manufactory*, 1858.
—— *Diary and Consultation Books of the Council, 1682–1685*; Pringle.
—— *Inscriptions on Monuments in*; J. J. Cotton, Madras, 1905.
—— *The Nabobs of*; H. Dodwell (Williams & Norgate), 1926.
—— *Vestiges of Old*; H. D. Love (John Murray), 1913.
*Metcalfe, Life and Correspondence of Charles, Lord*; Kaye.
*Military Transactions in Hindustan*; R. Orme, 1780.
*Mysore, Journey through*; F. Buchanan, 1807.
*Prince Charles Edward Stuart, Life of*; Norrie.
Regimental Histories; various.
Reminiscences, Personal; various authors.
*Sepoy War, History of the*; J. W. Kaye (Allen & Co.), 1878.
*Tippoo Sultaun, War with*; A. Beatson, 1800.
*Travancore, The State History of.*
*Wellington's Dispatches*; Gurwood, 1884–7.

And especially the Manuscript Records in the India Office.

# INDEX A

## OFFICERS AND OTHERS

# INDEX B

## PLACES

*(References to the Presidencies are not included)*

www.ingramcontent.com/pod-product-compliance
Ingram Content Group UK Ltd.
Pitfield, Milton Keynes, MK11 3LW, UK
UKHW041848190726
13854UKWH00002B/775